# NORTH-EASTERN
# BRANCH LINE
# TERMINI

# NORTH-EASTERN BRANCH LINE TERMINI

## KEN HOOLE

With Drawings by
John Addyman, C. Eng. M.I.C.E.
and
Andrew Pearson

## Oxford Publishing Co.

Typesetting by:
Aquarius Typesetting Services, New Milton, Hants.

Printed in Great Britain by:
Biddles Ltd., Guildford, Surrey.

Published by:
Oxford Publishing Co.
Link House
West Street
POOLE, Dorset

# ACKNOWLEDGEMENTS

Primarily, my thanks must go to John Addyman for his excellent drawings of five of the stations, and to Andrew Pearson for the fine drawings of the sixth, Guisborough. These have entailed a great deal of hard work and patience, as the official drawings spanning the life of the stations have proved none too reliable, and some of the details shown were conflicting and impossible to reconcile. In such cases the matter has been resolved by reference to old photographs or a visit to the station itself. At Alston, for instance, drawings exist for three different roofs but our considered opinion is that only two existed; the original of 1852 and the higher and longer version that lasted until BR days. There is no trace of the third shown in a York drawing. Middleton-in-Teesdale has also posed many problems as it developed from a small single storey building to a station with a large house for the stationmaster, and an extensive range of buildings for passengers. Even so, one building has not been fully documented, although it is known that its odd size and situation is due to the filling in of a gap left by earlier alterations.

I must also thank the members of the North Eastern Railway Association who have helped with the project in various ways; notably, P. B. Booth, C. B. Foster, C. A. Kimber, K. L. Taylor, L. Ward and C. J. Woolstenholmes, and in particular, J. F. Mallon for the use of items from his records and photographs of NER staff.

Thanks are also due to S. L. Rankin of the Public Affairs Department of British Rail at York, who has gone to a great deal of trouble to obtain copies of drawings we needed to view to settle various points.

Photographs have come from many sources and where the photographer is known, due credit has been given. Unfortunately with a collection of more than 200 albums of NER-related photographs, it is impossible to identify or trace the origin of many of them and these have been credited to 'Author's Collection', solely for that reason. To all known and unknown photographers may I express my thanks.

# INTRODUCTION

Of the six terminal stations chosen for this work, Richmond (1846), now a farm and garden centre, is the oldest, closely followed by Whitby (1847), Alston (1852) and Guisborough (1853), and all were built before the NER was formed. Middleton-in-Teesdale (1868), built by an independent company, has been rebuilt and extended, leaving Alnwick, new in 1887, as the only true North Eastern station. Only Whitby still accommodates trains, but only Guisborough has completely disappeared.

Alnwick, although having only two platforms, was the most imposing station, probably provided by the NER to impress the Royal visitors to the Duke of Northumberland at nearby Alnwick Castle. When King Edward VII opened the new railway bridge across the River Tyne between Newcastle and Gateshead in June 1906, he made Alnwick Castle his headquarters for three days and, in 1908, the Prince and Princess of Wales (later King George V and Queen Mary) stayed at the castle from 29th June to 6th July. These visits brought the LNWR Royal Train to Alnwick and during their stay local journeys were made by train.

Alston Station, serving the highest market town in England, managed to remain open until 1976, largely because of the unsuitability of the roads in the area. Unfortunately, the train shed had been demolished some years earlier, leaving a building looking quite attractive from the front but just the opposite from the back! Attempts by a preservation society to retain the track and operate a train service have proved unsuccessful, although the society has laid a stretch of narrow gauge track on the original formation north of Alston.

Guisborough with its unusual glazed end screens, was unique on the North Eastern Railway, to which it passed in 1863 with the remainder of the old Stockton & Darlington system. It was demolished in May 1967.

Middleton-in-Teesdale is now a caravan park but retains the station buildings, some adapted to their new use. Just across the road on the west side of the station is the long-disused Low Quarry; a silent reminder of the millions of tons of stone that passed along the Middleton branch in its years of operation.

Richmond Station, specially designed to fit in with its historic and picturesque surroundings, was one of the most attractive in North-East England and it is indeed fortunate that it has been possible to find another use for it, although the future of the one time engine shed is now in doubt.

Whitby, now with only one service, survives with a small staff and accommodation to spare, its Andrews buildings adding a touch of distinction to a motely collection of harbourside buildings. At one time it faced on to a small dock, long since filled in and now providing parking space for the railway's greatest enemy! Even the engine shed caters for another form of transport, as it houses a supplier of goods and equipment for the sailing enthusiast. However, it is a means of ensuring the survival of the building.

But what is the future of these buildings and others like them? A disused station a century or more old needs regular maintenance, although an enlightened attitude to preservation is making their future more secure. However, it does not seem right that British Rail alone should be saddled with the cost of maintaining them once the buildings have outgrown their use as stations.

Although the six stations originated at different periods, and from different companies, their latter-day fixtures and fittings became fairly standard, and such things as luggage barrows, notice and poster boards, and signs, etc. were common to all. Signals and signal boxes differed, depending on their Southern, Central or Northern Division ancestry. At Alnwick the signals were electrically lit from 1908, but at Middleton and Richmond they were gas lit, the former probably from the nearby town gasworks and the latter from the company's own gasworks in the station yard. Unfortunately, the period of use of these forms of lighting is not known.

The wages paid to the staff in 1914 at the stations under discussion appear negligible when compared with today's rates of pay. For instance, a signalman at Alnwick Station box received £1. 10s. 0d. for a 48 hour week, and at Shilbottle Colliery Junction box, £1. 7s. 0d. for a 60 hour week. Today's weekly rates for the lowest grade of signalman are £81.20 and the highest, £125.45. Class 1 passenger guards received £1. 12s. 0d. and Class 2, £1. 9s. 0d. again for a 60 hour week. Now, guards receive £86.35 per week.

Engine drivers on the top rate received £2. 5s. 0d. for a week of 54 hours, and firemen £1.10s. 0d. for the same hours, but cleaners worked one hour less and received £1.2s. At Middleton-in-Teesdale, Richmond and Guisborough the cleaners were paid an extra 1s. 0d. per week for lighting up the engine and raising steam. Now, drivers on their maximum are paid £110.40 per week, driver's assistants £89.70, and traction trainees £69.10, although from 19th April 1982 there is a minimum earnings level of £81.20 per week for staff aged 18 and over. At Whitby Shed, with several engines to maintain, additional staff employed included boiler washers and steam raisers, grades which have now disappeared from the railway scene.

In this work, the text has concentrated on those items which cannot be illustrated by photographs or drawings and thus refers mainly to the history of the station and the working of the trains and engines. This has enabled more drawings to be presented, often showing the buildings at various periods and these have been drawn to a uniform scale, except for Guisborough, which has been treated differently by a different draughtsman.

Also, rather than repeating the details common to all six stations, such as the size of the turntable, population, tickets issued and goods traffic, etc., these have been tabulated or summarised for easy reference, and they appear in the extensive Appendix.

The drawings have been prepared either from the originals or from microfilm copies, supplemented by site measurements (in certain cases taken some years prior to demolition), and details from NER records and ordnance survey sheets. Those for Alnwick, Alston, Middleton-in-Teesdale, Richmond and Whitby have been specially prepared by John Addyman at a scale of 4mm. = 1ft., reduced in printing to 2mm. = 1ft. to fit the page size, but the Guisborough drawings, by Andrew Pearson, were completed some years ago and are to a scale of 1/8in. = 1ft., reduced in printing to 1/16in. = 1ft.

Many surviving drawings date from later alterations that have been carried out on the buildings, and do not necessarily give all the information required to produce full plans, elevations, and sections of the subject; for example, only minimal roof details for Whitby Station have survived. The originals are by no means accurate even after allowing for shrinkage and distortion, some of them being more than a century old, and in that time having passed through the hands of many companies. Features that appear in three views can have three different sizes and positions, and quoted and actual dimensions can vary considerably. Similarly, drawings produced at different dates can give contradictory information and can be incorrect, even on such basic dimensions as length, height, width and roof angles, not to mention door, window and chimney details.

There is no guarantee that requirements given on the original drawing were faithfully carried out at the time of building, and it can be wrong to assume that because a later drawing, or the actual building, differs from the first design, a physical rebuilding has been carried out. The railway company's architect or clerk of works may have issued site instructions for revision, or permitted the contractor to deviate from the original plans for various reasons. At Alston, for example, the 1851 drawings show the house chimneys in clusters of four instead of three and two, and the goods shed roof 2ft. 3in. higher than it was later, but it is very probable that these amendments date from the outset. The alterations to the original designs were rarely added to the master drawings at the time of building, and must have caused embarrassment, if not expense, when later changes were planned on inaccurate data!

It was NER practice not to date drawings, and only if the signed contractor's copies are available is this information given. Smaller alterations were rarely subjects for new drawings and details of the proposals were usually executed as an amendment on an earlier drawing. This may have been carried out at any time in a fifty to sixty year span, although further research can often reduce the limit to within twenty years.

The drawings reproduced in this book have been corrected as far as possible for major errors by site measurements, or checking against photographs but, in some cases, average, or most probable, dimensions have had to be accepted. Some drawings contain anachronisms, either because the official drawings do not give all the later amendments or, following the NER's example, to keep the cost down by reducing the number of drawings needed. These anachronisms are pointed out in text or captions.

Few useful dimensions appear on the original drawings and sometimes only one minor dimension is given on a large and complex plan. However, on the new drawings, readers should have no difficulty in scaling off any dimension they require.

# CONTENTS

# CHAPTER ONE
# Alnwick

The present Alnwick Station buildings, now occupied by various industrial concerns, date from 5th May 1887, replacing an old station at the terminus of the line from Alnmouth which reached Alnwick in August 1850. When the new station was built, the platform of the old station was allowed to remain as part of the goods yard, where it became the cattle dock, and the old station building was converted to a goods shed.

An Act for the construction of the line from Gateshead to Berwick was obtained by the Newcastle & Berwick Railway on 31st July 1845, and this included powers to build certain branches, including one 2¾ miles long from Bilton (renamed Alnmouth in 1892) to the town of Alnwick, terminating 'at or near to the Coal Staith adjoining the turnpike road leading from Newcastle-upon-Tyne to Alnwick, or otherwise at or near the south Toll-bar upon the same road in the Township of Alnwick'. The 'coal staith' referred to in the Act was at the end of a

tramway from Shilbottle Colliery, three miles south of Alnwick, which opened in 1809 to carry coal for sale to the inhabitants of the town and district.

Construction of the main line took preference, and it was not until August 1848 that the contract was let for the construction of the Alnwick branch. In view of the Hudson revelations in 1849, it was decided to postpone or suspend certain works, but work continued on the Alnwick branch, which was formally opened on 5th August 1850, and publicly two weeks later, but only for passengers. Goods traffic commenced on 1st October 1850. In the 1850s, the Alnwick stationmaster was James Paterson, who had acquired some early transport experience with Pickfords, the road haulage organisation and, in 1860, he purchased a small carrier's business in London for £725, of which part was put up by Walter Carter, a carrier from Manchester, and Paterson's two brothers, John and Robert. The new concern took the name of

Milepost 3 (from Alnmouth) stood outside the roof. A Class D20 locomotive, No. 62381, prepares to depart with a train.

*W. A. Camwell*

Carter Paterson and Co. and set up in business on 1st November 1860 with six carts and eight horses. In 1933, the four British main line companies acquired an interest in Pickford & Co., and after many years of working together, especially on the parcels delivery side of the business, Pickfords and Carter Paterson amalgamated in 1946.

After the branch had been open for 35 years, Alnwick Town Council approached the North Eastern Railway regarding improved facilities, and plans for a proposed new station were considered by the NER Traffic Committee in January 1885. However, it was decided that 'as Bilton is necessarily the most important point, the expenditure on improved station accommodation at Alnwick should at present be limited to as small an amount as possible'. Exactly eight weeks later there was a complete reversal of this decision, and it was decided to go ahead with a new station! The reason for this about turn has not been discovered.

Considering the population of Alnwick was less than 7,000, the inhabitants of Alnwick were to be provided with a substantial and expensive new station, the estimated cost when authorised on 3rd September 1885 being £10,444. 10s. 7d. This included a larger signal box with extra height to allow a view over a nearby bridge, whereas the original had looked under the bridge. The successful tender for the construction of the station was submitted by Meakin & Dean at £11,500, with an additional £3,931 for engineering works.

The new station was built at the same time as the line from Alnwick to Coldstream, which was being built by Meakin & Dean at a contract price of £272,266. 15s. 3d. for the 35½ miles. This reflected the size of the stations on the branch which were larger than really necessary, especially considering the small amount of traffic that could be expected from the area through which it ran. For the Coldstream line, the NER purchased from W. Potts & Sons Ltd. eleven station clocks at £12. 10s. 0d. each, and twenty one signal cabin clocks at £3.10s. 0d. each and, on a more substantial note, Mr. Worsdell was authorised to accept the tender of Messrs. Cowans, Sheldon for one 50ft. engine turntable, to be delivered and installed at Alnwick at a price of £327.

Near the station, on the opposite side of the old Great North Road, is the 83ft. high column surmounted by a Percy lion. It was erected in 1816 in gratitude for the second Duke adjusting the farm rents to the hard times of the day. The column is known locally as 'The Farmers Folly'.

On the outskirts of Alnwick is Alnwick Castle, the seat of the Dukes of Northumberland, and no doubt the new station was built to a high standard to cater for the Duke and his Royal visitors. Even so, the station had only two platforms, each covered by a glazed roof span. The two main spans were supported by the outer wall on each side and the station buildings down the centre. As the buildings did not extend as far as the roof, this required two rows of columns to support the inner edges of the spans beyond the buildings, with the arcade between the spans covered by a smaller glazed roof similar in design to the

Alnwick Station stood on an imposing site on the south-west side of the old Great North Road. The footpath up to the station was flanked by two low pillars on which were mounted lamps, presumably gas, but the tops vanished years ago. The motor cattle wagon stands on the site of the coal depot and weigh cabin.

*J. F. Mallon*

Fortunately, when the station was built, it was photographed (together with the stations on the Coldstream line opened at the same time) for the NER Architect, William Bell. This is one of these 1887 views of the front of the station, with the top of the footpath seen in the previous picture, although there is a difference of 89 years between the two views.

*Author's Collection*

The front of the station in 1958. Little has changed, except that the second window to the right of the entrance has been altered to a door to give access to W. H. Smith's bookstall.

*J. F. Mallon*

A view looking along the front of the station, under the glazed awning, and over the Great North Road, to the base of the column erected in 1816 in honour of the second Duke of Northumberland.

*J. F. Mallon*

One of the lamp standards at the foot of the station approach.

*J. F. Mallon*

A detailed view of the railings and gate at the top of the station approach.

*J. F. Mallon*

A view looking into the station, with the booking office window on the left. Originally the booking office was on the right of the entrance, but a rearrangement of the accommodation was necessary to allow W. H. Smith & Son Ltd. to move into the front block. The bookstall was previously between the platforms beyond the station buildings and the refreshment room.

*J. F. Mallon*

larger spans. Glazed windscreens were provided at the outer ends of each of the three roof spans; for the centre span this extended down to platform level for its full length, but the screens to the large spans extended to platform level only for a width of five panes, although their size was later reduced when the lower sections were re-renewed.

A three bay glazed canopy supported on cast-iron brackets protected passengers alighting from carriages at the northern end of the station buildings, where a single storey stone-built office block, with slate roof, ran across the end of the platforms. A large clock (without maker's name) was mounted on two brackets to the left of the canopy.

The fine new station was opened on 5th September 1887, together with the branch to Coldstream.

*Locomotive and Train Working*

There are not many branches where it is known exactly which engine worked the line in the 1850s, but it is known that, in its early years, the Alnwick branch was worked by 2-4-0WT No. 73, which was originally built by R. & W. Hawthorn in 1840 as a 2-2-2 tender engine for the Great North of England Railway, where it was named *Ouse*. It had 5ft. 6in. driving wheels and 12in. x 18in. cylinders

but, in 1852, it was rebuilt as a 2-4-0WT with 4ft. 6in. wheels and 13in. x18in. cylinders. The regular driver was Bobby Douglas and the fireman, J. Weddell, who was born in 1832, retired from the NER in 1900, and died in 1913. The engine is reputed to have been stationed at Bilton Junction (later Alnmouth) for working the Alnwick branch, but other factors point to it being stationed at the Alnwick end. In October 1874, it was decided to build a new shed at Bilton, together with some cottages and, in January 1875, the estimated cost was £1,610 for a shed for four engines, and £410 for three cottages. On 18th April 1875, a tender was accepted for £2,090. 19s. 2d. By that time the most likely type of engine to be working the Alnwick branch was the Fletcher 0-4-4T of Class BTP.

In May 1887, it was decided to extend Bilton Shed to take a further two engines for working the Alnwick to Coldstream services and, in the following month, a tender of £1,029. 7s. 3d. was accepted. Unfortunately, the contractor had made a mistake in his sums and his contract was cancelled, to be awarded to the next lowest figure of £1,043. 17s. 3d.

The 1898 derailment at the catch points between Alnwick and Alnmouth shows that the Worsdell Class A 2-4-2T engines were working the line, but an earlier double collision at Chevington, on 25th October 1887, shows that No. 469 of the same class was involved whilst working the Amble branch passenger train. As this was an Alnmouth Shed duty, it is certain that No. 469 also worked between Alnmouth and Alnwick, and probably through to Coldstream

It so happens that the driver of No. 469 (the engine was only five months old when involved in the collision) was the John Weddell, who appears as the fireman in the old photograph of 2-4-0T No. 73. In fact, at one time, almost every train working between Alnmouth and Alnwick must have had a member of the Weddell family on the footplate as another J. Weddell joined the NER in May 1883, another J. in April 1911, J. H. in November 1916, and T. W. in 1918!

Normally, before 1914, engines from only four sheds visited Alnwick, with Gateshead and Heaton engines and men working in from Newcastle, and Tweedmouth engines and men from Berwick, via Coldstream and also via the main line; the latter working requiring a reversal at Alnmouth. As a point of interest, another Tweedmouth engine worked the first 'up' train in a morning and the last 'down' train at night between Berwick, Coldstream and Alnwick, with a trip to Newcastle and back during the day. A Tweedmouth BTP 0-4-4T worked to Alnwick on a single coach autocar, forming the 2.45p.m. from Berwick and the 5.17p.m. from Alnwick, both via Coldstream. Finally, of course, Alnmouth engines were to be seen on many of the trains, most of which were through from Alnwick to Newcastle, although on one turn the engine also worked from Newcastle to Albert Edward Dock on Tuesdays, Thursdays and Saturdays, and from Newcastle to South Shields on Mondays, Wednesdays and Fridays. The two Alnmouth engines working on the Alnwick to Coldstream service both turned round at Coldstream, and did not go on to Tweedmouth or Berwick, connections being given with Kelso trains at Coldstream.

An Alnmouth passenger engine worked the 9.15a.m.

The interior of the station showing the station buildings and 'down' (No. 1) platform in an 1887 view.

*Author's Collection*

No. 1 platform some 75 years later.

*C. B. Foster*

The new station was opened on 5th September 1887, together with the line to Coldstream, and a large crowd turned out to watch the trains on the first day, including this departure over the new line, headed by BTP 0-4-4T No. 199.

*J. F. Mallon Collection*

goods from Alnwick to Wooler, where it was due at 12.32p.m. to connect with the goods returning from Wooler to Tweedmouth. The Alnmouth engine returned on the 1.17p.m. goods from Wooler, spending an hour shunting at Alnwick before terminating at Alnmouth. Unfortunately, at this period (1908), it is impossible to say exactly what engines were stationed at Alnmouth, but some Class A 2-4-2T locomotives were still there, together with some of the older 2-4-0 tender engines, such as Class 1440 (Fletcher) and Class 1463 (Tennant).

In 1923, the first year of the LNER, Alnmouth Shed had twelve engines, all of which worked into Alnwick at one time or another:

*Passenger*

Class A 2-4-2T Nos. 21, 485 and 1160
Class F 4-4-0 No. 18
Class M 4-4-0 No. 1637
Class 1440 2-4-0 No. 220
Class 1463 2-4-0 Nos. 1478 and 1504

*Goods*

Class C 0-6-0 Nos. 1563 and 1820
Class U 0-6-2T No. 1667
Class 59 0-6-0 No. 565

Five Alnmouth passenger engines were rostered to visit Alnwick daily, some as many as four times.

By this time a working had been introduced which was to last for another 35 years or more; this involved the engine working the 2.25p.m. from Alnwick to Newcastle, which worked forward light engine to Low Fell. There it collected, from the 'up' siding, the empty Bristol mail TPO set, which it hauled to Newcastle Central for loading, the engine later returning home with the 8.55p.m. to Alnwick.

From 1925, Alnmouth Shed came to rely more and more on former North Eastern 4-4-0 engines and became well-known for its use of the Class D17/1 (NER Class M) locomotives, including the famous No. 1621, now in the National Railway Museum at York. These were followed by the similar D17/2 (NER Class Q) engines with their clerestory cab roof, and finally the D20 (NER Class R), which became a familiar sight at Alnwick. The first class D20 locomotive to move to Alnwick was No. 2029, from Tweedmouth on 21st October 1938, followed by Nos. 1078 and 2106 in November, and No. 2023 in December. By 1946, there were seven Class D20 engines at Alnmouth and they performed consistently until the last three, Nos. 62381 (ex-1042), 62395 (ex-1260) and 62396 (ex-1665) were withdrawn from Alnmouth Shed in November 1957.

Subsequently, Almouth Shed used a variety of more

13

*(Above):* A view of the south-east end of the station, with the glazed end screen and platform wind-screens.

*C. B. Fost*

Details of screens and a lamp standard. Note that the cast-iron standard carries the spiral design common to the entrance lamps.

*C. B. Fost*

*(Below):* Just beyond milepost 3, and at the foot of the south-west corner pillar the station, was the DP (distance or datum post). Alnwick, being a terminal statio should have had this post at the buffer stop end of platform 1, and a NER surv dated 1922 shows it as being correctly sited at that date. This view also shows th the glazed ventilator did not extend over the end bay of the roof, and the roof ladd is of particular interest.

*C. B. Fos*

A general view of the station and yard from overbridge No. 10, which spans the tracks outside the station. The platform in the centre, in use as the cattle dock, was the main platform of the 1850 station, which was replaced in 1887 by the present structure. The goods yard is on the left and the weighbridge and cabin are on the extreme right. Beyond the station is the monument erected to the second Duke of Northumberland surmounted by the Percy lion. An upturned loading gauge is seen in the foreground.

*British Rail*

modern types, such as Class J39 0-6-0s, K1 2-6-0s and V1 2-6-2Ts, although for some years a combined diesel multiple unit and steam-operated service was in force. Thus in 1962, three Alnmouth drivers were responsible for working South Gosforth diesel multiple unit sets on the Alnwick to Alnmouth and Alnwick to Newcastle services, with four through trains a day to and from Newcastle. At the same time, a Class J39 0-6-0 started its day by working the 6.50a.m. goods from Alnmouth to Alnwick. Dur-

ing the day, it worked five return passenger trips between Alnwick and Alnmouth and also found time to shunt, as required, at both Alnwick and Alnmouth in the morning and afternoon. The engine ended its days on the 10.17p.m. from Alnmouth to Alnwick and then retired to Alnmouth Shed for the night.

When the passenger service ceased on the Coldstream line, there were three trains to Coldstream; at 8.30a.m., 1.50p.m. and 6.45p.m. from Alnwick, with the afternoon and evening trains running through to Tweedmouth. Alnwick to Coldstream trains were allowed 87 minutes, stopping at all stations, but the trains in the opposite direction were allowed 91 minutes. Parcels and goods traffic continued, with a No. 1 braked parcels train running at the same times as two of the passenger trains, namely 1.50p.m. Alnwick to Coldstream and 4.35p.m. Coldsteam to Alnwick. In fact, the 1.50p.m. from Alnwick was retained until BR days, although the return from Coldstream was brought forward to 4p.m.

On 26th October 1949, the line was breached by flooding just north of Ilderton and the service was necessarily divided into two parts; Alnwick to Ilderton and Coldstream to Wooler. The Ilderton service was subsequently retimed to leave Alnwick at 11.20a.m., arriving back at 3.50p.m. after a booked stop of 85 minutes at Ilderton, but it ceased from 2nd March 1953. On the other hand, the Wooler service from the Tweedmouth end continued until 29th March 1965. The two sections of line were never rejoined.

Alnwick was a venue for day excursions, particularly from the Newcastle area and, until 1908, the platform at the old station was known as the excursion platform, before becoming the cattle dock. In 1898, the maximum number of coaches allowed on excursion trains between Alnmouth and Alnwick was twenty (four wheel and six wheel), but two engines were required if the load exceeded twelve coaches. At that time, the assistant engine could be attached at the front of the train engine or at the rear, but a few years later, this was altered so that any train carrying passengers and requiring assistance had to have the assisting engine attached at the front, although all trains not conveying passengers could have assistance provided at the rear. Excursions from the north, from the Wooler direction, were allowed nine four wheel coaches if worked by a passenger engine, or eleven four wheel or nine six wheel if worked by a goods engine. The maximum number of coaches allowed on the Coldstream line was eleven.

The loads of ordinary and excursion trains as laid down in 1908 were:

Around 1898, a wooden refreshment room was built at the outer end of the station buildings, between the two platforms. A diesel multiple unit bound for Newcastle stands in platform 2.
*C. B. Foster*

When the last Class D20 engines were withdrawn in November 1957, Alnmouth Shed acquired various classes as replacments, such as K1 2-6-0 No. 62011, photographed in platform 2 at Alnwick.
*Author's Collection*

| Class of Engine | Alnmouth to Alnwick | | Alnwick to Alnmouth | |
|---|---|---|---|---|
| | Number of vehicles | Load (Tons) | Number of vehicles | Load (Tons) |
| M1, Q | 14 | 196 | 16 | 224 |
| A, C1, F1, I, J, 901, 1463 | 11 | 134 | 15 | 210 |
| O and Goods (ordinary train) | 14 | 196 | 16 | 224 |
| O and Goods (excursion train) | 16 | 224 | 20 | 280 |
| Maximum load with assistance | 20 | 280 | 27 | 378 |

The number of coaches allowed was based on six wheel coaches counting as 1 unit, with 45ft. and 49ft. bogie coaches as 1½, and 52ft. bogie stock as 1¾ so that, for instance, an excursion train travelling to Alnwick with two engines could be made up to eight 52ft. coaches (14 units) and four 45ft. or 49ft. coaches (6 units).

Class D20 4-4-0 No. 62381 stands under the roof in British Railways' days. This class of engine, once the mainstay of the East Coast Main Line between Newcastle and Edinburgh, spent its final years working between Newcastle and Alnwick from the small two road shed at Alnmouth.

*Author's Collection*

Virtually any class of engine could arrive at Alnwick on specials and excursions. On occasions, when the main line was blocked between Alnmouth and Tweedmouth, the Alnwick to Coldstream line could be used as an emergency route, but this meant a reversal at Alnwick and another at Tweedmouth. For the whole of the distance off the main line, 4-6-2 Pacific Locomotives were restricted to 35m.p.h. World War II brought incidents worth recording, such as the occasion, on 8th March 1941, when the main line was blocked by a bomb near Belford. The 10.5a.m. York to Edinburgh train arrived at Alnwick at 3.18p.m., only seventeen minutes before it was due in Edinburgh, 92 miles away, behind Class A3 No. 2578 *Bayardo* and Class D20 No. 592. After running round its train at Alnwick No. 2578 departed at 3.46p.m., running tender first and still assisted by No. 592. However, the train did not get far out of Alnwick before No. 2578 slipped to a standstill and, after several attempts to restart, the guard walked back to Alnwick with the tablet to get assistance. This was at 5.37p.m. and, at 5.46p.m., Class D20 No. 2023 was sent to assist at the rear. What time the train eventually reached Edinburgh I do not know, but it must have been five or six hours late.

Other engines seen as a result of the war were USA 2-8-0s, in 1943/4, and strangers from not so far afield were the two ex-North British 0-6-0s stationed at Alnmouth

Nos. 9172 of Class J36 and 9046 of Class J37, which were both frequently used on the Alnwick to Wooler goods.

Post-war visitors were Class Q6 0-8-0s on ballast trains, a WD 2-8-0 on a sheep special and, on 5th June 1953, Class V2 No. 60949 arrived on a Coronation Pageant excursion from Newcastle; it had to go to Tweedmouth to turn.

Alnwick's most famous visitor was Class D17/1 4-4-0 No. 1621, which arrived almost daily for many years until it was withdrawn from service on 28th July 1945. This engine started life in 1893 and two years later it took part in the 'Races to Aberdeen' when fierce competition between the East Coast and West Coast routes led to high speed runs between London and Aberdeen. After it was withdrawn, No. 1621 was restored to the glory of its old North Eastern green and placed in the Queen Street Railway Museum at York. It now rests in the National Railway Museum at York as a reminder of the Victorian 4-4-0, as portrayed by the North Eastern Railway.

In 1932 the Alnwick-Alnmouth-Newcastle services were operated by five 'Composition A' sets of coaches, comprising two brake thirds with, in between, one composite lavatory and one third, all compartment stock. During their daily diagram the sets visited Middlesbrough, Saltburn, Blackhill, North Wylam, Ferryhill, Leamside, Pelaw, Darlington and Birtley. The Alnwick-

The old and new signal boxes in 1887. The standard NER signals of the period are seen with the lamp below the arm, and the line which the signal controls is painted on the arm. For instance, the single arm signal to the left of centre carries, on the arm level with the top of the bridge girder, the words 'Carriage dock'. Note that the signal wires to the gantry beyond the bridge are carried on pulleys mounted on posts, to retain height.

*Author's Collection*

The installation of colour light signals in 1965. The entrance to the 1887 box was above ground level, with access to the working floor by means of an internal staircase. There was also an external stairway (just visible to the left of the box) from the operating floor to the nearby road. The old box, minus its top, was converted to a shelter.

*Author's Collection*

A scene photographed from the box in 1953, showing track remodelling operations in progress.

*J. F. Mallon*

Alnmouth-Berwick trains serving the intermediate stations on the main line utilised three 'Composition C' sets, made up of two brake composites, each with one first class compartment, but one coach had four thirds and the other had five, according to the carriage roster.

The Alnwick-Coldstream-Tweedmouth parcels train was rostered for a six wheel brake van, which left Newcastle at 6.53a.m. on the Berwick parcels. On its return journey it was picked up at Alnmouth and finally arrived back in Newcastle at 8.56p.m. Between Alnwick and Coldstream the single van train was classed as a No. 1 braked parcels but, by 1939, it had become a No. 1 express parcels. It is understood that on summer Saturdays this service carried passengers to the camping coaches along the line at Whittingham, Glanton, Hedgeley, Wooperton, Ilderton, Akeld, Kirknewton and Mindrum, but this facility is not mentioned in the carriage roster or working timetable.

In the 1930s, LNER corridor stock was drafted on to many North Eastern Area services, replacing the NER bogie compartment stock, much of which was twenty years old or more. Thus, in 1939, the Alnwick to Newcastle trains were made up of a BTKLV(4), a brake third corridor lavatory with four compartments, a CKLV(3½-4), a composite corridor lavatory with 3½ first class and four third class compartments, a TKLV, third corridor lavatory, and a BT non-corridor, non-lavatory brake third, giving 21 first class and 126 third class seats with a set weighing 125 tons. The corridor brakes for these sets were slow on delivery and at first the trains ran with a non-corridor brake third at each end, but these were replaced as the new stock became available. Following World War II, some Alnwick to Newcastle sets used a Pullman brake third at each end.

*Signal boxes*
The 1908 Working Timetable Appendix lists five signal boxes under the control of the Alnwick stationmaster; namely:

*Willowburn:* This box opened in 1885 with Stevens dwarf frame. It was a wooden box on the 'up' side of the line, situated one mile from Alnwick on the Alnmouth line. Prior to closure it opened 'only when required for excursion trains' and closed completely in 1908.

*Shilbottle Colliery Junction:* This box was on the 'up' side and opened 27th October 1908 replacing an earlier box on the 'down' side of the Alnmouth line, ½ mile from Alnwick. In addition to the colliery sidings, this box also controlled the connection to the local gasworks under an Agreement dated 19th August 1881. All signals were on lattice posts. The box was renamed Alnwick East in 1923 because of the construction of a new Shilbottle Colliery box on the main line south of Alnmouth. Alterations were carried out in 1940 and a new diagram was provided in the box and dated 6th February 1943, covering the provision of a new Petrol Sidings ground frame brought into use on 14th April 1943. The box was closed on 14th February 1965.

*Station Junction:* This box controlled all the lines into the station and goods yard from the Alnmouth and Coldstream lines. It was opened in 1887, with the new station, and closed on 14th February 1965. It was fitted with a

Stevens 35 lever frame in August 1908 and the diagram was dated 8th August 1908, but this was amended in July 1918. A new diagram was provided on 30th November 1954. From the 1908 alterations, all signals were electrically lit, except for the three most distant, two on the Alnmouth line and one on the Coldstream branch.

*Alnwick North:* This box was situated 375yds. from Station box on the Coldstream line where the double track out of the station became single line. It was fitted with a Stevens frame in 1902 and it closed on 16th June 1930 when the single line was extended to Station box.

*Summit:* This box, four miles from Alnwick, was situated in the cutting at the top of the 3½ mile climb at 1 in 50 from the Alnwick direction, in the course of which trains climbed from 223ft. above sea level at Alnwick to 655ft. at Summit box. It was closed in 1911, when the staff section was altered to Alnwick North—Edlingham. A siding at Summit box could accommodate only nine wagons in addition to the engine and van. Marks on the side of the cutting where the box once stood can still be discerned.

At Alnwick the gantry on the Alnmouth side of the overbridge at the approach to the station carried four pairs of co-acting arms so that they could be seen above and below the bridge. The lower arms were of the upper quadrant variety utilising normal arms mounted inverted.

The following item appeared in the Signalling Alterations Notice:

**Sunday, 14th February 1965: Alnmouth, Alnwick East and Alnwick Station**

*Alnmouth:* The branch line Alnmouth to Alnwick will become a single line controlled from Alnmouth signal box. Points near the turntable at Alnwick will connect the passenger line to the freight line. The ground frame points leading to the Petroleum Siding will remain as existing but will be released from Alnmouth signal box. The existing 'down' branch line at Alnmouth will become a shunt spur.

*Alnwick East:* Signal box and all points and signals dispensed with.

*Alnwick Station:* Signal box and all points connected with the passenger line dispensed with. All points in Alnwick goods yard to be hand worked. All signals dispensed with.

*Alnmouth to Alnwick:* The signals for the single line between Alnmouth and Alnwick are electrically controlled to prevent opposing movements and to prevent more than one train being on the line between two stop signals, applicable to the same direction of travel, at the same time. The line is worked on the electric token block system so far as this is applicable, except that the line is controlled entirely from Alnmouth signal box and no token is provided.

Wrong line order forms will not be used. At Alnwick movements between the passenger and freight lines may be regarded as within station limits.

On Monday, 22nd February 1965, the contractor

Looking from overbridge No. 10, a train from Alnmouth is seen approaching, headed by Class J39 0-6-0 No. 64711. The two signals above the train and on the lower gantry were lower quadrant arms adapted for upper quadrant operation, even though the co-acting arms on the upper gantry were lower quadrants.

*E. E. Smith*

A view looking towards the station in 1958. The Coldstream line is on the left, Alnmouth lines are on the right, and the turntable line is in the centre.

*J. F. Mallon*

started to recover the former 'down' main line to Alnwick between the ½ mile and 2 ¼ mileposts. In January 1967, a contractor was engaged on removing redundant signal gantries, the turntable, and the water tank at Alnwick.

A strange accident occurred on the evening of 11th November 1898 when, due to an error by the Alnwick signalman and the careless misreading of signals by the driver, the 8.50p.m. from Alnwick to Alnmouth departed on the wrong line, running on the 'down' line instead of the 'up'. After leaving Alnwick the line dropped at 1 in 77 for 1½ miles and, to provide for any runaway wagons breaking away and running back from trains travelling towards Alnwick, catch points were installed on the 'down' line. The train was headed by Class A 2-4-2T No. 187 and, as it travelled towards Alnmouth, the driver and fireman were unaware that they were running on the wrong line, until the engine, running bunker first, was derailed at the catch points. It turned on its side and the driver fell on top of the fireman, who was sweeping the cab floor at the time! Fortunately neither was injured. The engine suffered only minor damage to the fittings on its left-hand side, and the green paintwork was defaced. The leading coach also turned over on to its side and the next three coaches were derailed. There were few passengers in the train and only one complained of injury, but the guard was 'hurt on the head'.

One of the most notable regular visitors to Alnwick in the 1920s and 1930s was Class D17/1 4-4-0 No. 1621, which took part in the 1895 'Races to Aberdeen'. It was stationed at Alnmouth from 1927 until it was withdrawn in July 1945. It can now be seen in the National Railway Museum, York in all the glory of its NER green livery.

*Author's Collection*

*Delivery Services*
In horse and cart days, Alnwick had three horse-drawn rulleys and rulleymen; Messrs Hood, Sproat and Wilson. By 1953, the cartage and delivery work was undertaken by six motor vehicles:

| Fleet No. | Regn. No. | Type | Driver | Note |
|---|---|---|---|---|
| WR7193 | HDN 57 | 5 ton Bedford | R. J. Purvis | 1 |
| EF2125 | DVY 474 | 1 ton Commer van | R. E. Hall | 2 |
| EF2168 | EVY 787 | 1 ton Commer van | G. R. Mason | 3 |
| HD6299 | EGT 857 | 3 ton mechanical horse | F. A. Clegg | 4 |
| KA6146 | EVY 756 | 3 ton Karrier Bantam | W. B. Charlton | 5 |
| KE6116 | GDN 327 | 3 ton Karrier Bantam | A. Rough | 6 |

*Notes:*

1: West goods and parcels. A trestle for overhanging loads of steel for Alnwick Foundry was used with No. WR 7193. This was kept beside the yard crane in Alnwick goods yard when not in use.

2: No. EF2125 was used on the mail service to Wooler and also carried newspapers. On return it delivered Alnwick local parcels.

3: No. EF2168 was used on Amble parcels (loaded at Acklington).

4: No. HD6299 was used on Alnwick goods traffic.

5: No. KA6146 delivered Shilbottle, Warkworth and Alnmouth goods and parcels, and Amble goods traffic.

6: No. KE6116 delivered goods and parcels to Longhoughton, Little Mill and Christon Bank stations, and generally east of the A1 road.

About 1930, a garage was provided for the motor vehicle used on the Wooler mail run, to ensure the vehicle could be started in winter! This later housed No. EF2125. A hand pump for petrol was provided adjacent to this garage, which was situated between the stables and Silcock's warehouse.

*Closure*
On 1st March 1966, the North Eastern Region announced that it was proposing to close Alnwick Station and to withdraw the passenger service to Alnmouth and Newcastle from 6th June 1966. In the formal notice, it was pointed out that alternative local bus services were available, including United Automobile Service's buses between Ashington—Amble—Alnwick, Alnwick—Bamburgh—Belford and Alnwick—Chathill—Seahouses. In addition, there was the joint United/Scottish Omnibuses services between Newcastle—Morpeth—Alnwick—Berwick—Edinburgh. As a sop to protesting passengers, additional buses were proposed between Alnwick and Alnmouth stations:

Cowans, Sheldon 50ft. turntable and parachute water tank in the restricted space between the Coldstream and Alnmouth lines. Cattle wagons stand in the sidings to the right.

*P. B. Booth*

Class D20 No. 62383 is turned on the turntable in June 1953.

*J. F. Mallon*

In the course of transfer between nearby collieries, NCB 0-4-0ST *Bella* was allowed to run from Alnmouth to Alnwick and back on 7th September 1953 to use the turntable. This was necessary because at its new home the engine was required to work the opposite way round.

*J. F. Mallon*

*Monday to Saturday:* A morning bus from Alnwick to connect into a commuter train to Newcastle, and an evening bus from Alnwick to connect into a train to Berwick; two evening buses from Alnmouth each connecting out of a commuter train from Newcastle.

*Saturdays only:* A lunch time bus from Alnwick to connect into trains to Berwick, and a lunch time bus from Alnmouth to connect out of a train from Newcastle.

Objections to the proposals were submitted, but after recommendations from the North Eastern Area Transport Users' Consultative Committee, the Minister of Transport (Mrs Barbara Castle) on 28th September 1967 gave her consent to the withdrawal of the Alnwick to Alnmouth service, but not until the proposed additional bus service had been authorised and implemented. On

18th January 1968, the Eastern Region announced that the passenger service would cease from 29th January 1968. The goods service continued until 7th October 1968.

Nearly forty years earlier, the Alnwick to Coldstream passenger service was withdrawn by the LNER. This was because of the decline in passengers and trains last ran on 22nd September 1930. The Coldstream line, through the heart of rural Northumberland, had opened on 5th September 1887, at the same time as Alnwick Station, but it had little prospect of ever paying its way or even recouping the initial cost.

Following the withdrawal of the goods traffic on 7th November 1968, the coal cells and weigh cabin were demolished and a large modern style warehouse has been built on to the outer wall of the 1887 station. This was followed in December 1975 by the removal of the remaining buildings from the 1850 station, which had survived in the yard.

A most surprising engine to work a three mile long branch would be a massive 2-10-0 locomotive; but that is what actually worked the last steam service between Alnmouth and Alnwick on 18th June 1966. The engine was No. 92099, specially cleaned for the occasion and seen here entering platform 2 at Alnwick.

*E. E. Smith*

# Notes on the Drawings — ALNWICK

### General

Due to the size and detail of this station, eleven sheets have been considered necessary to illustrate the various features. In addition, the retention of the 1850 passenger station building as a goods warehouse has been thought worthy of full coverage, together with the original goods shed (also circa 1850), and the second signal box opened with the new station in 1887. The stationmaster's house has also warranted a sheet of its own.

### Station *(Drawings 1 to 5)*

The 1887 station was built to the designs of the NER architect, William Bell. The roof comprised two 38ft. 10in. spans and a central 17ft. 3in. span. The station offices were grouped on each side of the entrance, and the passenger facilities were provided in a range of central buildings. The roof lights commenced at one bay from the open end of the station on all three spans, and the crown of the roofs on that bay were covered with lead sheet. The roof light on the centre span was interrupted by the pitched roof of the platform buildings. At the north end, the roof lights were closed by matching stonework but, at the south end, because of their position, wood sufficed.

The station underwent very little alteration in its eighty one years of railway use. The timber refreshment room was added some ten years after the opening of the station, and newspaper kiosk and a ticket collectors' cabin (latterly used by cleaners) were added soon after. The original drawing shows the end screens extending to 6ft. from the platform edge, with two 2ft. 6in. wide by 8ft. high doors in the middle of the small centre span screen. However, a photograph taken at the opening of the station shows that the screens were built to a modified design with nearly 8ft. clearance to the platform edge, retaining the doors but with a changed arrangement of glazing bars. In the drawings, the end screens are shown in their final condition, giving more than the 10ft. clearance to the platform edge required by Board of Trade standards.

The offices underwent some minor alterations and, in 1938, as an economy measure, the booking office was transferred across the entrance passage and combined with the parcels office. The vacated room was later used as the station bookstall and a door replaced a window in the front elevation to provide access from outside the station.

## ALNWICK STATION PLAN 1888–1938
### HALF SCALE

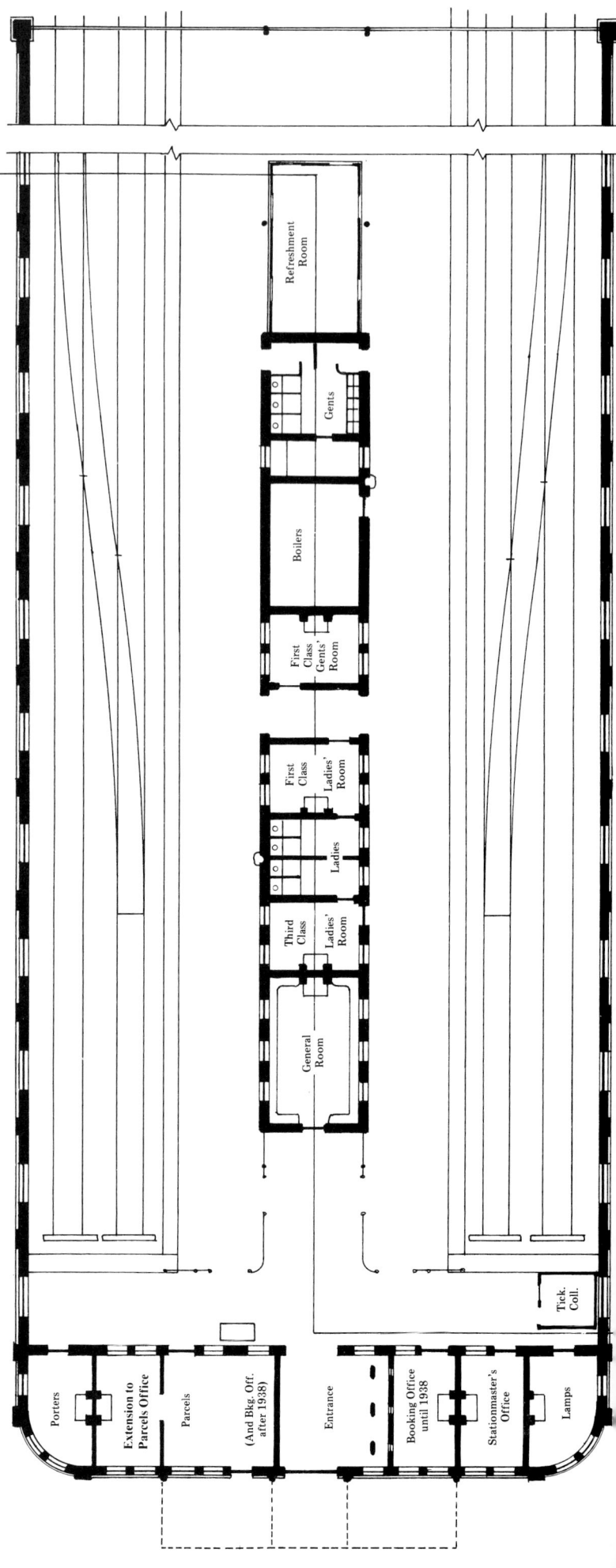

24                                   *Fig. 1*

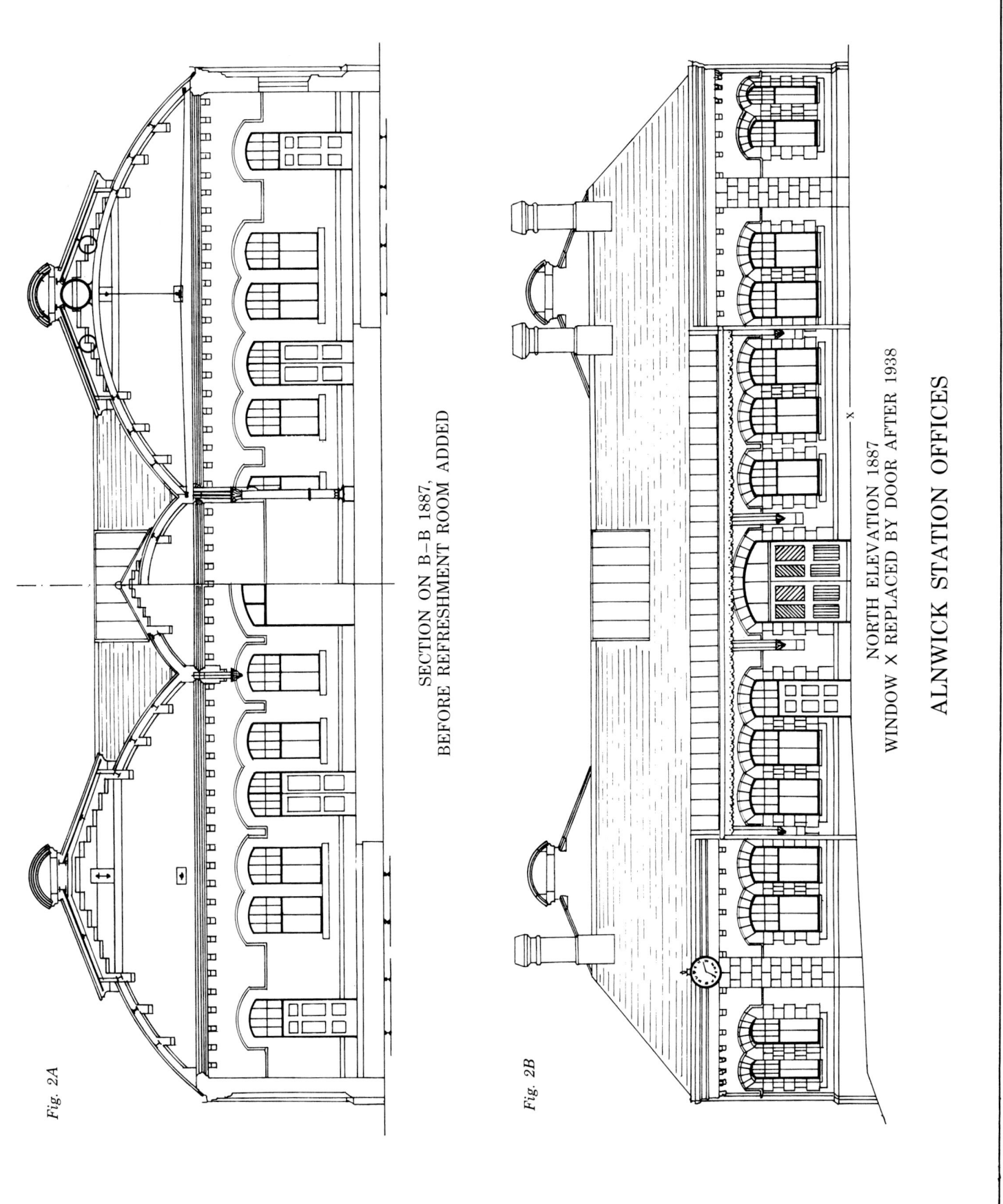

*Fig. 2A*

SECTION ON B–B 1887,
BEFORE REFRESHMENT ROOM ADDED

*Fig. 2B*

NORTH ELEVATION 1887
WINDOW X REPLACED BY DOOR AFTER 1938

ALNWICK STATION OFFICES

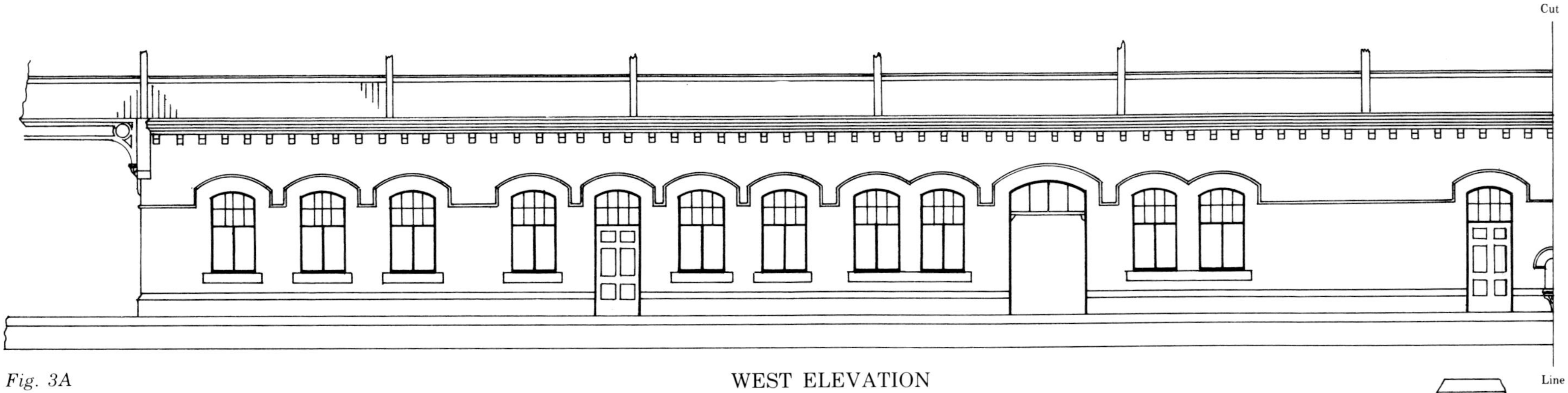

WEST ELEVATION

*Fig. 3A*

Cut

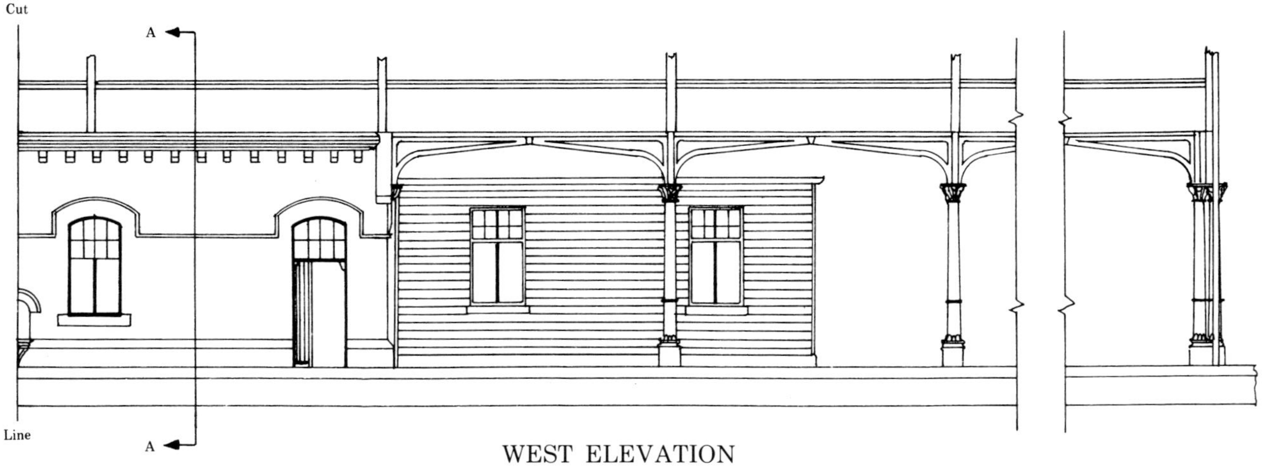

Line

WEST ELEVATION

A

A

Cut

Line

*Fig. 3B*

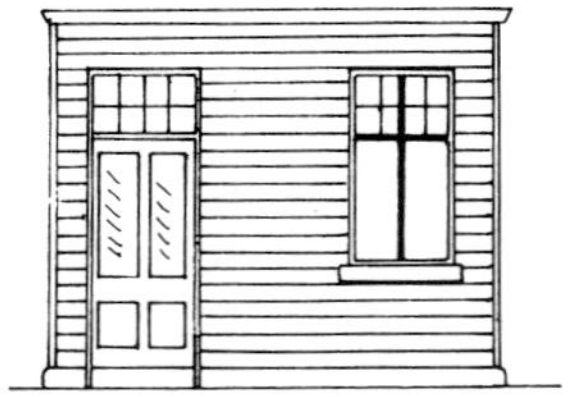

END ELEVATION OF
REFRESHMENT ROOM

*Fig. 3C*

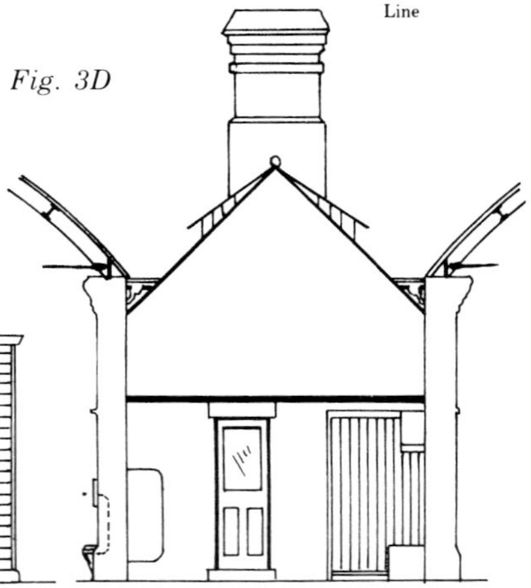

SECTION A–A

*Fig. 3D*

ALNWICK STATION PLATFORM BUILDINGS

*Fig. 4A*

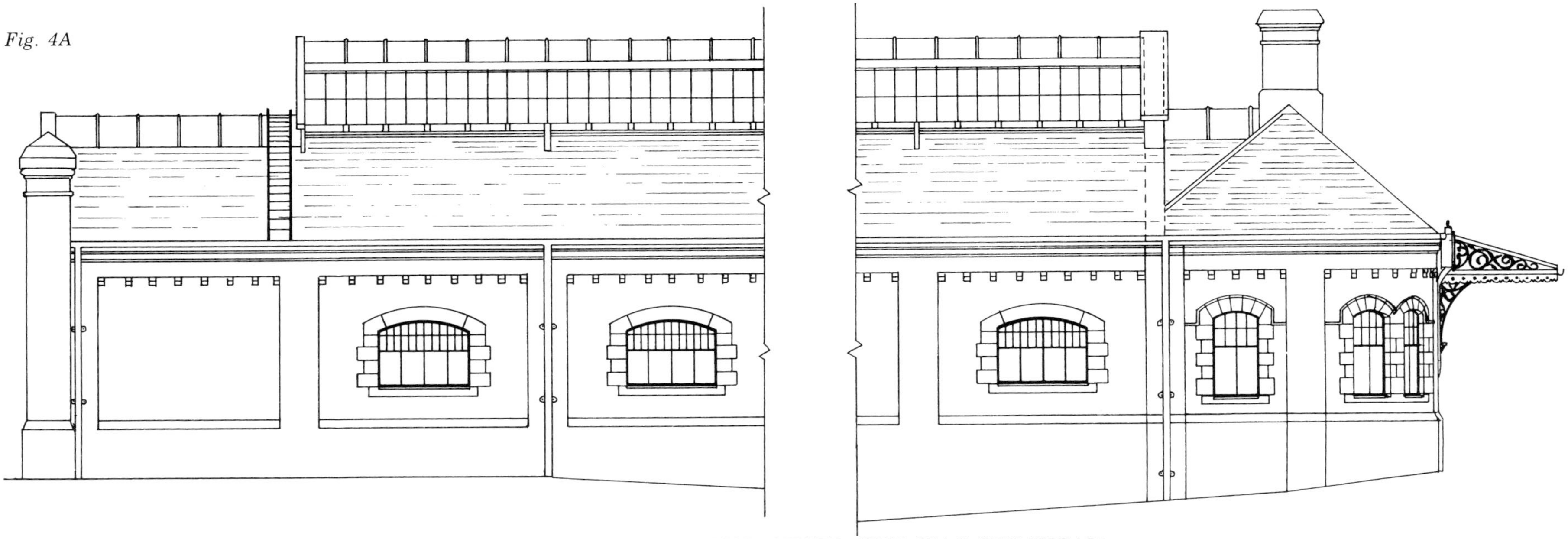

EAST SIDE ELEVATION (OTHER SIDE WAS IDENTICAL)
(NO KNOWN ALTERATION TO THIS VIEW)

ALNWICK 1887

The station after closure, with ramps to the former platforms to give access
to the storage area under the 1887 roof.

*J. F. Mallon*

Fig. 5A

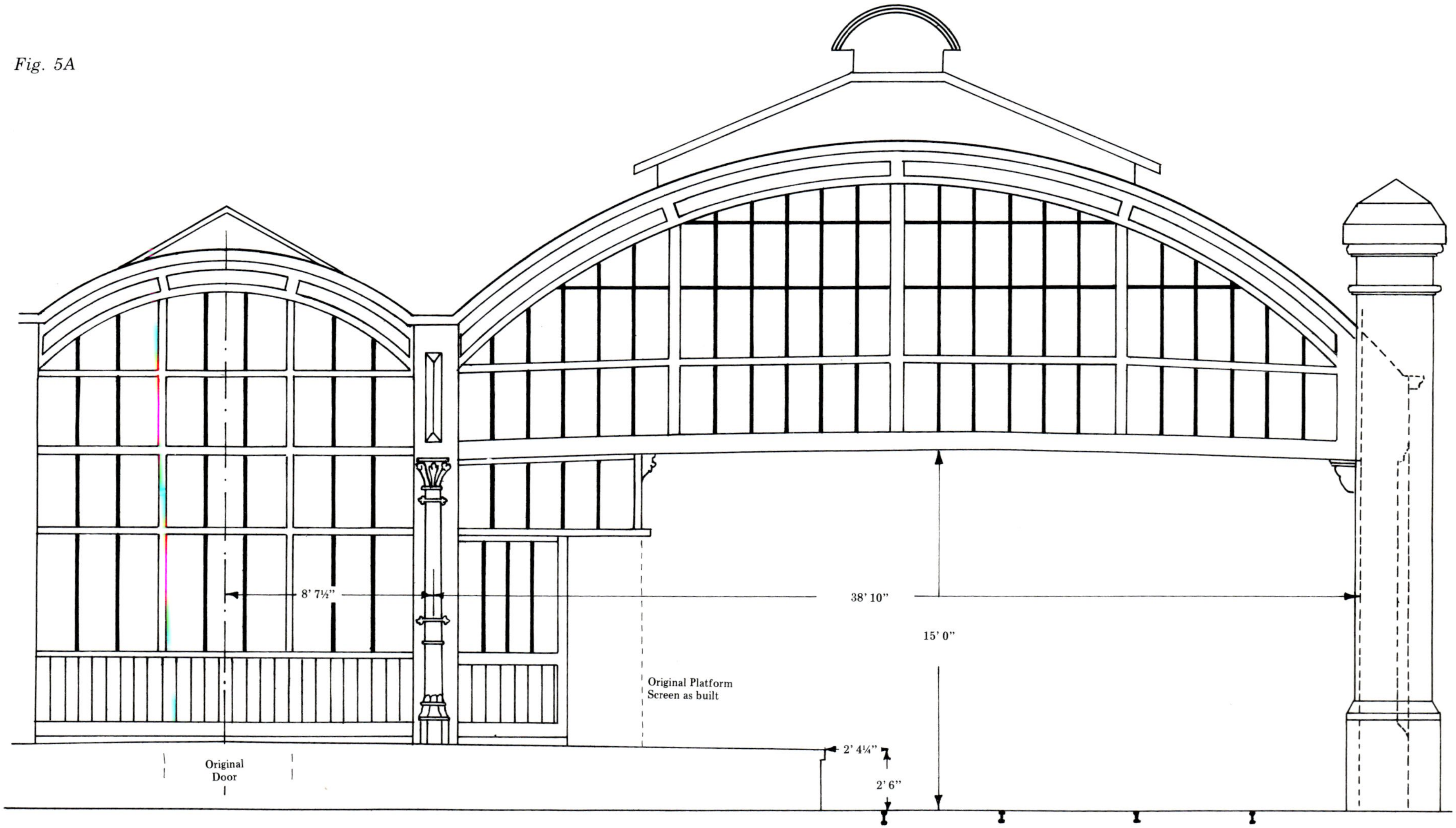

8' 7½"

Original
Door

Original Platform
Screen as built

38' 10"

15' 0"

2' 4¼"

2' 6"

FINAL END ELEVATION
(Twice Scale)

ALNWICK STATION

Fig. 6C

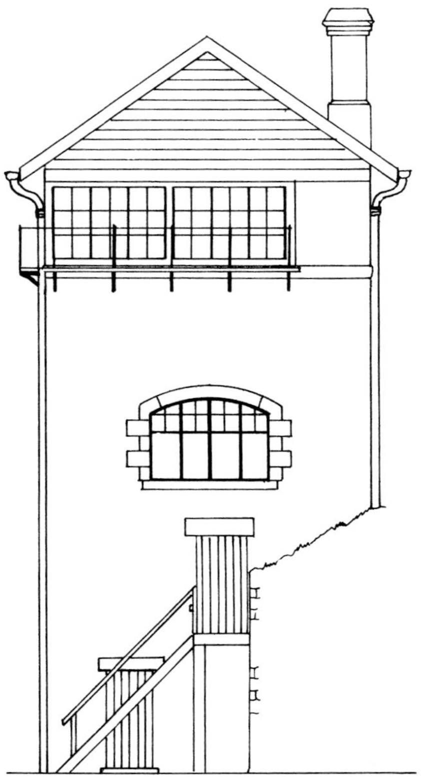

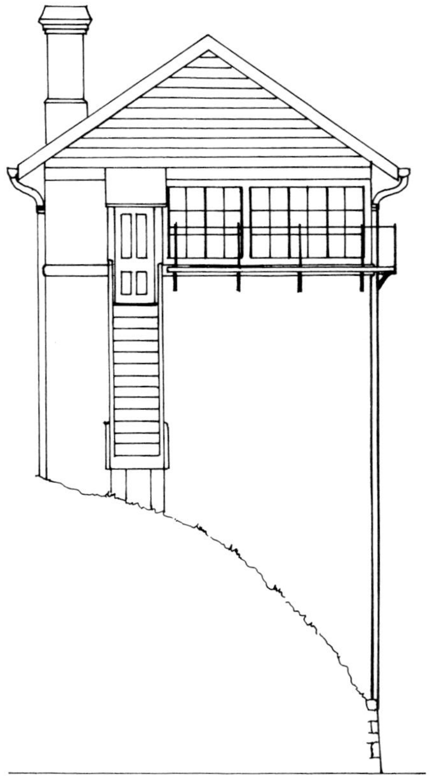

Fig. 6B

Fig. 6A

SOUTH END ELEVATION

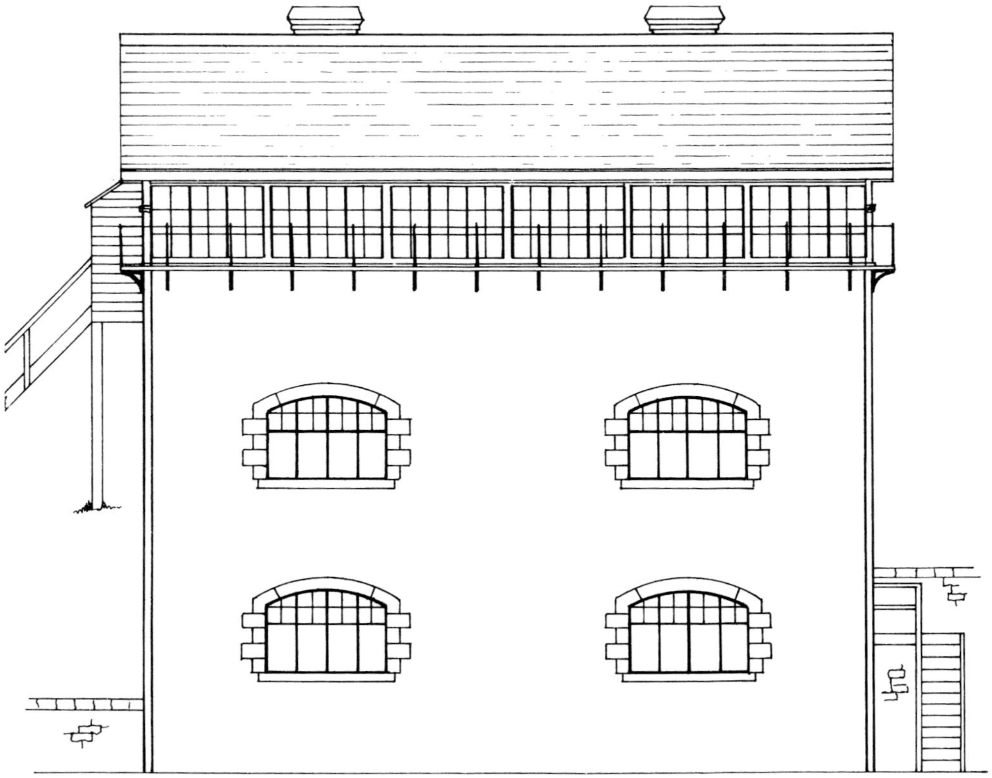

FRONT ELEVATION

NORTH END ELEVATION

ALNWICK SIGNALBOX 1887

**Signal box** (*Drawing 6*)
This three storey structure, built in stone, was built so that the signalmen could have a good view of approaching and departing trains over the nearby road bridge. Originally, access to the working floor was gained by internal stairways, but at a later (unknown) date, a short flight of steps from the south end of the box gave access to a wooden gangway to the road.

Also under the control of the Alnwick stationmaster was Alnwick East box, renamed from Shilbottle Colliery Junction in 1923, and photographed in September 1956. The box controlled the siding serving Alnwick gasworks (under an Agreement dating from 1881) and a 1927 siding for the Co-operative Wholesale Society which were both situated on the 'down' side (left). On the 'up' side (right), an old established siding was provided for the Shilbottle Colliery Company, but in 1925 this was taken over by the Anglo-American Oil Company.

*J. F. Mallon*

The interior of Alnwick box in 1956.

*J. F. Mallon*

**Goods sheds and stables** *(Drawings 7 to 10)*

The original shed probably dates back to the opening of the Alnmouth to Alnwick branch in 1850, and it is shown in a side view in its 1888 condition *(Fig. 10a)* and in end views *(Figs. 9a & 9b)* in its final condition. The stable and the offices may have been added after 1850. At first, the only access to the office was by means of a sliding door from the warehouse, but in 1914 it was altered to have an outside door at the north corner. This displaced the fireplace to the centre of the east wall and, in turn, required the window to be replaced by two smaller windows. By 1938, the former south end stable had been extended to the full size of the main warehouse, but the west wall was of timber construction only.

In 1888, anticipating the increased goods traffic likely to be generated by the new Alnwick to Coldstream branch, the original 1850 passenger station was converted into a warehouse. The building was gutted, the front door was widened, the roof was strengthened to take a 2 ton crane, the two doors on to the platform were blocked, and the end walls were pierced to accommodate the through siding.

At the same time a stable block was added, linked to the original building by a mash house *(Figs. 7a & 7b)*. The original drawings meticulously detail the quoins on the old building, but show none on the new stables, so it may have been intended to build them in brick. By 1938, the original station building had been demolished and the mash room upgraded to a mess room. A motor garage and Silcock's trader's store were built partly on its site, and the siding was shortened by approximatey 60ft.

A view looking south-east in the goods yard, with the old station building in use as a goods warehouse in the centre and the 1888 stables on the left. The original goods shed is seen on the right. About 1930, the old station building was demolished and a motor garage was erected on the site to accommodate the vehicle used on the Wooler mail run, with a petrol tank and pump nearby. At a later date, a prefabricated warehouse for Messrs Silcocks was erected to the south, followed in 1954 by a similar store from Messrs Bibby.

*J. F. Mallon Collection*

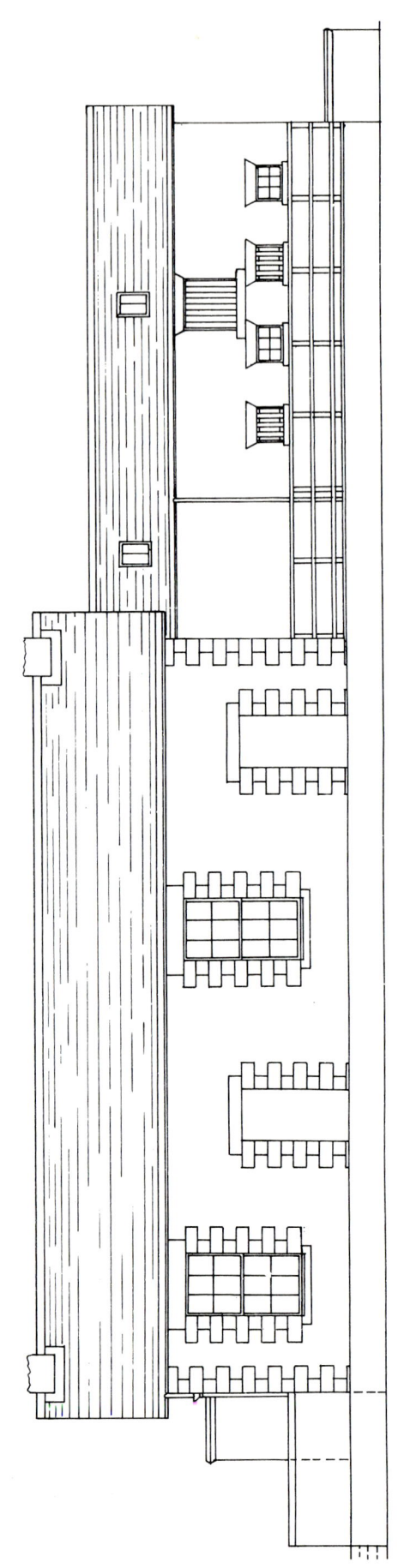

Fig. 7A

1888 STABLES AND MASH HOUSE          ORIGINAL 1850 STATION CONVERTED TO WAREHOUSE

FRONT ELEVATION

Fig. 7B

PLATFORM ELEVATION OF 1850 STATION AND
1888 STABLES

ALNWICK

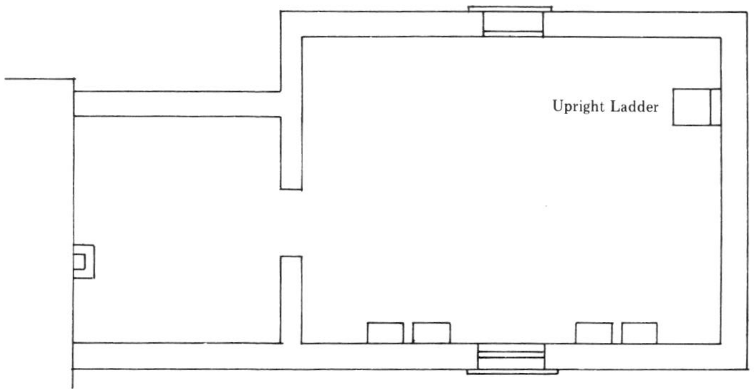

PLAN OF HAYLOFT ABOVE STABLES

Upright Ladder

Fig. 8B

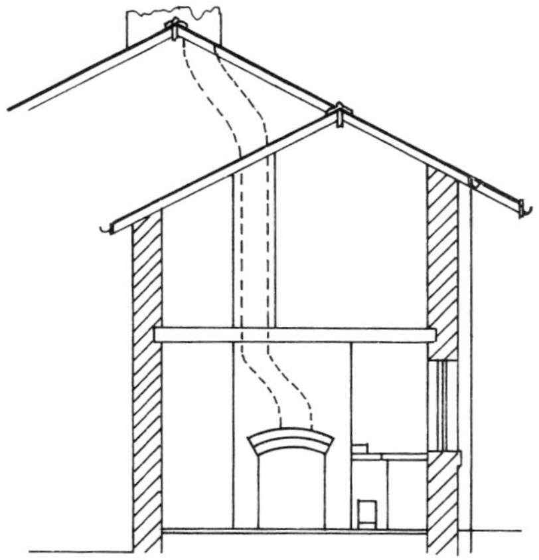

SECTION OF MASH HOUSE

Fig. 8A

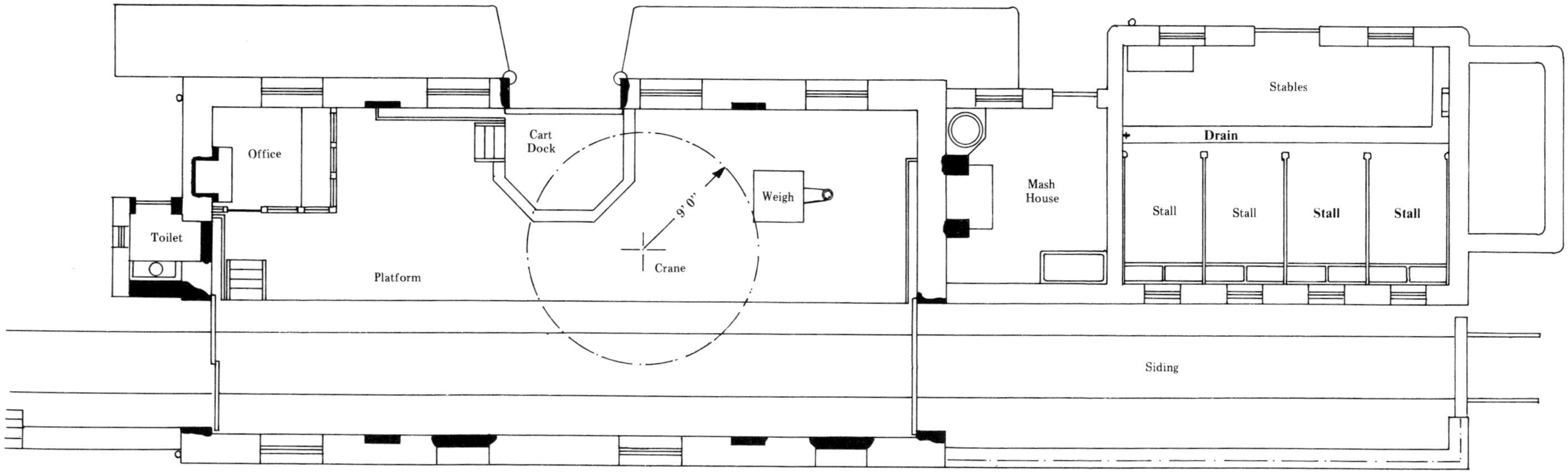

GROUND PLAN OF CONVERTED STATION AND
1888 STABLES AND MASH HOUSE

ALNWICK

Stables

Stall

Stall

**Stall**

Stall

**Stall**

**Drain**

Siding

Mash House

Weigh

Crane

0.6

Cart Dock

Platform

Office

Toilet

Fig. 8C

Looking in the opposite direction, Stationmaster Carlisle and the goods staff stand outside the 1850 warehouse, seen on the left, circa 1906. The rear of the stationmaster's house is in the background, with the 1888 stables on the right.

*J. F. Mallon Collection*

The north-west end of the warehouse, and the goods office.

*C. B. Foster*

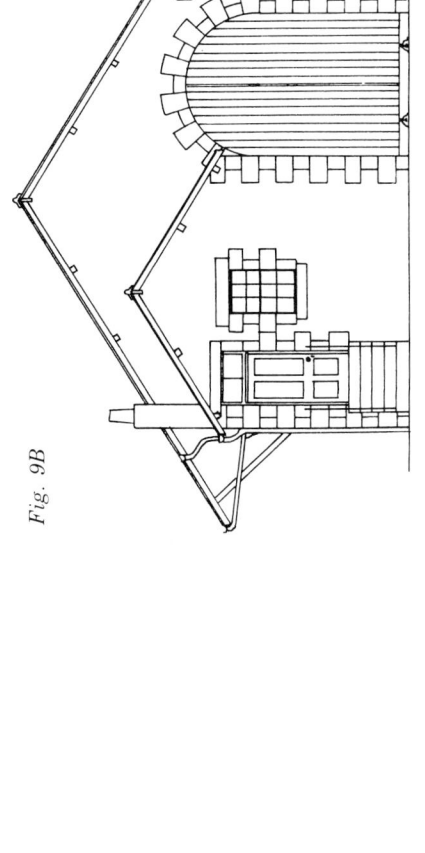

Fig. 9A

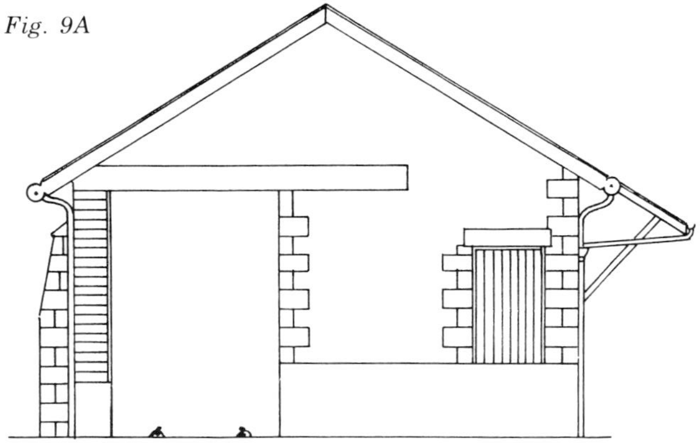

FINAL SOUTH ELEVATION OF
ORIGINAL WAREHOUSE

Fig. 9B

FINAL NORTH ELEVATION OF
ORIGINAL WAREHOUSE

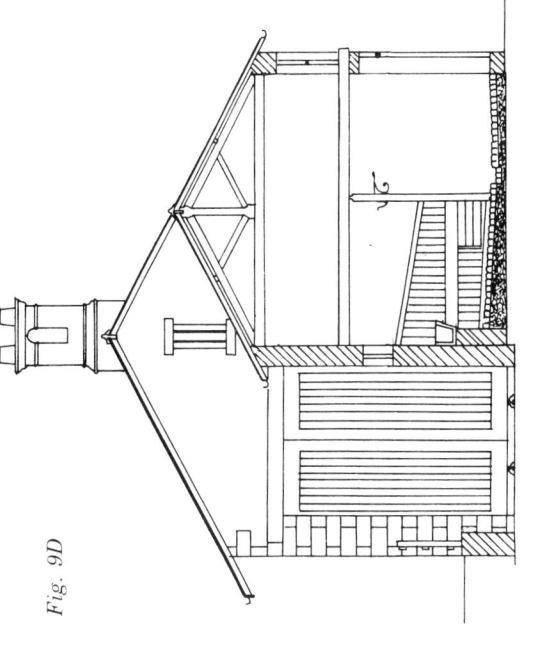

Fig. 9C

Office
(No details)

SECTION OF OLD STATION AFTER
CONVERSION TO WAREHOUSE

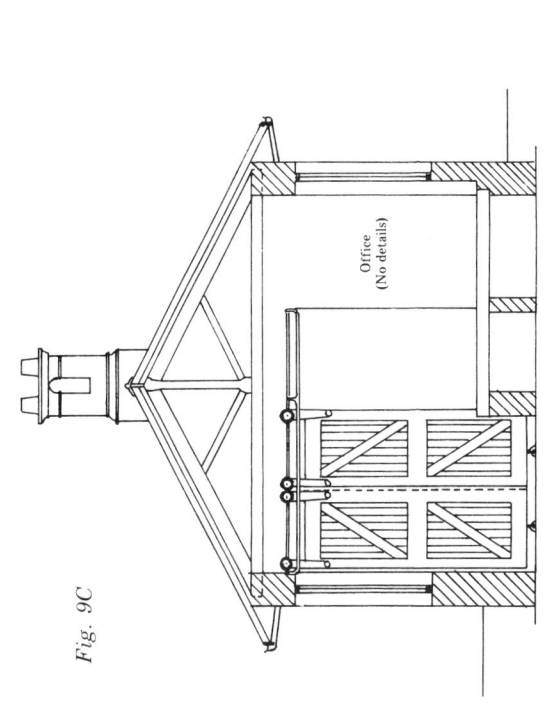

Fig. 9D

SECTION OF 1888 STABLES

ALNWICK

A van body used as a store, with the goods office in the background. The large privately-owned granary is seen on the right.
*M. Ridley*

The former goods office and warehouse after closure of the station. Part of this building has been re-erected at Beamish Open Air Museum.

*J. F. Mallon*

The south-east end of the warehouse, with two yard cranes in the foreground. Bibby's prefabricated store is seen on the right, and beyond is the gable end of the stable block.
*C. B. Foster*

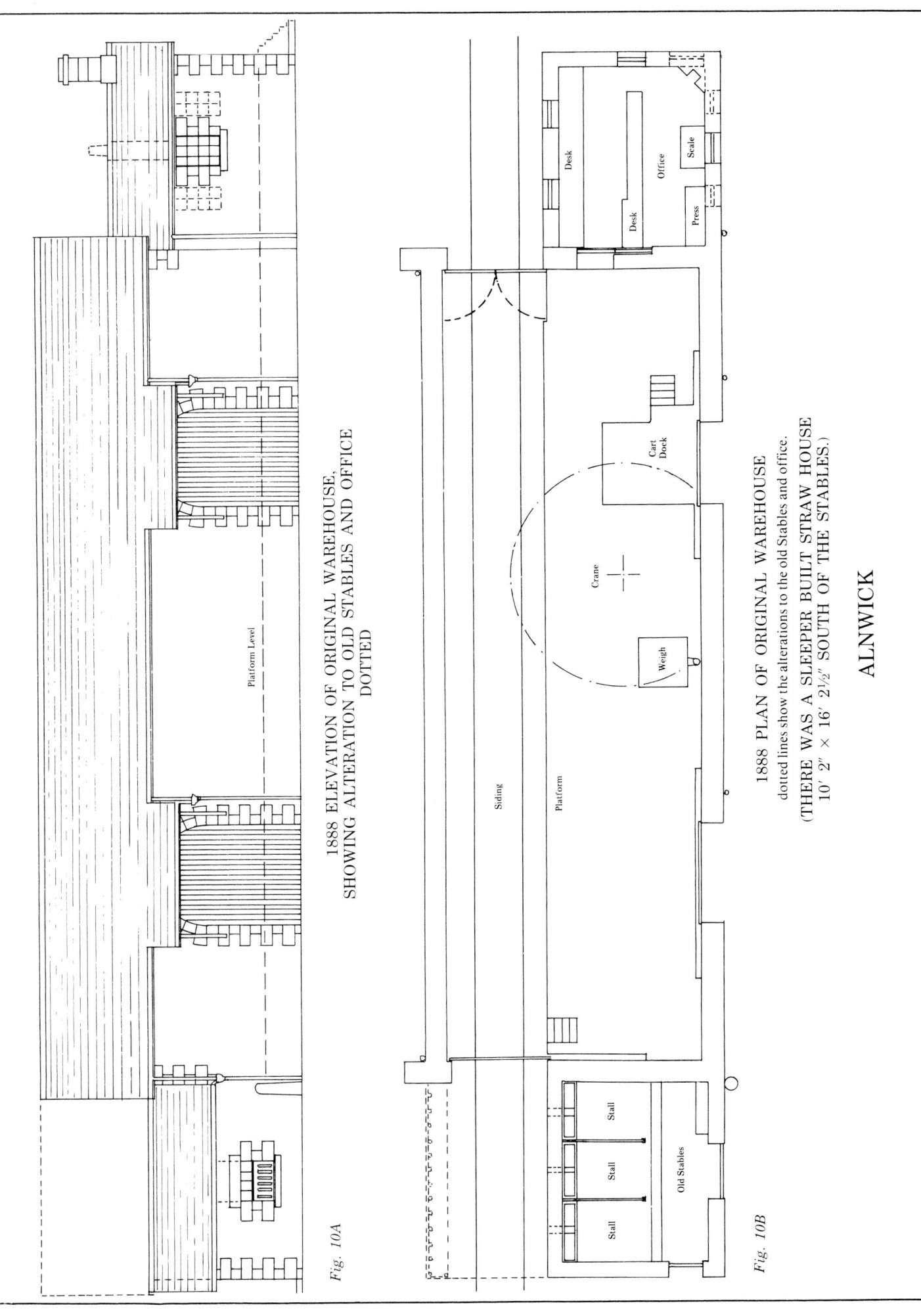

Platform Level

*Fig. 10A*

1888 ELEVATION OF ORIGINAL WAREHOUSE,
SHOWING ALTERATION TO OLD STABLES AND OFFICE
DOTTED

Desk

Desk

Office

Scale

Press

Cart Dock

Crane

Weigh

Siding

Platform

Stall

Stall

Stall

Old Stables

*Fig. 10B*

1888 PLAN OF ORIGINAL WAREHOUSE
dotted lines show the alterations to the old Stables and office.
(THERE WAS A SLEEPER BUILT STRAW HOUSE
10′ 2″ × 16′ 2½″ SOUTH OF THE STABLES.)

# ALNWICK

The granary on the west side of the goods yard. The corner of the warehouse is on the extreme right.
*C. B. Foster*

The weigh cabin, with the 1887 signal box in the background.
*C. B. Foster*

The coal depots, and weigh office with enlarged windows. Note that three cells have been extended.
*C. B. Foster*

*(Above):* This 3 ton mechanical horse No. HD6299 (Regn. No. EGT 857), pictured in 1954, was used on local 'smalls' delivery service in Alnwick.

*J. F. Mallon*

*(Left):* The weigh office and an end view of the coal cells.

*C. B. Foster*

(Below): Another Alnwick-based vehicle was 1 ton Commer No. EF 2125 (Regn. No. DVY 474) seen here with Driver R. E. Hall. The day return fare between Alnwick and Newcastle was 5s. 7d. (28p) in 1954, as can be seen on the side of the vehicle.

*J. F. Mallon*

**Stationmaster's house** *(Drawing 11)*
Again, this probably dates from 1850 as it bears a family resemblance to the Tweedmouth to Kelso line buildings which were opened in the previous year. The bathroom was added in 1904 and, at the time of writing, the house survives virtually unchanged. Two other stations in this work had detached stationmasters' dwellings; Whitby and Richmond. Richmond still stands but no drawings are available, and Whitby was demolished to make way for a United bus station.

Three female porters at Alnwick in 1920.

*J. F. Mallon Collection*

Brake composite coach No. 2014 was built in 1909 to Diagram 145 for use between Alnwick and Coldstream, although it was actually plated 'Aln'k & C'hill'. It was 52ft. over headstocks, 8ft. 6in. wide (9ft. over duckets), and seated 8 first class and 40 third class passengers. It was converted for use in an ambulance train supplied to the Government in 1917 and did not return to NER service.

*British Rail*

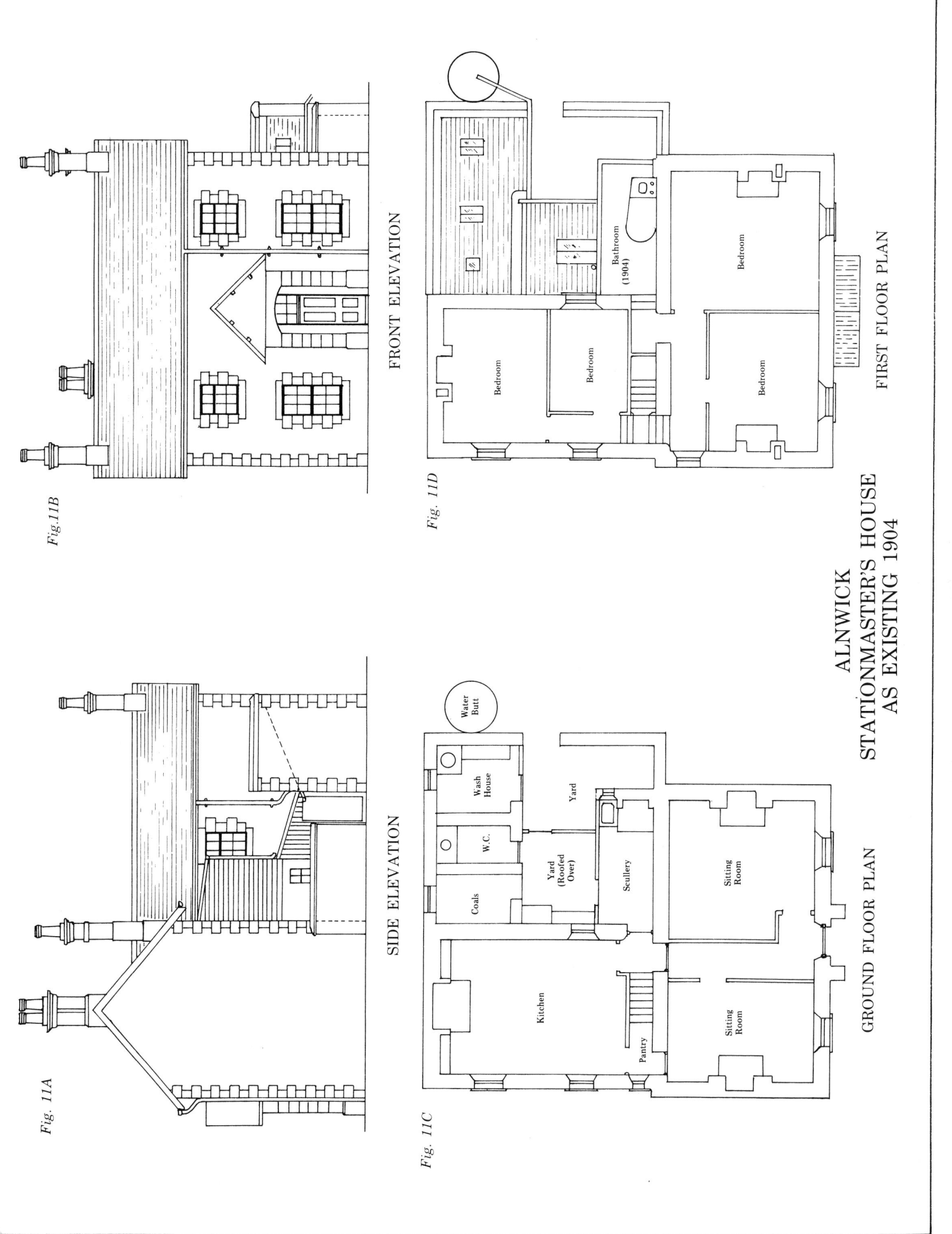

Fig.11B

FRONT ELEVATION

Fig. 11A

SIDE ELEVATION

Fig. 11D

Bathroom
(1904)

Bedroom

Bedroom

Bedroom

Bedroom

FIRST FLOOR PLAN

Fig. 11C

Water
Butt

Wash
House

W.C.

Coals

Yard
(Roofed
Over)

Yard

Scullery

Sitting
Room

Kitchen

Pantry

Sitting
Room

GROUND FLOOR PLAN

ALNWICK
STATIONMASTER'S HOUSE
AS EXISTING 1904

Stationmaster Carlisle (in top hat) and his staff at the front of the station, circa 1900.

*J. F. Mallon Collection*

Stationmaster R. Reid and his staff, circa 1945.

*J. F. Mallon Collection*

# CHAPTER TWO

# Alston

A general view of the station from above the gasworks. This view must have been photographed in the early years of this century as it shows the old signal box which was replaced around 1905. The goods shed had a rooflight in the end, later removed, and the goods office had not yet been added. A goods train has just arrived, and another engine is about to draw off the brake van and wagons prior to placing them in the goods yard. The River South Tyne is seen in the background. Some time later a siding passed under the road from Hexham, shown in the foreground.

*Author's Collection*

The station buildings at Alston were to the design of Benjamin Green, with a train shed 125ft. long and a 34ft. 6in. span, supported by the west wall of the station house and offices on one side and the east wall of the engine shed on the other, although as the engine shed was not as long as the station roof, a plain supporting wall had to be built at the south end. There were two tracks inside the train shed; one serving the platform and the other forming a carriage siding. The station platform was originally 12in. high but it was later raised to 30in., necessitating steps down into the offices lining the platform; a feature to be found at many early North Eastern Railway stations where the original buildings survived.

The original roof was replaced in the 1870s and, at the same time, the springing of the span was raised by 16in., from 12ft. 10in. to 14ft. 2in., the new roof (which remained in use until the 1960s) being of the Mansard pattern. At the same time, the roof was extended 25ft. at the northern end. The cost of these alterations, authorised on 15th May 1872, was £446. 13s. 4d.

The single road engine shed adjoined the station on the west side. Originally, its length was 60ft., with its north end in line with the end of the station roof, but the length of the engine shed was increased by 25ft. to correspond with the lengthening of the train shed. The original shed included an inspection pit, 36ft. long, but this was increased to 70ft. when the shed was extended.

Adjoining the west wall of the engine shed were two buildings, each 17ft. square. That to the south was a store house, with a water tank on top, and that to the north was the smiths' shop. When an additional building was added at the north end to match the extension to the engine shed, this 25ft. long addition became the smiths' shop, and the former shop became a time office and mess room, although it may have had other uses in between. The new smiths' shop had a set of double doors, suitable only for foot traffic, at its north end, with a short siding for coal wagons ending just outside. A standard NER. water column stood between the engine shed road and the coal siding.

43

A view looking past the station buildings towards Haltwhistle, with Alston signal box in the distance. A lean-to building housing a scullery has been added to the end wall of the stationmaster's house. This originally reached only as high as the string course, but it was later raised to the centre of one of the sitting room windows.

*L. Ward*

Early in the century additional accommodation was provided at the north end of the station. A gentlemen's toilet adjoining the booking office (and the full depth of the main building) was added, and beyond that was an entrance to the platform. This was followed by the porters' room-cum-lamp room and a boiler house, probably for foot warmers. Almost immediately, between 1904 and 1908, the open space between the north wall of the gentlemen's toilet and the south wall of the porters' room was converted into the 'gents' so that the former 'gents' could become the new booking office, allowing more office space to be used for parcels. This view shows the old booking office entrance plated for 'PARCELS & ENQUIRIES' (on left) and the open door which gave access to the replacement booking hall, with the porters' room, etc. beyond.

*Author*

The platform line and the engine shed line both ran through their respective buildings to end at a 42ft. 4in. locomotive turntable at the south end of the station platform, which also served a track running round the western extremity of the buildings. This allowed the engine of an incoming train to run round its coaches without removing the coaches from the platform.

The stone-built warehouse, or goods shed, in the yard on the east side of the station, had a hipped roof. One track ran through the building on its west side, and two cart loading bay entrances were in the east wall. A lean-to office was added at the south end in 1866. A wide loading dock with a track on each side was provided between the goods shed and the station platform, with the east side of the dock earmarked for cattle traffic. There was also a track giving end loading facilities.

A bank of sixteen coal cells in two rows of eight was provided in the yard, with a gated entrance on each side. Latterly, each road had a substantial buffer stop at the south end but their designs differed. On the western track the construction was of massive timbers for the uprights and the rear supports, but on the eastern track the uprights were of timber, but the supports were of cast iron, and triangular in shape.

Under an Agreement dated 21st September 1908 between the NER and the Alston Limestone Co., a new siding was constructed. This branched off the track lead-

ing into the goods shed and ran between the shed and the coal cells to the south-east limit of the yard. It then passed under a bridge carrying what is now the A686 road to Hexham and ended at a timber-built bench used for loading the stone from the nearby quarry.

A photograph of the station taken around 1900 shows a gable-ended signal box, but the box that survived until the 1960s was of the standard Northern Division pattern, apparently dating from about 1905. At the end of a short siding terminating on the south side of the box there was, at one time, a shed for a snowplough. The shed was probably of wooden construction and although photographs of the signal box are available, not one shows the snowplough shed. However a number of views do show a plough standing in the open on the site of the shed.

Trap points in the shed line protected the running line near the signal box, and it was here that a mishap occurred in 1920 when an engine, standing at the north end of the shed, set off on its own accord early one morning. The trap points led to the NER boundary alongside the River South Tyne, but the engine was no respecter of property and it went over the boundary, down a low bank and into the river! The engine, BTP 0-4-4T No. 69, was recovered and was noted at Gateshead on 28th June 1920 minus its chimney, and with a badly damaged cab.

The completion of the Newcastle & Carlisle Railway in 1838 gave rise to various schemes for connections,

The south end of the station in August 1951, with the engine shed on the left. Class G5 0-4-4T No. 67315 had just arrived from Haltwhistle but had to back its set out and run round, as the turntable in the foreground was out of use and awaiting removal. Note the lean-to building which was added to the stationmaster's house, with a fire appliance cupboard on the platform wall. The building on the extreme right was a coal store.

*T. J. Edgington*

usually via Alston, to lines further south, and the lead mining activities in the Alston area also demonstrated the need for a railway. Consequently, on 26th August 1846, the Newcastle & Carlisle Railway obtained an Act of Parliament for a branch running south from its main line at Haltwhistle to the market town of Alston, although it had originally been planned to continue further south to Nenthead. A further N&CR Act of 13th July 1849 authorised diversions at six locations on the branch, especially in the first mile south of Haltwhistle, and the line was eventually opened in stages, the date of opening throughout being 17th November 1852. After crossing the River South Tyne, immediately after leaving Haltwhistle, the line remained on the east bank until it crossed to the west bank between Coanwood and Lambley, on the striking Lambley Viaduct. Finally, the line crossed back to the east side of the river ½ mile short of Alston Station and terminated on the north bank of the River Nent, which joins the South Tyne adjacent to the station.

The branch had four intermediate stations and, in addition to the local goods traffic handled at Alston, there were at various times, coal mines and stone quarries along the line, notably at Featherstone Colliery, between Featherstone and Coanwood, who had a Sidings Agreement with the NER dated 18th November 1886. This colliery closed on 26th January 1905, although the north and south ground frames, giving access to both ends of the colliery yard were left in place until 1908.

Coanwood Colliery and coke ovens were situated immediately south of Coanwood Station but, about 1905, appear to have passed into the hands of the Burnhouse Coal Co., which operated the mine as Burnhouse Colliery. Coanwood Whinstone Quarry, ½ mile south of Coanwood Station, had a siding installed in 1891 and worked for about twenty years.

At Lambley, a mile long branch went off to the north to serve Lambley Colliery and Lambley Fell goods depot. This branch also connected with the Brampton (or Kirkhouse) Railway; a private mineral line with numerous branches which ran across the hills to Brampton, 7½ miles away. At Slaggyford there was a siding dating from 1913 serving the Barhaugh Anthracite & Limestone Company's screens and ropeway, but this was closed around 1935.

Approaching Alston, the four sidings on the 'down' side were used by the Alston Lime Co. (W. Benson & Sons), the Alston & Nentforce Quarry Co., and the Vielle Montagne Zinc Co. (1916 to 1922), with spouts and gantries for loading stone, lime and ores into railway wagons.

The traffic from the various collieries and quarries affected the amount of freight and mineral traffic on the branch and, in 1904 for instance, there was a morning pick-up goods from Blaydon to Alston and back, followed by a smiliar train from Carlisle. In addition, there was an 'if required' mineral empties train from Carlisle to Lambley, returning with traffic from Featherstone and Lambley collieries.

In 1909, Plenmeller Collieries Ltd. arranged with the North Eastern Railway for a siding to serve its new pit

The north end of the station with Class G5 No. 67315 ready to depart for Haltwhistle.

*Author's Collection*

After standard BR diesel multiple units had been working the line for six years, it was decided to try 4-wheel rail buses, but they were not a success. No. E79963 was photographed at York Shed in August 1965 on its way to South Gosforth for trials on the Alston branch.

*Author's Collection*

The two Alston engines are seen working the midday train from Haltwhistle to Alston so that the Class J21 0-6-0 could change crews. It spent most of its day shunting at Haltwhistle, until it was transferred to Northallerton at the end of 1948.

*E. E. Smith*

at Plenmeller, ¾ mile south of Haltwhistle, and a dwarf ground frame was installed. This was followed in 1916 by an Agreement covering the working of workmen's trains between Haltwhistle and Alston, specifically referring to a train at 4.45a.m. from Haltwhistle. Next came an Agreement dated 4th June 1919 regarding the erection of a halt near Plenmeller Colliery, and the running of workmen's trains between Alston and the new halt. This had a notable effect on the branch working as it meant that the line had to open around 3a.m. to pass the trains carrying the early shift on duty, and the night-shift off duty and back home to Alston. The service consisted of a train from Alston at 3.05a.m., arriving at Plenmeller Halt at 3.39a.m. The train then ran empty to and from Haltwhistle, picking up the night-shift at the halt at 4a.m., arriving at Alston at 4.34a.m. Because of the night-time activity, three sets of footplatemen were required at Alston shed, each working eight hours and booking on at 2.05a.m., 9.45a.m. and 1.45p.m. Some of the daytime passenger trains called at Plenmeller Halt, but the service was never advertised in the public timetable. The colliery closed in 1931 but the night service had ceased some time before. The colliery reopened in the 1940s, with a ground frame controlling the entrance to reception sidings, but a start on removing the connections was scheduled to take place on 9th August 1965.

*Locomotive and Train Working*

At the Grouping, Alston Shed housed a single Class G5 0-4-4T (No. 2097), but this was soon replaced by Class F8 2-4-2T No. 1599, followed by No. 172 of the same class. A Class G5 returned in September 1925, this time No. 1838, and later the same year the G5 was joined by Class J25 0-6-0 No. 2131 for the goods traffic between Alston and Haltwhistle. In September 1930, No. 1838 was moved to Gateshead and No. 2131 to Borough Gardens, with Class N8 0-6-2T No. 863 being moved from Hartlepool to Alston to handle both the passenger and goods traffic. After less than three years No. 863 was replaced by another Class G5 locomotive, this time No. 1788 from Gateshead, but in January 1936, this engine was moved to Neville Hill and Class J21 0-6-0 No. 51 from Gateshead took its place. The J21 spent more than four years at Alston, shuttling backwards and forwards on the branch, but in May 1940, it was joined by six engines under the Evacuation Scheme, Class G5 locomotive Nos. 1755 from Heaton, 1795 from Gateshead and 2086 from Rothbury; Class D49 4-4-0s Nos. 211 *The York and Ainsty* and 362 *The Goath-*

The north end of the station in LNER days, with the timber coaling stage for the locomotives seen alongside the shed line.

*Author's Collection*

*land*, both from Gateshead, and Class C7 4-4-2 No. 2211 from Heaton.

The two D49 locomotives were moved to Tweedmouth in November 1940 and No. 2211 went to Gateshead at the same time. Two of the G5s, Nos. 1755 and 1795, left in May and June 1941 respectively, leaving Nos. 2086 and 51 to handle the passenger and goods traffic, but because of the war, the shunting work increased to such an extent that additional power was required, and Sentinel locomotive Y1 No. 106 was transferred from Hull to Alston for shunting at Alston and Haltwhistle. Another Class G5, No. 405, replaced the Sentinel in May 1942 but left in January 1943 and, at the same time, Class J21 No. 51 was replaced by No. 1122 of the same class.

For some years, the Alston goods engine spent most of its time shunting at Haltwhistle and at midday, so that the early and late turns crew could change over, it had to return to Alston. For this purpose it was attached to the branch passenger train, giving the unusual sight of a Class J21 piloting a G5, or two J39s, on the two coach branch set.

The J21 No. 1122, by then renumbered 5100, was transferred to Northallerton at the end of 1948 and replaced in January 1949 by J39 No. 64851. This in turn was replaced by another Class J39, No. 64812, four years later. However, after only a few months at Alston, No. 64812 departed, accompanied by Alston's last G5, No. 67315 (formerly 2086), which had been shedded at Alston for 13 years. The two replacement engines were 4MT 2-6-0s Nos.

### Engine Working Alston, — Summer 1908

*Weekdays*

|  | arr. | dep. |
|---|---|---|
|  | a.m. | a.m. |
| Alston | - | 7.15 |
| Haltwhistle | 7.50 | 8.20 |
| Alston | 8.55 | 10.00 |
| Haltwhistle | 10.35 | 11.40 |
|  | p.m. | p.m. |
| Alston | 12.15 | - |
| Alston | - | 2.15 |
| Haltwhistle | 2.50 | 4.15 |
| Alston | 4.50 | 6.30 |
| Haltwhistle | 7.05 | 7.32 |
| Alston | 8.07 | 8.25(SO) |
| Haltwhistle | 9.00 | 9.15(SO) |
| Alston | 9.50 | - |

*Crews change at Alston at 1p.m.*

**Sundays**

|  | a.m. | a.m. |
|---|---|---|
| Alston | - | 7.20 |
| Haltwhistle | 7.55 | 8.50 |
| Alston | 9.25 | - |
|  | p.m. | p.m. |
| Alston | - | 6.20 |
| Haltwhistle | 6.55 | 7.25 |
| Alston | 8.00 | - |

*First set 6.20a.m. to 1p.m.; second set 5.20p.m. to midnight*

### Passenger Engine Working Alston, — Spring 1939

*Saturdays excepted*

|  | a.m. | a.m. |
|---|---|---|
| Shed | — | 6.55 (Light engine) |
| Alston | — | 7.10 |
| Haltwhistle | 7.41 | 8.10 |
| Alston | 8.42 C | 10.15 |
| Haltwhistle | 10.41 S | 11.35 |
|  | p.m. |  |
| Alston | 12.07 | — (Light engine) |
|  |  | p.m. |
| Shed | 12.10 * | 3.40 (Light engine) |
| Alston | — | 3.55 |
| Haltwhistle | 4.26 | 5.05 |
| Alston | 5.37 C | 7.00 |
| Haltwhistle | 7.31 S | 9.10 |
| Alston | 9.42 | — (Light engine) |
| Shed | — | — |

*C = Coal engine   S = Shunt goods yard   * = Change enginemen*
*First set 6.10a.m. to 2.10p.m.; second set 2.55p.m. to 10.55p.m.*

*NOTE:* Carlisle No. 5 engine worked the 1.35p.m. passenger from Haltwhistle to Alston, the 2.30p.m. Class D goods from Alston to Haltwhistle, the 6.20p.m. passenger from Haltwhistle to Alston, and the 8.20p.m. passenger from Alston to Haltwhistle. Carlisle No. 7 engine worked the 9.45a.m. Class D goods from Haltwhistle to Alston and the 12.35p.m. passenger from Alston to Haltwhistle.

### Passenger Engine Working Alston, — Summer 1948

*Weekdays*

Alston No. 1 Passenger. (Class G5 engine)

|  | a.m. | a.m. |
|---|---|---|
| Shed | — | 5.10 (Light engine) |
| Alston | — | 5.25 |
| Haltwhistle | 6.00 | 6.18 |
| Alston | 6.53 | 7.12 (Assisted) |
| Haltwhistle | 7.47 S | 9.45 |
| Alston | 10.20 | 10.50 |
| Haltwhistle | 11.25 | 11.45 (Assisted) |
|  | p.m. | p.m. |
| Alston | 12.20 * | 2.00 |
| Haltwhistle | 2.35 S | 3.25 |
| Alston | 4.00 | 4.20 |
| Haltwhistle | 4.55 | 5.40 |
| Alston | 6.15 | 6.50 |
| Haltwhistle | 7.25 | 8.10 |
| Alston | 8.45 S | — (Light engine) |
| Shed | 9.05 | — |

*S = Shunt as required   * = Change enginemen*
*First set 4.25a.m. to 12.35p.m.; second set 1.35p.m. to 10.15p.m.*

Alston No. 1 Goods. (Class J21 engine)

|  | a.m. | a.m. |
|---|---|---|
| Shed | — | 7.02 (Light engine) |
| Alston | — | 7.12 (Assist above) |
| Haltwhistle | 7.47 | 8.00 |
| Alston | 8.35 | 8.50 |
| Haltwhistle | 9.25 S | 11.45 (Assist above) |
|  | p.m. |  |
| Alston | 12.20 S* | — |
| Alston | — | — (Goods) |
| Haltwhistle | — | — (Goods) |
| Alston | — | — (Light engine) |
| Shed | — | — |

*S = Shunt as required   * = Change enginemen*
*First set 6a.m. to 2p.m.; second set 12.10p.m. to 8.10p.m.*

43126 and 43128, but No. 43126 was replaced by the BR version, No. 76024, in April 1954. Both Nos. 43128 and 76024 were moved away in 1955 and yet another class arrived at Alston for the branch service. This was 3MT 2-6-0 No. 77011 and it remained at Alston until the shed closed on 27th September 1959.

This short review of the engines at Alston deals only with those actually stationed there on a permanent basis. Obviously for repairs and overhaul these engines were absent for various periods and usually another engine of the same class was borrowed, so that there are photographs of other engines working the branch.

After steam locomotives had disappeared from the branch passenger trains, the service was provided by diesel multiple units based at South Gosforth, but during the summer of 1965, railbuses Nos. E79963 and E79964 were tried on the branch, having been obtained on loan from Cambridge.

*The Long Delayed Closure*

The first proposals to close the Alston branch were made in the late 1950s and, on 9th December 1959, the North Eastern Transport Users' Consultative Committee reported that after representations had been made about the unsuitability of the roads in the area, British Rail had agreed to keep the line open. There was no direct road from Alston to Haltwhistle. Again, on 19th June 1962, the North Eastern TUCC recommended to the Central TUCC that withdrawal of the Haltwhistle to Alston service would result in undue hardship, and again the unsuitability of the roads was given as one of the main reasons.

In March 1963, Dr Beechings's massive list of closures was issued, but on 24th July 1963 Mr Ernest Marples, then Minister of Transport, announced that after studying all the circumstances he had decided to accept the recommendations of the North Eastern and Central TUCC that the Alston branch should not be closed. Closure was proposed yet again in 1970 and in 1973 consent was given but with the stipulation that the line should remain open until May 1975 to allow road improvements to be carried out. In the notice of consent, it was pointed out that the 1972 grant for the line was £77,000 and the receipts for the year were £4,000, an annual deficit of £73,000!

Finally, on 22nd March 1976, British Rail announced that the line would close on 3rd May 1976, with the last trains running on Saturday 1st May. This turned out to be an extremely wet, windy and cold day, but many enthusiasts turned up at Alston to pay their last respects to this line which had been many years in passing. The new road was formally opened by Viscount Ridley on the following Monday, 3rd May.

Following the withdrawal of goods facilities on 6th September 1965, the layout at Alston was reduced. In October of that year, contractors were demolishing the engine shed and in the following month a start was made on removing the loading dock sidings.

In 1966, alterations were made to the level crossings on the branch, at Featherstone Park and Slaggyford, making them into open crossings without signals or gates, suitable for 'one engine in steam' working, which replaced the electric token working in October. From the same date, the signal boxes at Lambley and Alston were closed.

## Notes on the Drawings — ALSTON

### General

If the station was built in accordance with the drawing then the east elevation remains virtually unchanged, b the west underwent considerable rebuilding due to (a) t raising of the platform level by 1ft. 6in. and (b) t reconstruction of the station roof. The lifting of the pla form to 2ft. 6in. above rail level required the doorwa and the large bay window to be rebuilt to new levels, a steps to be provided down into the rooms leading off t platform.

### Station (Drawings 1 to 3)

The 1851 drawings indicate that the station roof w supported beside the station buildings by only a 3½i projection of the masonry string course and, if it was bu in that way, it is not surprising that it survived for on twenty years. The roof was reconstructed and extend northwards by 25ft. (making it 150ft.), with the arch ri adjacent to the house built into the first floor wall abo the string course level. This must have required the lar windows (matching those in the east elevation) to blocked up.

The first roof cladding followed the 22ft. 6in. radius the arch ribs, but during reconstruction it was design to follow a Mansard shape. It is probable that the 18 roof did not have an end screen at the north end. All liable evidence suggests that the top of the string cour was built at 12ft. 4in. above rail level, although it w quoted as 12ft. 10in. on the 1851 drawings. The 18 drawing for the new end screen assumed that the heig from platform level was 12ft. 10in. and another 12 were added to give the height above rail level, making total dimension of 13ft. 10in. The designer then added camber of 4in. to the end screen to give a theoreti clearance of 14ft. 2in. above the track of the platform li when it was actually 12ft. 8in. *(see Fig. 3a)*.

The reduction from 12ft. 10in. to 12ft. 4in. was n noted on the 1851 drawing, nor is there any indicati on the 1872 drawing as to the modifications required achieve 14ft. 2in. by reducing the depth of the screen. is hoped that the mistake was discovered before the fir locomotive entered the station!

In 1905, a new drawing was prepared entitled 'Alst as at present' and it shows the recently added outbui ings, which consisted of the coal shed and scullery at t south end, and the gents', porters' room, and lamp roc at the north. This drawing, unfortunately, includes a co siderable amount of fiction! The height and shape of t roof and end screens are so incorrect as to suggest th there was a second roof reconstruction, but considerab research indicates that this was not so. Also the numbe and positions of windows vary and these have been c rected as far as possible, with reference to the earli drawings.

Almost immediately after the alterations were co pleted, it was decided to provide a parcels office with the booking office, and the new arrangement effective blocked the east entrance. The position of the entran and the gents' were transposed and a ticket window w provided in the new entrance passage. The drawings sh the final form. Another minor alteration was the raisi of the scullery roof level at the south end of the hou from string course level to half way up the first flo window. The overall roof was removed in the 1960s.

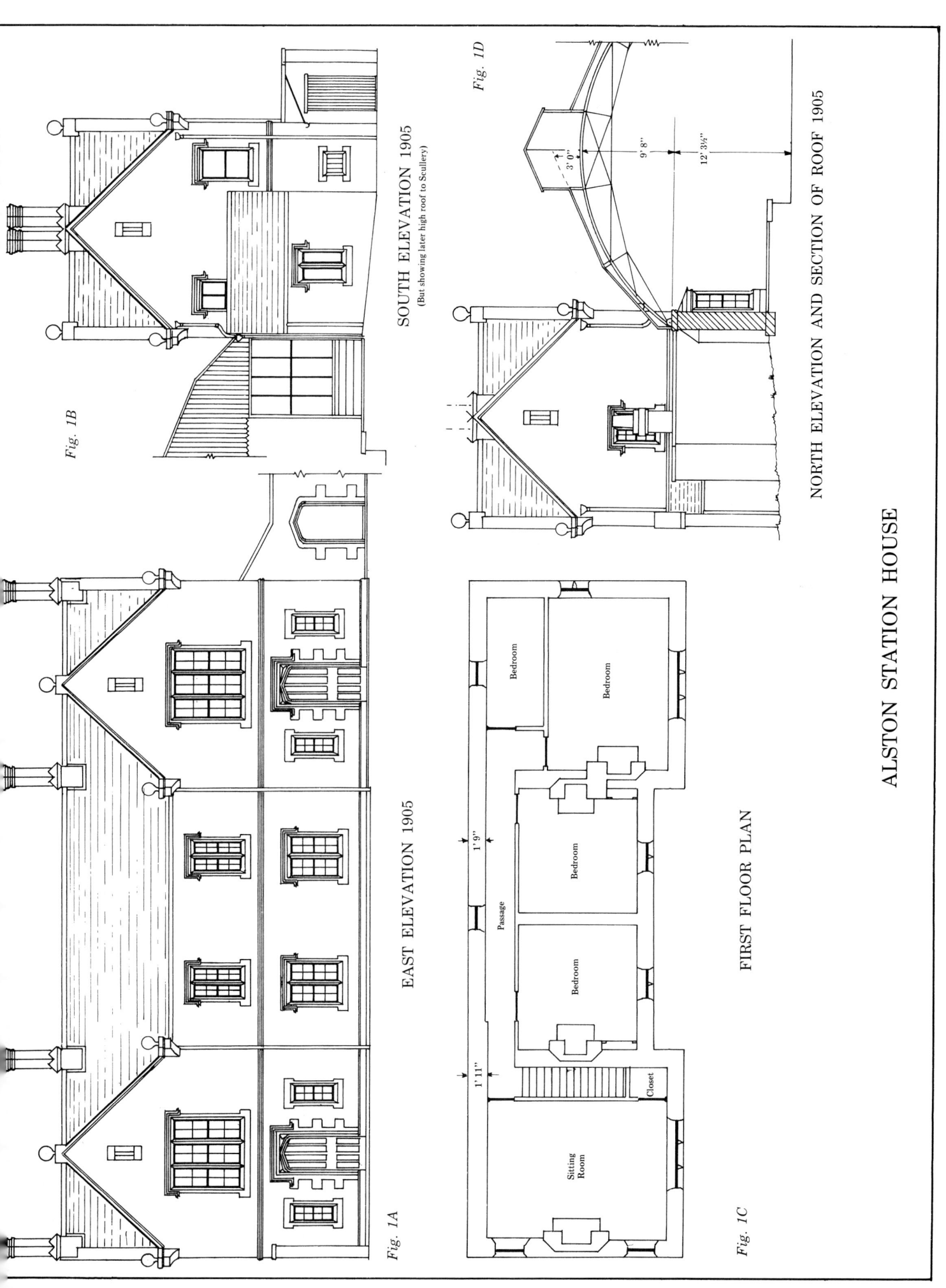

*Fig. 1B*

SOUTH ELEVATION 1905
(But showing later high roof to Scullery)

*Fig. 1A*

EAST ELEVATION 1905

*Fig. 1D*

NORTH ELEVATION AND SECTION OF ROOF 1905

3' 0"

9' 8"

12' 3½"

*Fig. 1C*

FIRST FLOOR PLAN

Bedroom

Bedroom

Bedroom

Passage

1' 9"

Bedroom

1' 11"

Sitting Room

Closet

ALSTON STATION HOUSE

Fig. 2A

WEST (PLATFORM) ELEVATION 1905

(But showing higher Scullery Roof)

37' 0"

Fig. 2B

Meter

W.C.

Pantry

Lobby

Scullery (1904)

Closet

W.C.

Stairs

Ladies' Waiting Room

General Waiting Room

Parcels Lobby (1905)

Booking Office (after 1905 alteration)

Entrance New (1905) position

Gents New (1905) position

Lamp Bench

Porters' and Lamp Room (1904)

Boiler

Boiler House (1904)

Shed for Sawdust etc. 15' 0" X 10' 0"

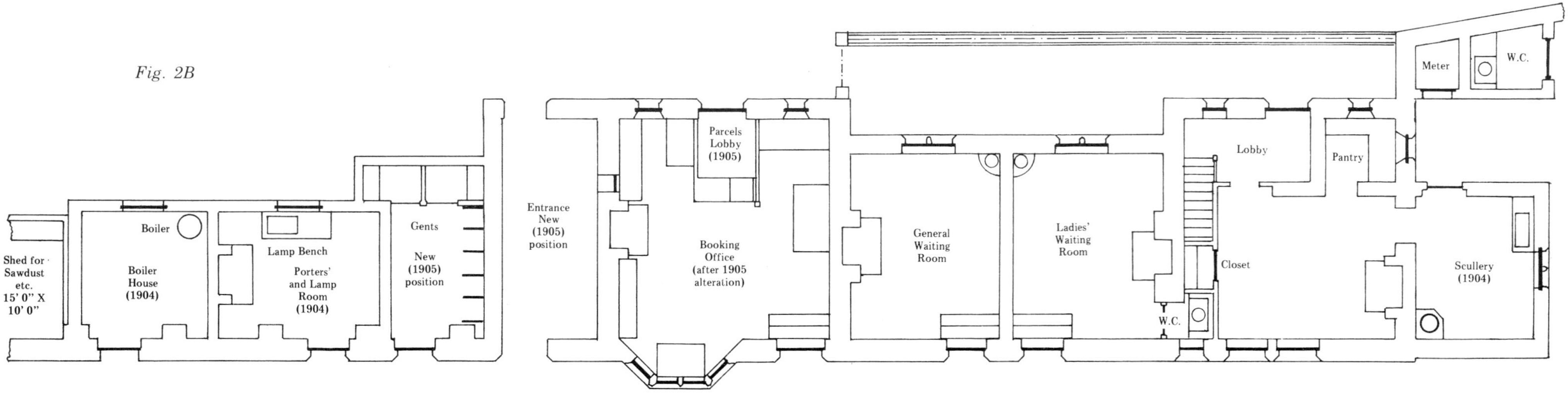

PLAN AFTER 1904–5 ALTERATIONS

ALSTON STATION HOUSE

The intermediate stage, with the roof partially dismantled.
*L. Ward*

The final stage as seen on 27th July 1971! The station roof, engine shed and associated buildings have been removed.
*R. B. Parr*

The west side of the building exposed. The lean-to building on the right has had a window put in the platform wall, and the extension to the same wall, to give more headroom, can be seen. It is presumed that both gables facing on to the platform originally had large windows, matching the east elevation.
*L. Ward*

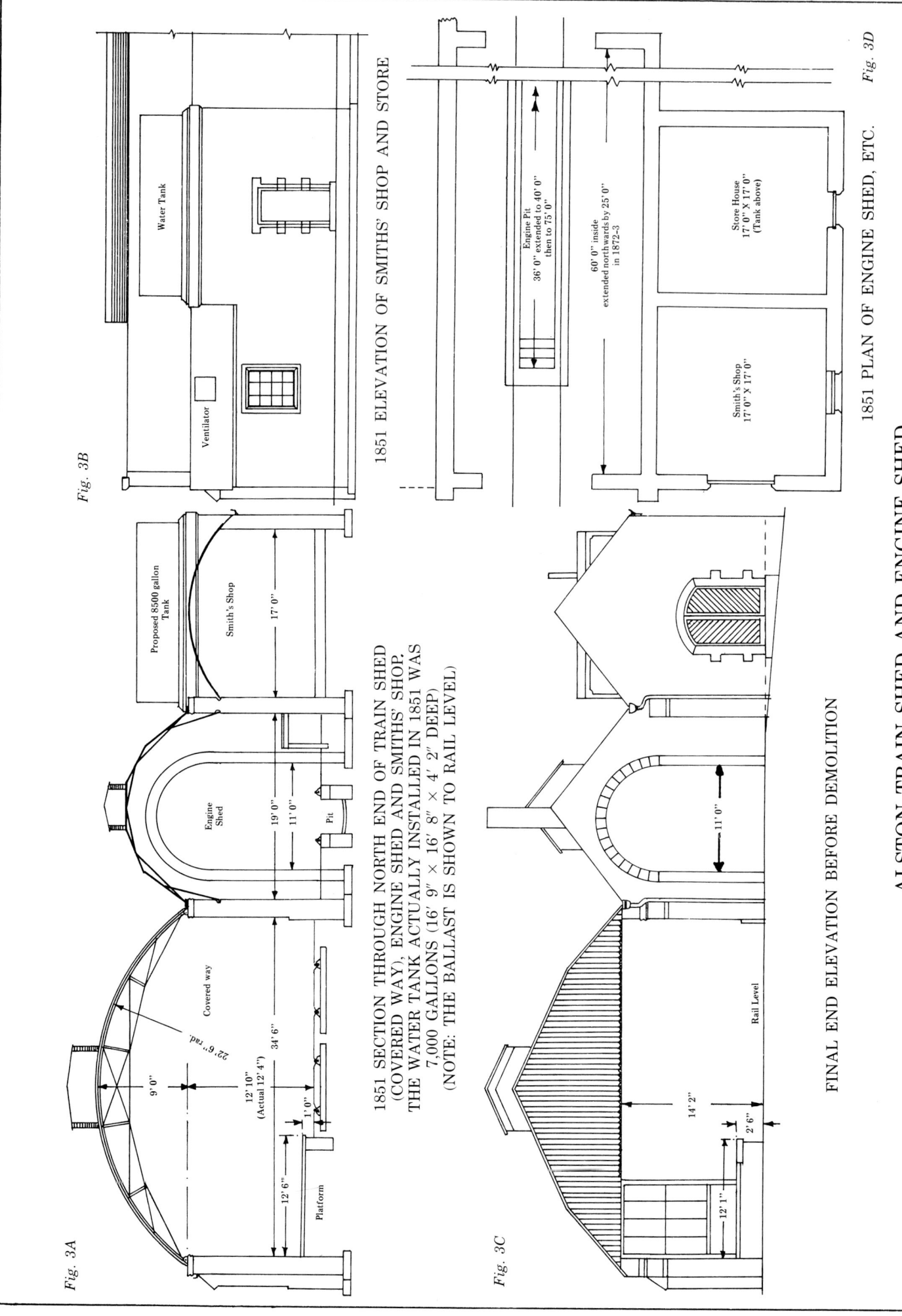

*Fig. 3B*

*Fig. 3A*

*Fig. 3C*

*Fig. 3D*

Water Tank

Ventilator

1851 ELEVATION OF SMITHS' SHOP AND STORE

Engine Pit
36' 0" extended to 40' 0"
then to 75' 0"

60' 0" inside
extended northwards by 25' 0"
in 1872-3

Store House
17' 0" X 17' 0"
(Tank above)

Smith's Shop
17' 0" X 17' 0"

1851 PLAN OF ENGINE SHED, ETC.

Proposed 8500 gallon
Tank

Smith's Shop

17' 0"

Engine
Shed

19' 0"

11' 0"

Pit

Covered way

22' 6" rad.

9' 0"

12' 10"
(Actual 12' 4")

34' 6"

1' 0"

12' 6"

Platform

1851 SECTION THROUGH NORTH END OF TRAIN SHED
(COVERED WAY), ENGINE SHED AND SMITHS' SHOP.
THE WATER TANK ACTUALLY INSTALLED IN 1851 WAS
7,000 GALLONS (16' 9" × 16' 8" × 4' 2" DEEP)
(NOTE: THE BALLAST IS SHOWN TO RAIL LEVEL)

11' 0"

Rail Level

14' 2"

2' 6"

12' 1"

FINAL END ELEVATION BEFORE DEMOLITION

ALSTON TRAIN SHED AND ENGINE SHED

**Engine shed** *(Drawing 3)*

The only surviving drawing of the shed is the sparsely-detailed 1851 version reproduced in *Figs. 3b, 3c & 3d.* At some time the shed was extended northwards by 25ft. and the Mansard iron-framed roof was replaced by a timber 'A' framed roof. It is probable that these alterations were carried out in 1872/3, when the station roof was rebuilt and extended, as both roofs shared a common support wall.

The LNER shed diagram of 1930 gives the usage of the outbuildings from north to south as (a) fitters' and smiths' shop, (b) time office and mess room, and (c) plate-layers (under tank). It must be remembered that a third outbuilding was added when the roof of the engine shed was extended. The same diagram also quotes the shed as being 8ft. longer than it actually was. The engine pit in-side the shed was extended twice *(see Fig. 3d)* and a further pit was provided outside the shed.

*(Top):* A post-World War II scene when all LNER engines had been renumbered. One Alston engine, Class G5 No. 7315, is waiting to depart for Haltwhistle, and the other, Class J21 No. 5100, has probably come up from Haltwhistle to change crews.
*W. A. Camwell*

*(Lower):* Alston signal box, and snowplough No. 900568 (ex-NER No. 14) pictured on 29th May 1953. There are references to a snowplough shed at this point but no photograph has been traced.

*R. B. Parr*

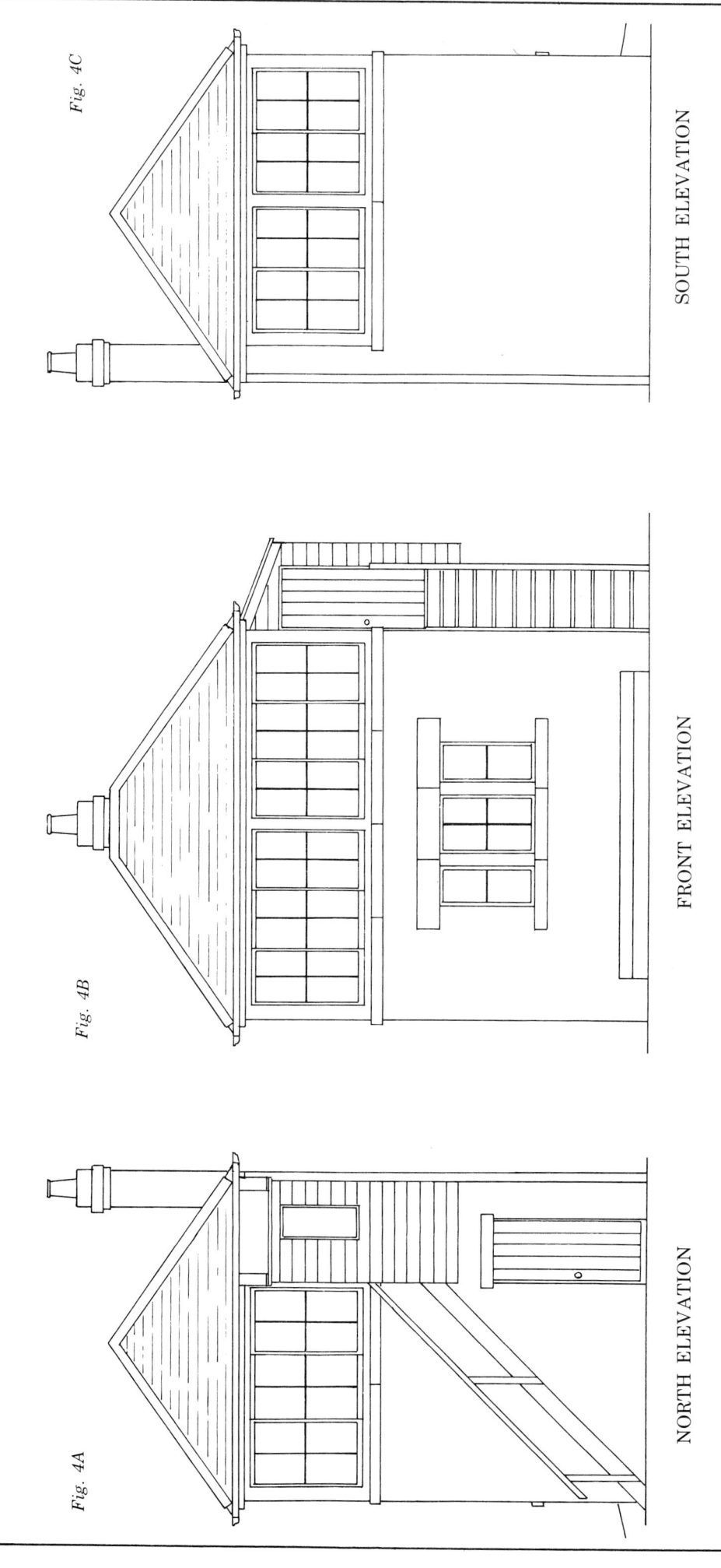

Fig. 4C.

SOUTH ELEVATION

Fig. 4B

FRONT ELEVATION

Fig. 4A

NORTH ELEVATION

## ALSTON SIGNALBOX c.1904

**Signal box** (*Drawing 4*)

The first signal box was a gable-ended two storey structure, in masonry and timber, which was replaced by the new brick box between 1900 and 1904. Apparently, the new box was built alongside the old, which was demolished when the new box was commissioned. The second box was of the standard style used extensively in the Northern Division of the NER, but it was unusual for such a small box to have a horizontal ridge section in the roof.

*(Above left):*   A view of the signal box from the front.

*Author's Collection*

*(Above right):*   The north side of the signal box, showing the steps and entrance porch.

*L. Ward*

*(Left):* Milepost 13 (from Haltwhistle) on the 'down' side at the approach to Alston Station. Note the raised 'dolly' controlling access to the running line from the goods yard.

*L. Ward*

*(Lower left):*   A view looking towards Haltwhistle, with the 'down' sidings seen in the distance. High in the trees on the river bank (left) are the signals governing the entrance to Alston, so placed as to be visible round the left-hand curve when approaching from the north.

*L. Ward*

*Lower right):* The signals in the trees as mentioned above. These are of the NER slotted post pattern.

*L. Ward*

*Fig. 5A*

EAST ELEVATION
APPROXIMATE POSITION OF FINAL ROOF LIGHTS
SHOWN DOTTED. ORIGINAL OFFICE CHIMNEY
DEMOLISHED *c.*1907.

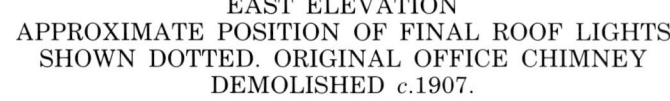

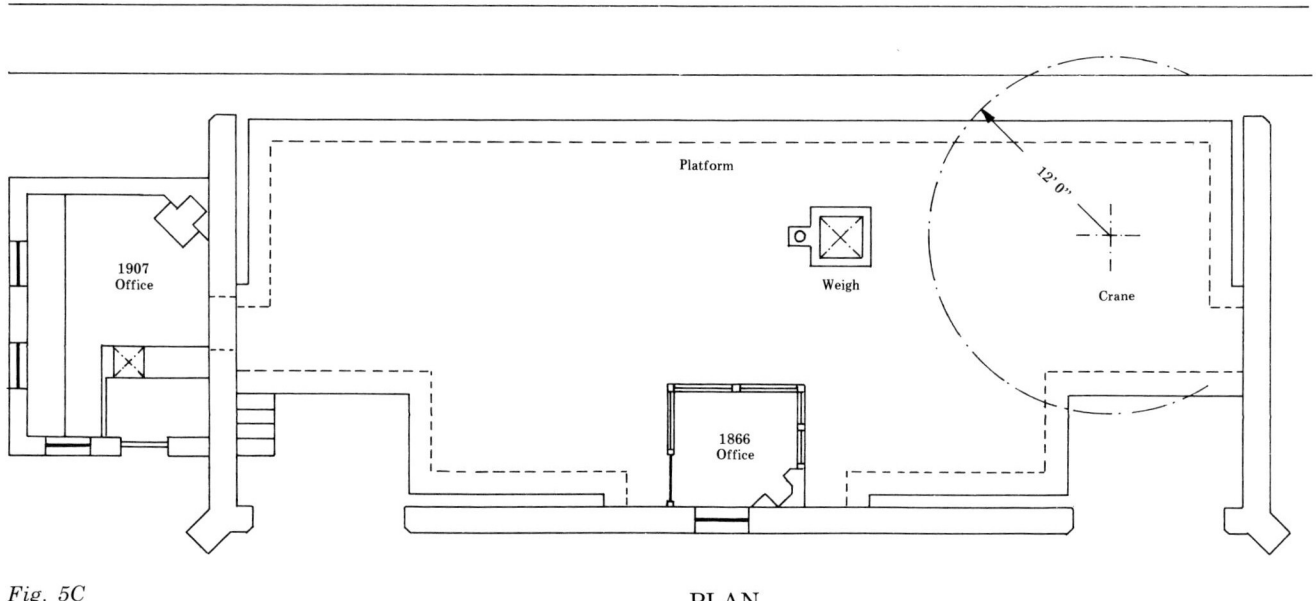

1907
Office

Platform

Weigh

12'0"

Crane

1866
Office

*Fig. 5C*

PLAN

# ALSTON WAREHOUSE

**Goods shed and coal depots** *(Drawings 5 & 6)*
Drawings of the goods shed are available for 1851, when built, 1866 for the new internal office, and 1907 for the new external office (which replaced an earlier one). The drawings, as reproduced, combine information from all three. The two later drawings agree the roof to be 2ft. 3in. lower than the original and this seems to be correct. The side windows are shown in the 1866 drawing but not in the original. Neither of the later drawings give the modified roof-lights and their approximate position is shown dotted; the proposed 1851 roof-lights are shown in full.

They were removed in the late 1940s. A sleeper-built lean-to stable existed on the north wall from about 1866.

The coal depots are from the July 1851 drawing and the later additions of the fencing and the platform for buffer stops are shown dotted on the drawing. The dwarf wall above rail level at the rear was removed, probably when the waybeams first became due for renewal, and the tracks spaced to nearer the standard 6ft. interval. Most NER stations had coal cells, and the majority of them had pier centres of 12ft., as at Alston, to utilise standard length cast girder rails of varying carrying capacity.

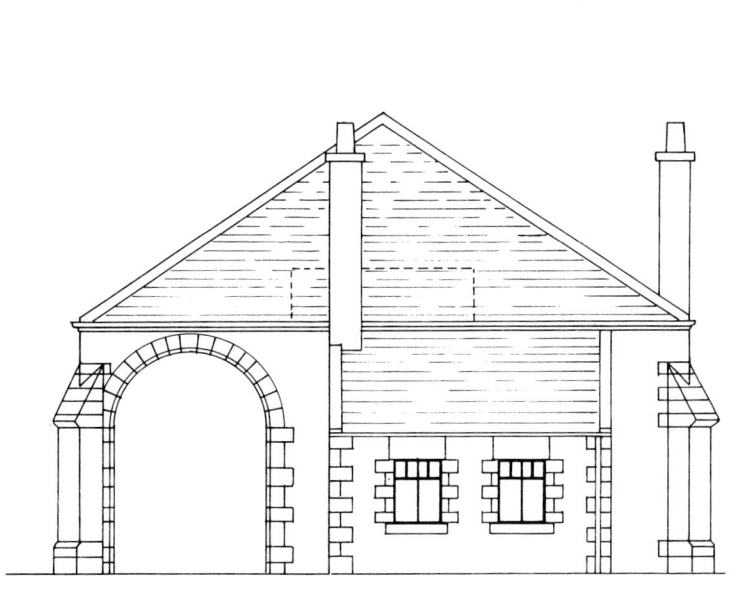

Fig. 5B     SOUTH ELEVATION

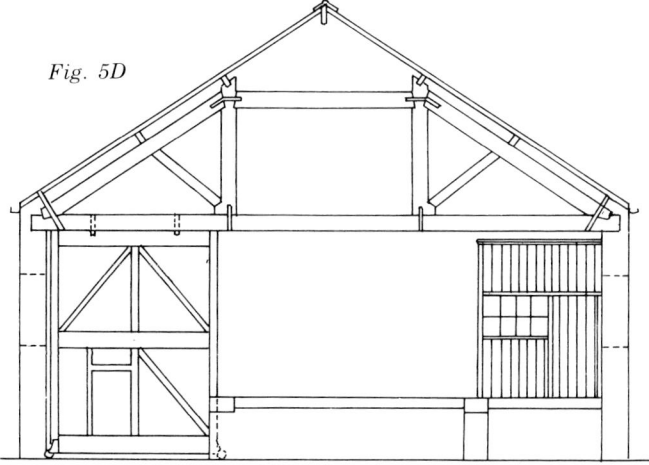

Fig. 5D

SECTION WITH ROOF DETAILS FROM 1866 DRAWING

*(Above):* The south end of the goods warehouse with the former goods office in use as a coal and coke order office. The signal box is seen in the left background and the end of coal depots are on the right. Note the roof-lights have been removed in the goods shed.

*L. Ward*

*(Below):* The 4 ton hand crane outside the south end of the warehouse. The photographer has placed a 5ft. surveying rod against the crane with a view to modelling it. The wooden weigh cabin is in the background.

*Ian Holloway*

North end of the warehouse. Beyond the second wagon on the left can be seen the bridge carrying the Alston to Hexham road over an extended siding. The sleeper-built stable is seen against the end wall.

*L. Ward*

The east side of the goods warehouse with the two cart entrances giving access to the loading bench.

*Author's Collection*

The south end of the coal cells. The different types of buffer stops are of interest.

*Author*

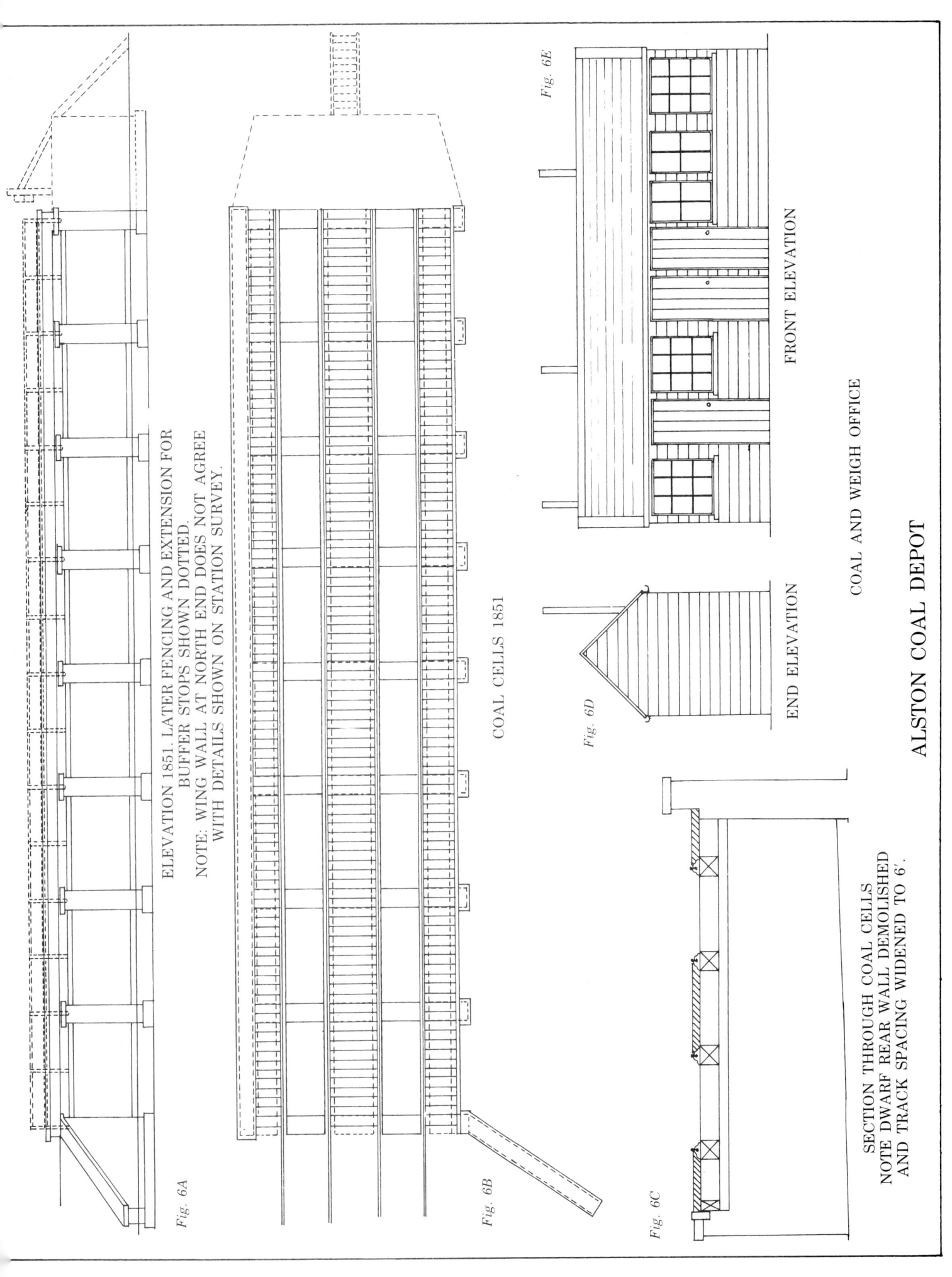

Fig. 6A

ELEVATION 1851. LATER FENCING AND EXTENSION FOR
BUFFER STOPS SHOWN DOTTED.
NOTE: WING WALL AT NORTH END DOES NOT AGREE
WITH DETAILS SHOWN ON STATION SURVEY.

Fig. 6B

COAL CELLS 1851

Fig. 6C

SECTION THROUGH COAL CELLS
NOTE DWARF REAR WALL DEMOLISHED
AND TRACK SPACING WIDENED TO 6'.

Fig. 6D

END ELEVATION

Fig. 6E

FRONT ELEVATION

COAL AND WEIGH OFFICE

ALSTON COAL DEPOT

The wooden weigh cabin and coal office on the east side of the yard, again with a convenient guide to the height.

*Ian Holloway*

The north end of the engine shed and workshop, with a standard NER water crane, and a wagon of 'Loco' coal. Engines were coaled manually, from wagon to tender or bunker, using the wooden coal stage.

*P. B. Booth*

*(Left):* The engine shed in its final days, with the signal box in the distance. These are the remains of the replacement roof, probably dating from 1872/3.

*L. Ward*

*(Below):* In 1920, BTP 0-4-4T No. 69, which had been left outside the shed, moved off unattended. Trap points near the signal box stopped it from encroaching on the running lines, but diverted it towards the river bank where it ran off the rails, knocked down a low wall, and fell on to the rocks and boulders bordering the River South Tyne, landing on its right-hand side. Here it has been righted ready for lifting to rail level, where the tool vans and a steam crane are standing.

*South Tynedale RPS*

A view taken in the late 1950s, with the station roof partly dismantled.

*L. Ward*

**Looking north** through the station, a diesel multiple unit is seen arriving.

*L. Ward*

# CHAPTER THREE
# Guisborough

The line to Guisborough was opened by the Middlesbrough & Guisborough Railway in 1853, with the backing of the Stockton & Darlington Railway, who worked the line from the outset and took it over in July 1858. When, in 1857, the Stockton & Darlington Railway decided to number its houses, this building was included and was allocated the number B12. The letter indicated the area and the figures the serial number in the area, and these were displayed by means of a black and white ceramic tile. Here it can be seen under the eaves on the corner nearest the camera. The entrance to the station is beyond the stationmaster's house. The station closed on 2nd March 1964 and it was demolished in 1967.

*Author*

Guisborough Station was built at the eastern end of the Middlesbrough & Guisborough Railway, which opened for mineral traffic on 11th November 1853, and for passenger traffic on 25th March 1854. The Middlesbrough & Guisborough Railway was backed by the Stockton & Darlington Railway (which had reached Middlesbrough in 1830) and the Pease family (who wished to develop ironstone deposits on the route of the railway), and Guisborough became the centre of a very busy ironstone mining area. Within a few years, the Cleveland Railway also appeared on the scene to serve the area, and the proximity of these lines led to the unusual layout of the lines south of the town.

The station itself has disappeared, but various earthworks show where the lines once ran, although these too are gradually disappearing under car-parks and housing developments.

The Middlesbrough & Guisborough Railway received its Act on 17th June 1852, and this lists amongst the subscribers five members of the Pease family, the Darlington based Quakers who were the power behind the Stockton & Darlington Railway. Henry Pease of Pierremont, Darlington, was elected one of the first Directors of the Middlesbrough & Guisborough Railway. Two branches were also authorised but only the Cod Hill branch was built to serve ironstone mines near Hutton Low Cross, south of Guisborough.

At Guisborough, the line terminated on the south-east side of the town, with a single platform in a train shed. The glazed end screens were unusual for the North-East in having a sun's rays design.

The realisation of the size of the ironstone field around Guisborough brought others eager for a share of the spoils, leading to the formation of the Cleveland Railway, with plans to build a line from the River Tees, east of Middlesbrough, to Loftus. The section between Guisborough and Loftus was authorised by the Cleveland Railway Act of 23rd July 1858, and, while this line was being built, the promoters were also going ahead with the section from Guisborough to the River Tees, but as a wayleave line for which Parliamentary sanction was not required. Thus when the Cleveland Railway did eventually receive its Act for the Guisborough to Tees section (on 22nd July 1861), it was already well on the way to completion and it was opened on 23rd November 1861.

The Cleveland Railway crossed over the Middlesbrough & Guisborough route some 200 yards outside the latter's Guisborough Station, and a connection between the two lines was also opened on 23rd November 1861. Over the next four years the Cleveland Railway gradually extended eastwards towards its goal at Loftus, eventually reaching as far as Carlin How on the western escarpment of the Kilton Valley.

In 1863, the Stockton & Darlington Railway was taken over by the NER, and the Cleveland Railway followed in 1865. This meant that the two routes from Guisborough to the River Tees were now under one ownership and the North Eastern Railway decided to abandon the Cleveland route (except for a section at its northern end), and to concentrate traffic on the M&GR route. Because of the connection put in between the two lines at Guisborough in 1861, mineral traffic from the east on the former Cleveland line could pass on to the former M&GR line, and travel to Middlesbrough, via Nunthorpe.

Until 1875, a passenger service did not operate east of Guisborough, but then a Guisborough—Saltburn—Loftus service was introduced, reversing at Hutton Junction, where there appears to have been a short-lived station. As there was no nearby habitation, this station may have been solely for interchange purposes. Eventually, the Middlesbrough to Guisborough service was connected with the Guisborough to Saltburn service, to provide a Middlesbrough—Guisborough (reverse)—Hutton Junction (reverse)-Brotton(reverse)-Saltburn West Junction (reverse)-Saltburn service. Special permission was given at Guisborough for a pilot engine to draw Middlesbrough to Saltburn trains out of the station, as far as Hutton Junction, and to draw Saltburn to Middlesbrough trains from Hutton Junction into the station, both with the train engine at the rear, thus reducing the delay.

The position was eased with the introduction of autocars in 1905 when a reversal required only the driver to change ends. A similar method of working continued with the Sentinel steam railcars, the LNER push-and-pull units, and finally with the BR diesel railcars. Permission to propel trains conveying passengers from Guisborough Station to Hutton Junction was given about 1901. This referred to eastbound trains, but in the opposite direction only autocars were allowed to run into Guisborough Station without an engine leading, and thus westbound trains could not reverse into the station. However, this latter restriction was eased in 1931 when Middlesbrough-bound trains of up to three coaches were allowed to be propelled from Hutton Junction into Guisborough Station, provided the platform line was clear to the buffer

A pre-World War I view of Guisborough Station (west end) and its goods warehouse.

*Langbaurgh Museums*

Because of the reversals necessary to work the services around Guisborough, the NER autocars were particularly useful. These consisted of a BTP 0-4-4T locomotive between two coaches, each having a driving compartment at its outer end. The fireman remained on the engine but the driver controlled the train from which ever end was leading. This World War I view shows the bay platform outside the train shed.

*Langbaurgh Museums*

stops, that the guard rode in the leading vehicle which had to be one in which he had access to the automatic brake handle, and that speed did not exceed 10m.p.h.

From 16th March 1932, as an economy measure, Guisborough box was abolished and Hutton Junction box was renamed Guisborough. The two tracks from the newly-named Guisborough box to the station became two single lines, one (the former 'up' line) for the passenger trains to and from the station, and the other (the former 'down' line) for the goods trains to and from the goods yard. A three lever ground frame controlled by Guisborough box was provided at the outer end of the station platform to operate the points for the bay platform and the engine shed. The points in the goods yard were hand-operated.

Late in 1933, no doubt because of the increased traffic brought about by changing the terminus of the Scarborough service from Saltburn to Middlesbrough, the Middlesbrough-bound trains were allowed to reverse from Guisborough box to the station platform when consisting of up to seven coaches (or 420ft. in length), again provided

the platform line was clear to the buffers, and the guard had access to an automatic brake valve. To assist drivers, a marker board lettered 'seven' was provided near the platform starting signal.

Guisborough Station had a long platform serving a track which passed through the train shed to end in a buffer stop not far short of the Guisborough to Whitby road. At the west end of the station, outside the train shed roof, the south face of this platform formed a short bay. The section of the main platform inside the train shed was of wood.

A house for the stationmaster adjoined the south-east wall of the train shed, with a goods warehouse on the north-west side, both house and warehouse being built in stone. Just below the eaves of the house, on the north-east wall, was one of the Stockton & Darlington Railway house number tiles lettered and numbered B12. These tiles, 9¼in. wide x 10⅞in. high, were introduced in 1857 at the request of the Company's rent collector, who was authorised 'to divide the line into sections under letters, and the

Forty years later, and the last day of steam working on the lines around Guisborough. This view was taken from the footplate of BR Standard 2-6-4T No. 80116 working the 11.40a.m. Scarborough to Middlesbrough train.

*Author*

A general view of Guisborough Station looking towards the buffer stops in the 1930s. By this time Guisborough Station signal box had been closed and the working was controlled from the former Hutton Junction box, renamed Guisborough, by a ground frame (visible beyond the signal post) at the platform end. The engine shed is on the right.

*Author's Collection*

buildings and houses to be numbered'.

When approached from the road, the stationmaster's house was passed, and then came two single storey gabled buildings at right angles to the train shed, with a glazed canopy between them. The gabled building adjoining the house was contemporary with the train shed, having the same pattern of sun ray glazing over the entrance, whereas the other building had stone above the windows. The entrance gave into a large gabled booking hall, naturally lit by glazed panels in the roof. This was also at right angles to the train shed and with more sun ray glazing above the entrance to the platform.

*Locomotive and Train Working*
One engine and two sets of men were stationed at Guisborough for working to Middlesbrough, Loftus and Saltburn and, in 1908, this duty was performed by a steam autocar, a BTP 0-4-4T with a coach at each end, which left Guisborough for Middlesbrough at 5.17a.m. On most days, the engine retired to the shed after arriving back at Guisborough at 8.47p.m. but on Wednesdays and Saturdays, it was not due back until 11.15p.m. By 1922, the working had changed little, although with the introduction of the eight hour day, a Middlesbrough crew had to work the autocar in the middle of the day as the day's work could not be encompassed in two consecutive eight hour shifts by the Guisborough crews. This was largely due to the early departure of the first train.

Because of their age, the BTP engines used for the autocar workings were rapidly disappearing in the 1920s,

and Guisborough Shed had a succession of different engines. Thus, No. 226 was withdrawn from Guisborough on 10th May 1929, followed by No. 595 on 29th July 1929, and No. 1436 on 23rd November 1929. No. 1436 was actually the last BTP engine to remain in LNER stock, although some of the class, which were rebuilt as 0-6-0T locomotives, lasted well into British Railways' days. As no other push-and-pull engines were available, the trains worked by Guisborough Shed had to revert to normal operation, and for this, Class F8 2-4-2T No. 685 was transferred to Guisborough on 29th July 1929. Drawings were prepared at Darlington Works in 1926 to fit this class with push-and-pull control equipment, but the scheme was dropped due to the widespread introduction of Sentinel steam railcars in the North Eastern Area of the LNER. However, it was not until 1930 that Guisborough received a Sentinel railcar, this being the first of the new twelve cylinder variety with Woolnough boiler, purchased specially to work the hilly lines in the North Riding. Thus, in June 1930, No. 2281 *Old John Bull* commenced working from Guisborough, starting each day on the 5.14a.m. to Middlesbrough and ending on the 9.40p.m. arrival (Wednesdays and Saturdays excepted), 10.28p.m. (Wednesdays only) and 11.32p.m. (Saturdays only). On some workings, the Sentinel car hauled one of the Clayton lightweight trailers which were specially built for such duties. Sister car No. 2283 *Old Blue* was shedded at Middlesbrough to work some of the duties on the line and, in fact, changed places with *Old John Bull* in November 1930, although the latter car returned to

The 1963 RCTS and SLS 'North Eastern Five Day Tour' at Guisborough, with 4MT No. 43129. Note the standard NER 45 degree wooden fencing.

*T. J. Edgington*

Whitby Shed received 4MT 2-6-4T engines Nos. 80116-20 in 1955 for working to Malton, and for the Scarborough to Middlesbrough service. No. 80118 halts at Guisborough ready to propel its train back to the junction, there to reverse again and set off for Brotton and Loftus. The east end of the goods warehouse and the office are visible in the right background.

*Langbaurgh Museum*

Guisborough in May 1931 when *Old Blue* went on trial to other areas of the LNER. It went to St. Margaret's (Edinburgh) in May 1931, then south to Norwich in September 1931. Five days later, it moved to Ipswich, and after only two days there it went to Cambridge, before returning to Guisborough on 26th September 1931.

Saltburn and Stockton six cylinder Sentinel cars also visited Guisborough each day in the 1930s, and the Armstrong-Whitworth diesel-electric railcar *Tyneside Venturer* called daily on its way to Scarborough (6.25 a.m. from Middlesbrough) and on the return journey (11.45a.m. from Scarborough), as well as during the afternoon and evening on local workings from Middlesbrough.

The railcar *Old Blue* was withdrawn in September 1941 and *Old John Bull* in November 1941, and Guisborough Shed regained a locomotive on 15th September when Class G5 0-4-4T No. 1883 was transferred from West Hartlepool to work a two coach push-and-pull unit. This was the LNER version, using vacuum control gear, but the coaches were those originally used on the NER autocars with mechanical gear.

A Class G5 locomotive was used until 20th September 1954 when the long-established early morning train at 4.55a.m. from Guisborough was withdrawn and the first departure became 8.19a.m. The Guisborough Class G5 engine, No. 67281 (ex-1883) was transferred to Stockton and the shed closed.

On 5th May 1958, the steam-worked Middlesbrough to Scarborough service, via Guisborough and Whitby, was withdrawn south of Loftus, and henceforward Guisborough was served by a Middlesbrough to Loftus service, using railcars, but even this was reduced on 2nd May 1960 when it was cut back to a Middlesbrough to Guisborough service. Even this was withdrawn from 2nd March 1964.

<table>
<tr><td colspan="3">Engine Working Guisborough, — Summer 1908</td><td colspan="3" align="center">Passenger Engine Working Guisborough, — Spring 1939<br>(Saturdays excepted)<br>(Carriage Roster 434 for Sentinel coach, twelve cylinder)</td></tr>
</table>

| | | | | | |
|---|---|---|---|---|---|
| *Weekdays* | | | | *a.m.* | *a.m.* |
| | | | Shed | — | 5.04 (Empty) |
| *Engine and coach each end* | | | Guisborough | — | 5.14 |
| | | | Middlesbrough | 5.36 | 5.50 (Empty) |
| | *a.m.* | *a.m.* | Guisborough | 6.13 | 6.43 |
| Guisborough | — | 5.17 | Middlesbrough | 7.07 | 7.42 |
| Middlesbrough | 5.42 | 6.20 | Guisborough | 8.09 | 8.25 |
| Loftus | 7.15 | 7.25 | Middlesbrough | 8.49 LD | 9.33 |
| Saltburn | 7.54 | 8.04 | Guisborough | 10.00 | 10.13 |
| Guisborough | 8.33 | 8.37 | Middlesbrough | 10.37 | 10.50 |
| Middlesbrough | 9.02 | 9.42 | Stockton | 11.02 | 11.20 |
| Saltburn | 10.38 | 11.21 | | | *p.m.* |
| | *p.m.* | *p.m.* | Middlesbrough | 11.32 * | 12.03 M |
| Middlesbrough | 12.26 | 12.53 | | *p.m.* | |
| Guisborough | 1.20* | 1.30 | Guisborough | 12.30 | 1.13 M |
| Brotton | 1.45 | 2.30 | Middlesbrough | 1.37 | 2.03 M |
| Guisborough | 2.47 | 3.23 | Battersby | 2.31 | 2.42 M |
| Middlesbrough | 3.48 | 4.52** | Middlesbrough | 3.07 * | 3.33 |
| Saltburn | 5.58 | 6.21** | Brotton | 4.20 | 4.24 |
| Guisborough | 6.46 | 6.48** | Middlesbrough | 5.07 | 5.33 |
| Middlesbrough | 7.13 | 7.16** | Guisborough | 6.00 | 6.43 |
| Stockton | 7.30 | 8.02** | Middlesbrough | 7.07 | 8.03 ** |
| Middlesbrough | 8.14 | 8.20** | Loftus | 9.02 | 9.11 ** (Empty) |
| Guisborough | 8.47 | 10.08 (WSO) | Guisborough shed | 9.32 | — |
| Middlesbrough | 10.33 | 10.48 (WSO) | | | |
| Guisborough | 11.15 | — | | | |

*\* = Change enginemen — \*\* = Steam train on Saturdays*
*First set 4.22a.m. to 2.22p.m.;*
*Second set 2.10p.m. to 12.10a.m. (sic)*

*LD = Loco duties*
*\* = Change enginemen*
*\*\* = Steam train Fridays only*
*M = Worked by Middlesbrough enginemen*
*First set 4.34a.m. to 12.45p.m;*
*Second set 2.11p.m. to 10.11p.m.*

## A Sudden End

When compared with the delay in closing the Alston branch, which took more than fifteen years, the closure of the line to Guisborough was extremely rapid, as the following timetable of events shows:

| | |
|---|---|
| 14th June 1963 | Proposals for closure announced |
| 23rd August 1963 | Public enquiry held in Middlesbrough |
| 27th November 1963 | Consent to closure given by Minister of Transport |
| 13th February 1964 | Date of closure announced |
| 29th February 1964 | Last trains ran |

Following the closure, three of the former Guisborough to Middlesbrough and Newcastle trains started from Nunthorpe, and two from Newcastle terminated at Nunthorpe. The additional buses put on between Guisborough and Middlesbrough stopped at Hutton Gate Station in both directions. Later a Guisborough to Middlesbrough 'Easyway' bus-train commuter service was introduced, using a bus between Guisborough and Nunthorpe and a train between Nunthorpe and Middlesbrough, with one ticket covering the full journey. What a pity the railway was not not there to carry the passengers throughout!

The goods service to Guisborough continued until 31st August 1964, when rail traffic at Guisborough ceased completely. The whole station site was cleared in May 1967 and a health centre took the place of the station. However, a small memento of Guisborough's railway era remains in the yard of a nearby works, where some of the coal cells can still be seen.

An ex-NER 15 ton 6 wheel van used for storage purposes at Guisborough in BR days. It had been renumbered 040008.

*L. Ward*

# Notes on the Drawings — GUISBOROUGH

### General
The drawings concentrate on the station block of buildings, namely the train shed, goods shed, engine shed and coal depot. Also included is an unidentified crane in the warehouse.

### Station *(Drawings 1-5)*
This block of buildings, situated not far from the centre of Guisborough, was built to a design not used elsewhere on the Stockton & Darlington Railway, and presumably owes its inception to the Middlesbrough & Guisborough Railway. Although the goods shed was dated 1853, the date of opening of the line, it has been impossible to establish with certainty that the train shed was built at the same time.

*(Below):* A general view of Guisborough Station as seen from the approach road. The east end of the train shed roof is on the right and the starting signal at the outer end of the platform is on the left.

*C. B. Foster*

The interior of Guisborough Station looking east towards the buffer stops. Note the wooden platform inside the train shed and the sunray design repeated over the exit on the right. The weighing machine is in front of the wooden office.

*Author's Collection*

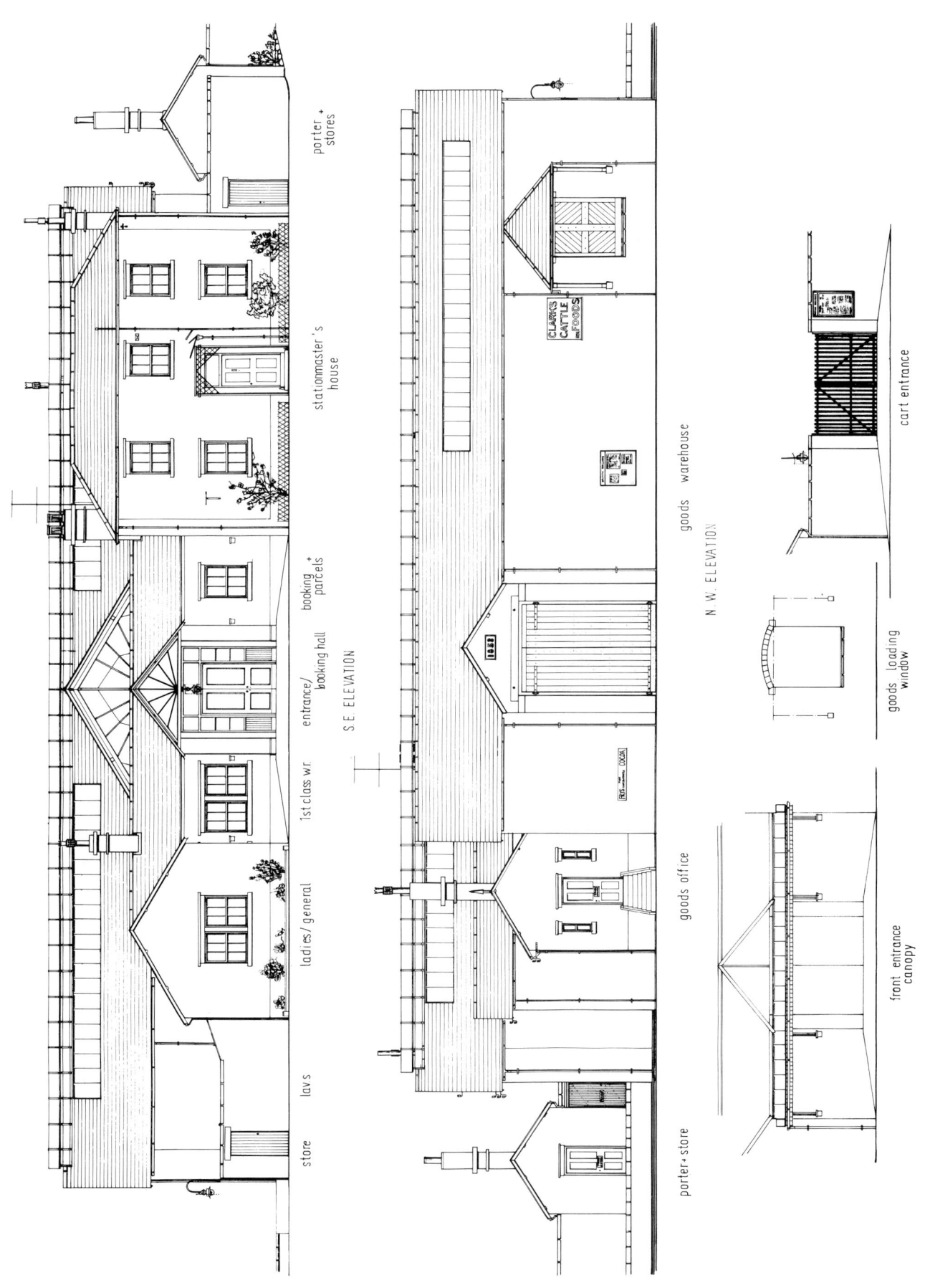

porter + stores

stationmaster's house

booking + parcels

entrance/ booking hall

S.E. ELEVATION

1st class w.r.

ladies/general

store        lavs

goods warehouse

CLARKS CATTLE FOODS

N.W. ELEVATION

cart entrance

goods loading window

goods office

front entrance canopy

porter+store

GUISBOROUGH

*Fig. 1*

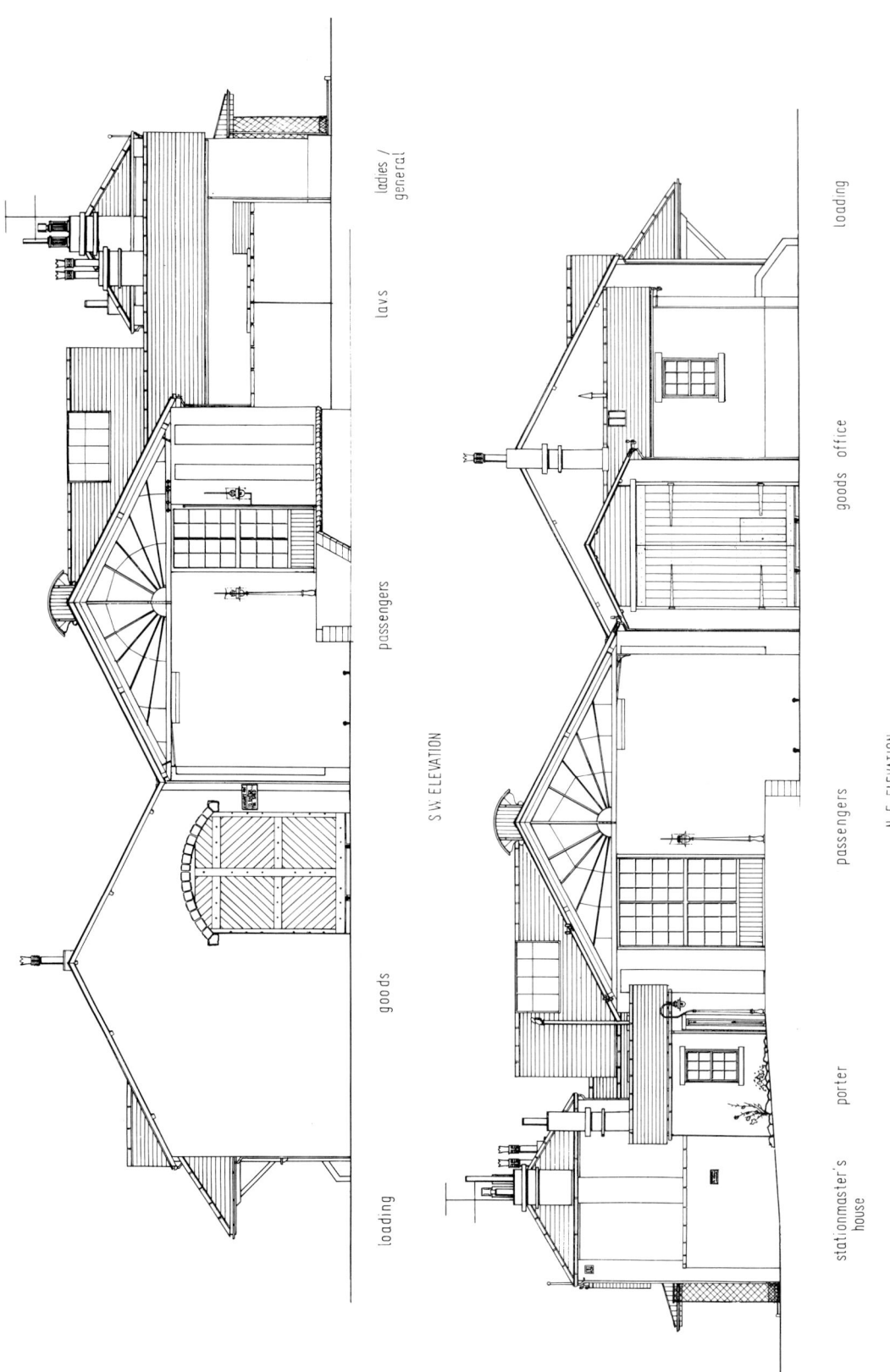

GUISBOROUGH

*Fig. 2*

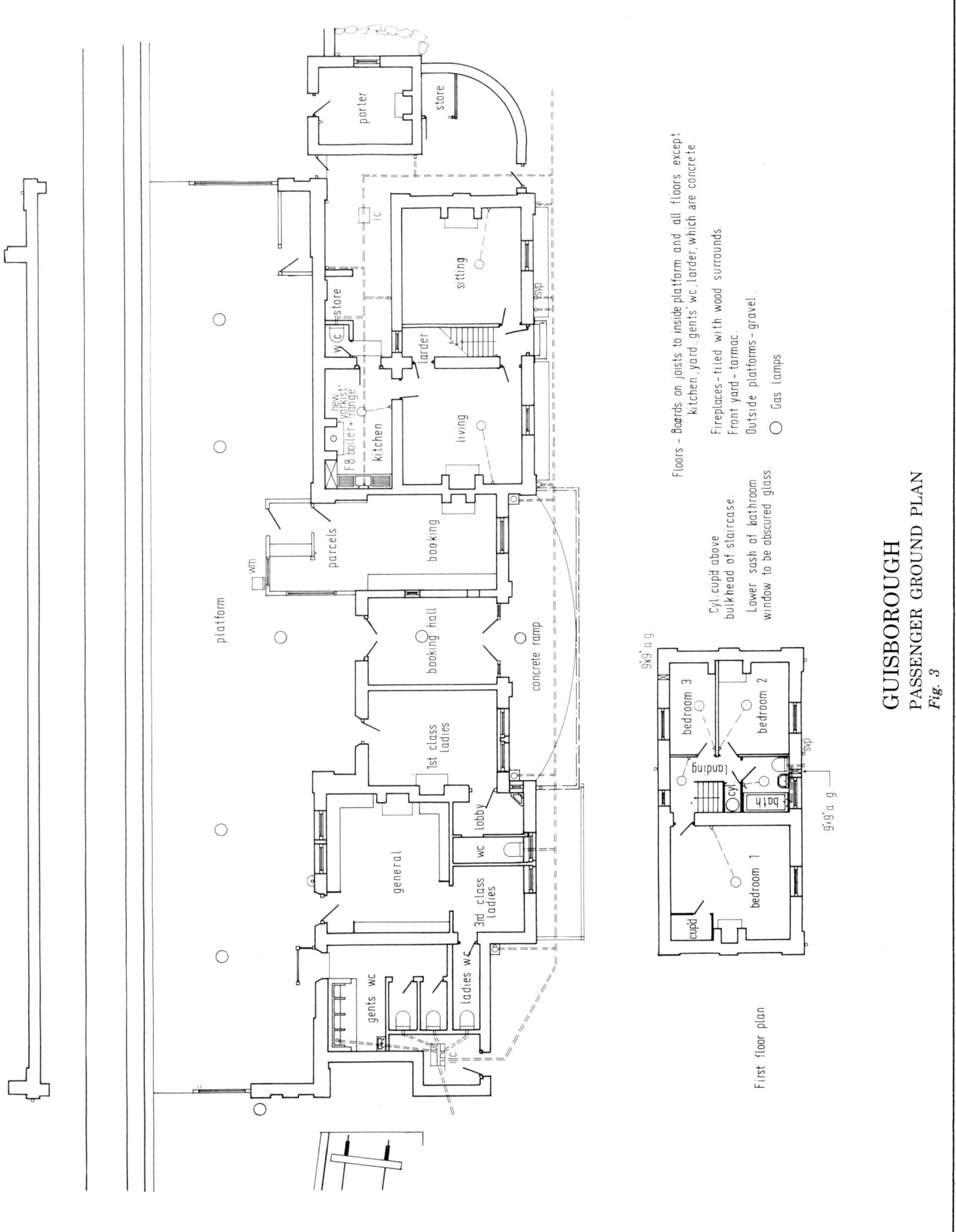

Floors - Boards on joists to inside platform and all floors except
    kitchen, yard gents' wc, larder, which are concrete.

Fireplaces - tiled with wood surrounds.
Front yard - tarmac.
Outside platforms - gravel.

○ Gas lamps

Cyl.cupd above
bulkhead of staircase.

Lower sash of bathroom
window to be obscured glass

First floor plan

**GUISBOROUGH**
PASSENGER GROUND PLAN
*Fig. 3*

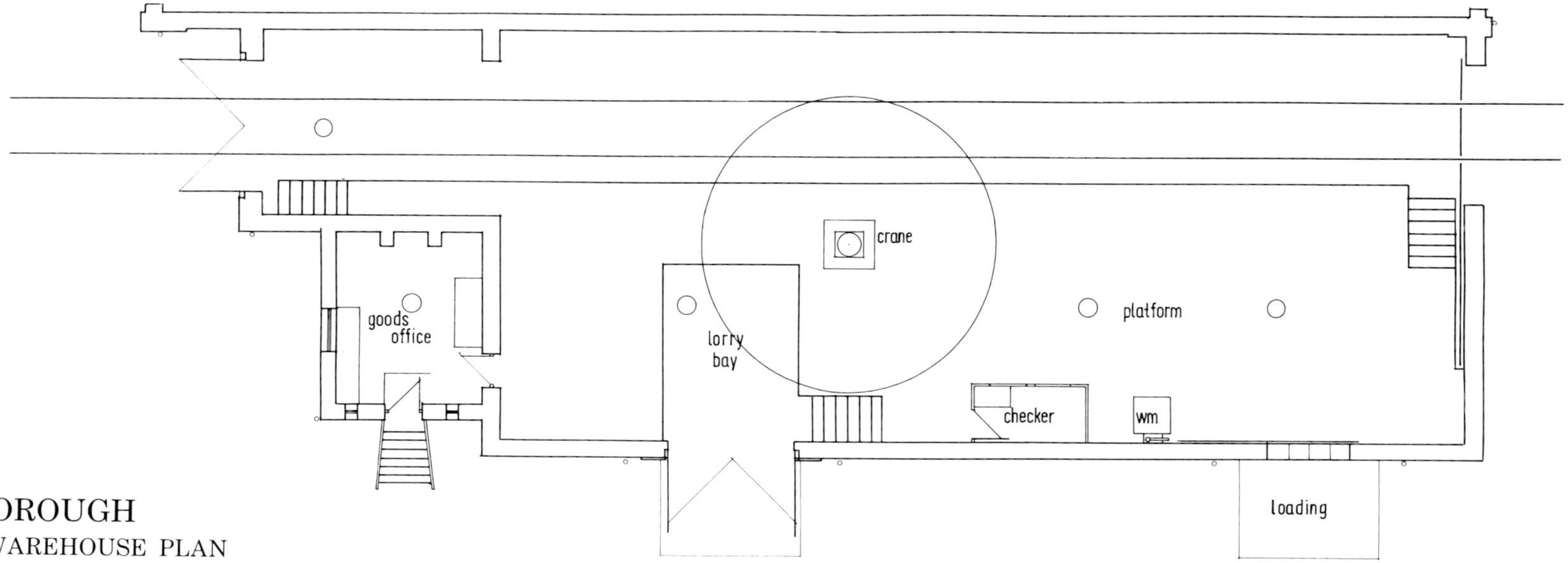

## GUISBOROUGH
### GOODS WAREHOUSE PLAN
*Fig. 4*

loading

platform

wm

checker

crane

lorry
bay

goods
office

The east end of the goods buildings.

*C. B. Foster*

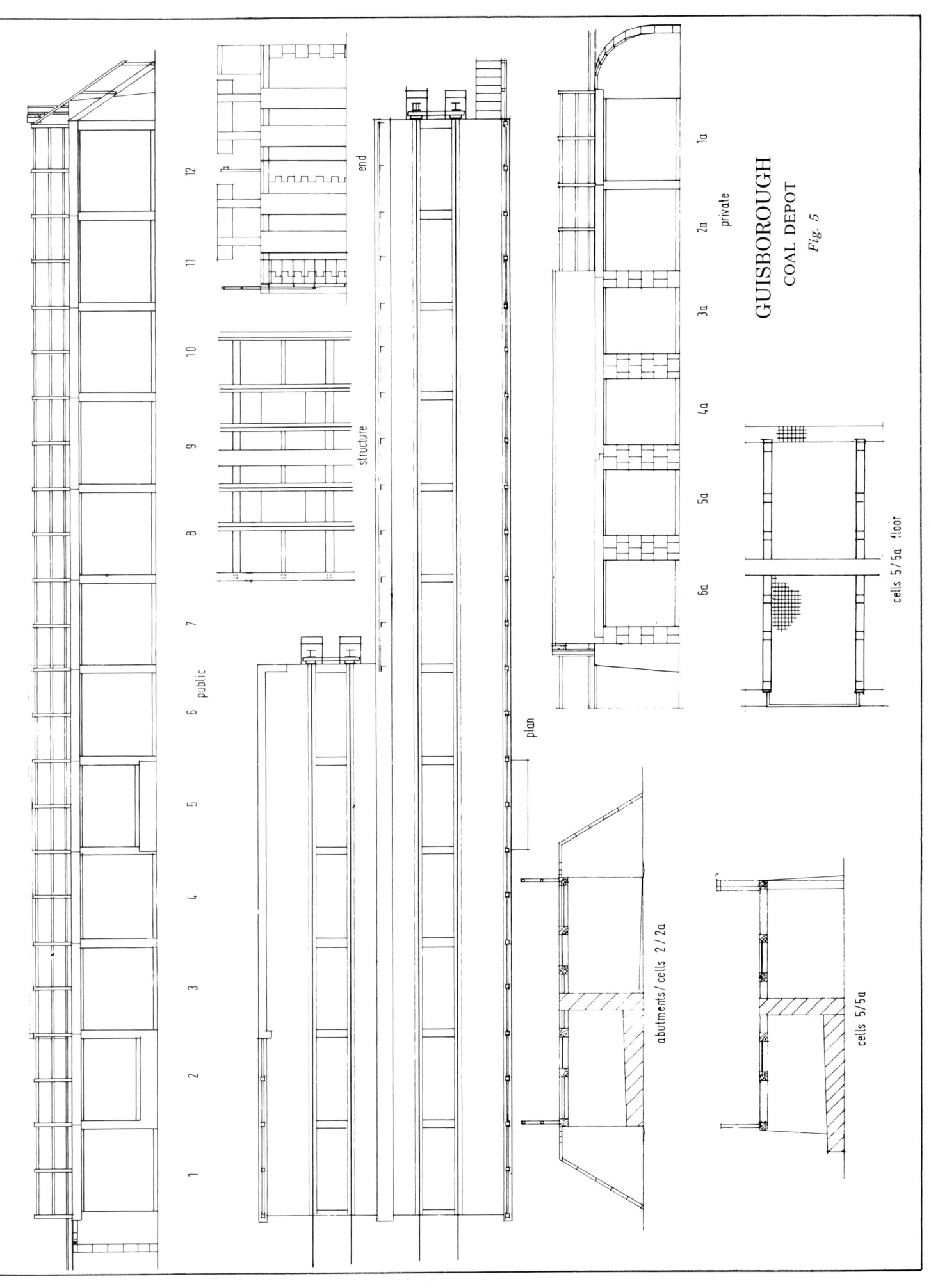

GUISBOROUGH
COAL DEPOT
*Fig. 5*

end

structure

plan

public

private

1a    2a    3a    4a    5a    6a

cells 5/5a floor

abutments/cells 2/2a

cells 5/5a

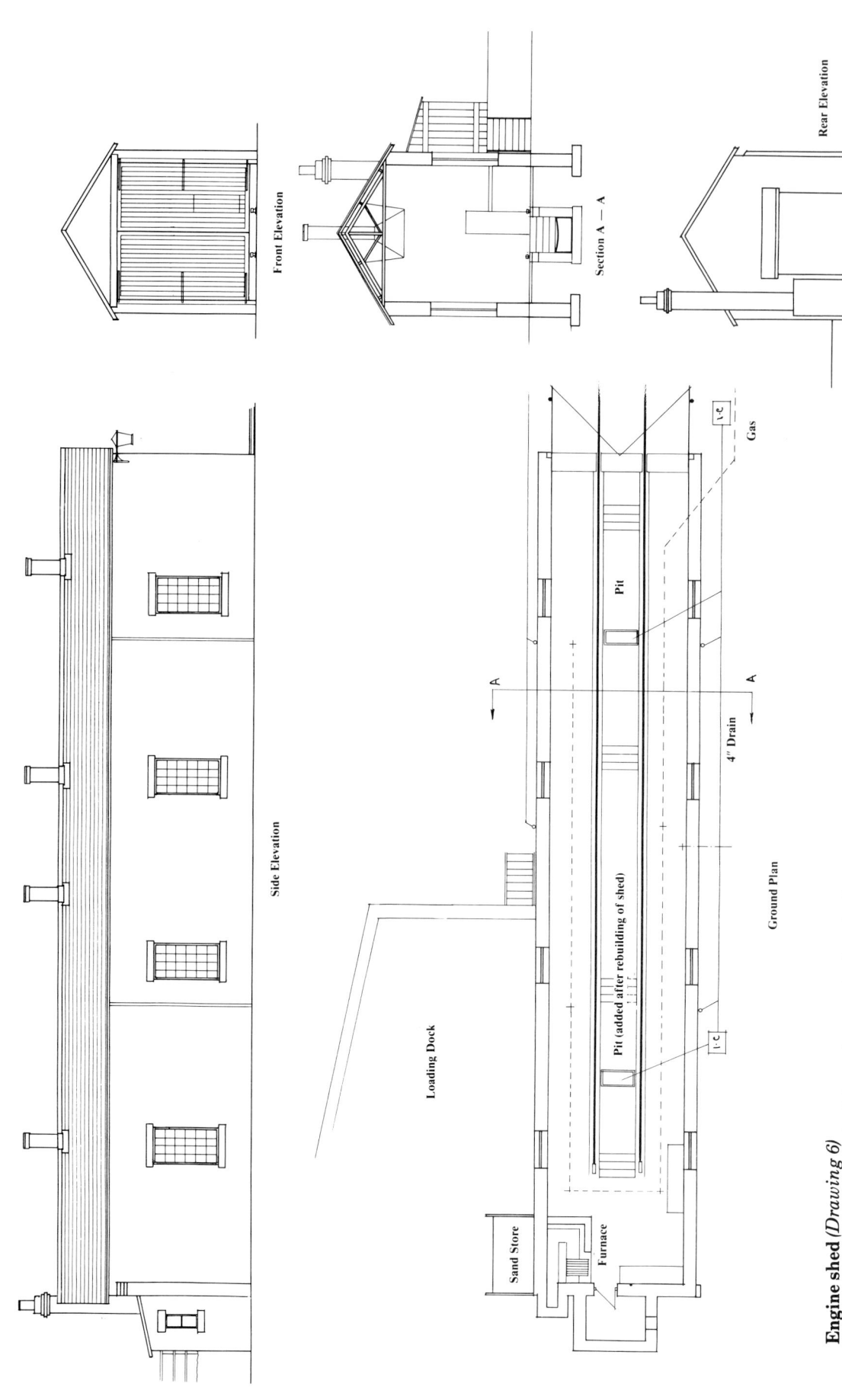

**Front Elevation**

**Section A — A**

**Rear Elevation**

**Side Elevation**

**Loading Dock**

**Sand Store**

**Furnace**

**Pit (added after rebuilding of shed)**

**Pit**

**Ground Plan**

**4" Drain**

**Gas**

w.c.

w.c.

**GUISBOROUGH**
**LOCOMOTIVE SHED**
*Fig. 6*

**Engine shed** (*Drawing 6*)
This was a very long building for a single platform terminus. The usual accommodation was for one engine and, in fact, that was the usual allocation for the shed, at least in late NER and LNER days. The origins of the shed are not known, although it is recorded as being destroyed by fire on 27th February 1903, but a replacement was not authorised until 1908, at an estimated cost of £504. 5s. 11d. Such fires were fairly common on the North Eastern Railway, and they usually destroyed the timber-beamed roof and left the walls standing, so that they could be used again, and this is what appears to have happened at Guisborough.

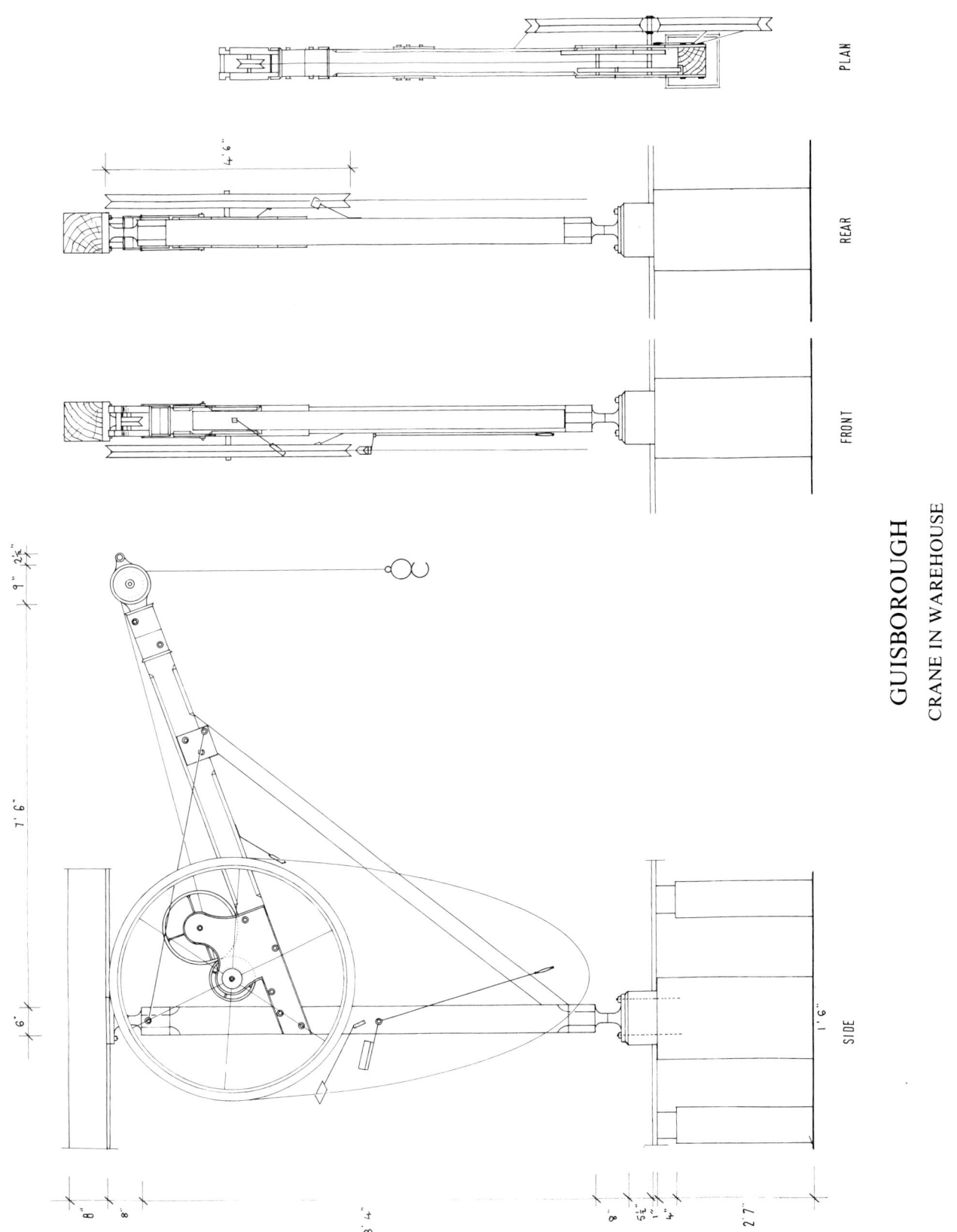

PLAN

REAR

FRONT

SIDE

GUISBOROUGH

CRANE IN WAREHOUSE

*Fig. 7*

*(Below):* The layout at Guisborough w
unusual, due to the combination of tw
distinct lines; the Middlesbrough & Gui
borough and the Cleveland. In this vie
the tracks on the left lead to Guisborou
Station and those on the right are to Brotto
The bridge over the Guisborough lines carri
a footpath, and running in front of it,
an embankment, is the course of the Clev
land Railway, which formerly crossed t
Middlesbrough & Guisborough line on
way to the River Tees. The Cleveland Ra
way eventually reached Carlin How and t
tracks on the extreme right were put in
join the Middlesbrough & Guisborough a
Cleveland Railway to allow through runnin
thus enabling the north end of the Clevela
line to be closed. Now all the tracks in t
area have been lifted and a housing esta
covers the area on the right. Guisborou
Station has also disappeared.

*Auth*

*(Above):* Guisborough box (formerly Hutton Junction) controlling the two single lines, one for passenger trains and one for goods trains, to Guisborough (left). The line seen directly ahead is double track towards Brotton and the view was photographed in May 1959.

*Author*

*(Left):* BTP 0-4-4T No. 1436, the la of the class to run, was withdra from Guisborough Shed in Novemb 1929 and it is seen at Middlesbrou earlier in the same year.

*Author's Collecti*

*(Right):* Sentinel 12 cylinder steam railcar *Old John Bull* was built in April 1930 and two months later it took over the Guisborough, Middlesbrough and Saltburn services, working from Guisborough Shed. It was relieved on occasions by sister car *Old Blue* and both were withdrawn in 1941.

*Author's Collection*

# CHAPTER FOUR
# Middleton-in-Teesdale

The original (1868) station buildings at Middleton-in-Teesdale.

*Author's Collection*

Middleton-in-Teesdale was one of the North Eastern stations where the station itself was in one county and the village in another (Yorkshire and County Durham respectively in this example) with the boundary defined by the River Tees.

After the towns in the north-east had been linked together by railway in the 1840s and 1850s, the thoughts of promoters turned to lines serving villages and market towns, where the smaller populations promised smaller returns, and many schemes were proposed for lines which had little chance of success, however attractive they appeared on paper. The thousands of acres of wild moorland on the Pennine slopes provided few passengers, but the South Durham & Lancashire Union Railway, across the barren heights between Barnard Castle, Kirkby Stephen and Tebay, was assured of a better future as it had a good flow of traffic in both directions; Durham coke going westwards, and Barrow ore going eastwards. The South Durham line was opened in 1861 and gave rise to schemes for a line across similar country from Barnard Castle and Middleton-in-Teesdale to Alston, the main attraction being the mineral deposits in the area, there being a decided lack of villages or towns which could provide passengers.

To appreciate the area the Middleton to Alston line would have traversed, it is necessary to travel the twenty miles of the lonely B6277 road, which follows the con-

tours, as it runs first along the valley of the infant Tees, and then along the valley of the South Tyne; two rivers which hereabouts flow in opposite directions although, eventually, the waters of both flow into the North Sea. Along the road are signs of long-abandoned workings, mainly for extracting lead, which had to be carried to the nearest railhead on the backs of pack-horses.

As might have been expected, the support for such a line was not encouraging and the scheme was modified to merely a line from Barnard Castle to Middleton. A company was formed (the Tees Valley Railway) and an Act of Parliament was obtained on 19th June 1865. The line, when completed, was 7 miles 55 chains long and it was formally opened on 12th May 1868; the public opening took place on the following day. In addition to the terminus at Middleton, there were originally two intermediate stations, at Cotherstone and Mickleton, the third, at Romaldkirk, not being ready at the opening date, was opened a few months later.

The Tees Valley Railway branched off the South Durham line at the appropriately-named Tees Valley Junction signal box, 1 mile 6 chains west of Barnard Castle, but the two lines ran parallel for another mile before the line to Kirkby Stephen turned to the south to serve Lartington and to cross Deepdale Viaduct. The Middleton line kept to the Yorkshire bank of the Tees for the whole of its length, and it was single throughout.

A 1956 view of the station. The office and waiting-room block dates from 1888/9. It can be seen that the clock has lost its gabled mounting in the centre of the block.

*Author's Collection*

The rear of the original office and waiting-room block, largely replaced in 1888/9, although the right-hand section (with chimney) was allowed to remain as the stationmaster's office. The house was originally single storey and must have been extended between 1868 and 1888.

*Author's Collection*

The fact that the Middleton to Brough road runs on the west side of Middleton-in-Teesdale Station at a higher level, has led to numerous photographs being taken from this viewpoint, and this was helped by the single station platform facing west. In this view, a train of 6 wheel coaches stands at the platform, with the single road engine shed in the left foreground, and Middleton-in-Teesdale itself in the background.

*Author's Collection*

The Act for the Tees Valley line was a straightforward document and, as might be expected, at the incorporation of the company the Directors included members of the Pease family, although by this time the Stockton & Darlington Railway had been taken over by the North Eastern Railway. Nominally the Tees Valley Railway was an independent concern, although Section 40 of the Act gave authorisation for the North Eastern Railway to become a shareholder to the extent of £25,000, out of an authorised share capital of £30,000! The company could enter into working arrangements with the North Eastern Railway for:

(a) Maintaining and managing the Tees Valley Railway.
(b) Use and working of the Tees Valley Railway, the conveyance of traffic thereon, and the provision of rolling stock.
(c) Fixing, collecting and the apportioning of tolls, rates, charges, receipts and revenues.

The Tees Valley Railway was not financially successful and was soon seeking to be taken over completely by the North Eastern Railway. Agreement was finally reached in 1880 and this was ratified by the Act of 19th June 1882, with the NER agreeing to settle the outstanding debts up to £22,000 and to purchase the line for £25,188. The line

was then incorporated into the Central Division of the NER.

Middleton-in-Teesdale Station always consisted of only one platform, with a run-round loop to release the engine of incoming trains, but it appears that the platform was widened at the time of the 1888 alterations. Beyond the loop was the engine shed, two water tanks and an engine turntable of 45ft. diameter. Further over were Ord & Maddison's Sidings, with a loading gantry for stone and, in the background and at a higher level, the original Low Quarry, which provided the stone traffic in the early days of the branch.

Originally, the station consisted of a single storey block of buildings, housing the stationmaster, the offices, and an open-fronted waiting shed, to a design obviously from the same architect that designed the stations on the South Durham & Lancashire Union (Barnard Castle to Tebay section) and the Eden Valley (Kirkby Stephen to Penrith). Thus, as built, Middleton was a smaller and simpler version of the stations at Ravenstonedale, on the former, and Kirkby Thore on the latter.

Extensive alterations were authorised on 1st March 1888, when the NER's Engineer submitted an estimate of £1,419, 14s. 11d. for a new station at Middleton. Photographs show that, by 1888, the station house of the 1868 building had already been considerably extended to provide a sizeable house for the stationmaster. In the 1888 alterations, part of the old waiting shed adjoining the house was left in place to form an office for the stationmaster. At a distance of 15ft. 2in. beyond the office, a single storey wood and glass fronted block, 98ft. 1in. long, was erected, housing booking office, waiting-rooms, toilets, etc., with the station clock mounted in a small dormer in the centre. The work appears to have been completed in 1889. At a later date (as yet undiscovered, but probably between 1895 and 1905) a long narrow building with a large skylight was erected between the stationmaster's office and the 1889 block. At the rear, this building was entered through sliding doors in the wall which was in line with the rear wall of the stationmaster's office. On the platform, the new building projected 12ft. 2½in. beyond the waiting-room block. A sliding door was fitted in the south-east side wall of the building to give access to the platform.

Immediately adjoining the back of the platform was the stone goods shed and, beyond that, the goods yard, with loading docks, cattle dock and coal cells.

The signal box was on the 'down' side of the line some distance outside the station, so that it could control the entrance to the goods yard on the far side of the running lines, and to Ord & Maddison's private sidings on the same side as the box; the two entrances to the latter being protected by wooden gates. Beyond the box, also on the 'down' side, was the London Lead Company's timber siding, subsequently used by various timber merchants after the London Lead Co. withdrew from Middleton.

At the buffer stop end of the station was a ground frame controlled by the signal box, 275 yards distant. The ground frame operated the points giving access to the run-round loop after the engine had run forward from its train and reversed at the buffers. Running round could also be performed without using the ground frame, with the engine propelling its empty coaches from the platform to stand on the running line near the signal box. The engine could change ends by using one of the tracks leading to the goods shed and then propel its train back into the platform. Use of the engine release loop meant the engine crossing over the turntable.

At one time, Middleton Station was beautified by attractive gardens on the platform, and a lily pond on the approach road, but when Mr E. W. Archer was appointed stationmaster in 1954, he found the gardens overgrown and the lily pond full of stones, broken branches and thick slime. His wife, Mrs Joy Archer, realised the possibilities and, over the years, with the help of the local staff, transformed the appearance of the station with flower beds, rockeries, a waterfall and a fountain, so that Middleton-in-Teesdale Station once again became notable for its floral beauty.

*Private Sidings and Stone*
Unfortunately, the original Agreement between the railway company and Ord & Maddison, the quarry owners, which must have dated from the 1870s, was not recorded by the NER, but intensive quarrying in the area appears to have started when the railway provided the means for getting the stone away. First to be developed was Low Quarry, opposite the station, but on the other side of the Middleton to Barnard Castle road (now B6277). The whin-

stone extracted from this quarry was, in 1871, reported to be 'practically inexhaustible, yielding a stone invaluable for the paving of streets and, we are informed, the product of these quarries is sent to every part of the kingdom. The enterprising proprietors have spared no expense in fitting up machinery of the best construction to facilitate their operations'.

Also in 1871 it was reported that ironstone 'of superior quality' had been discovered, and this outcropped to the surface and could be worked with comparative ease. This ironstone was actually at Holwick, three miles north-west of Middleton, where the large basaltic Holwick Scars and Crossthwaite Scars are local landmarks. To carry the ironstone from Holwick to the NER a tramway was laid, but the ironstone traffic did not develop and the main stone obtained was whinstone, supplementing the output from the original Low Quarry. Traffic from the various quarries was worked by Ord & Maddison's steam locomotives, using, at first, a Manning, Wardle 0-6-0ST (No. 126 built in 1864) and a second-hand 0-4-0ST by T. D. Ridley. On 19th April 1929, the LNER sold, to Ord & Maddison for £250, Class Y7 0-4-0T No. 898, which had latterly been employed as yard pilot at the North Road Locomotive Works at Darlington. It was built by the NER at Gateshead in December 1888 and put to stock with a book value of £1,061. Six months later, on 19th March 1930, a similar engine was purchased at the same price, £250. This was LNER No. 1302, also built at Gateshead, in September 1891 which, until withdrawal, had worked from Hull (Dairycoates) Shed.

In 1951, it was decided to abandon the rail link between the quarries and Middleton and, after working wagons of lifted rails and chairs down to Middleton, the two ex-NER engines were cut up there in 1952, followed by the removal of the Ord & Maddison Sidings and the demolition of the loading gantry in March 1953. However, Park End Quarry at Crossthwaite continued to work using road transport although, by that date, Ord & Maddison Ltd. had been succeeded by Tarmac Roadstone Ltd., who employed a reduced staff of sixteen quarrymen, a female clerk, and a manager.

Whinstone was also obtained from Lunedale Quarries, served by a siding ½ mile outside Middleton Station in the Mickleton direction, but here again the date of the NER Sidings Agreement is not recorded. In World War I, the Lunedale Whinstone Co. was succeeded by George Hodsman & Sons Ltd. and the siding tenancy was transferred to them from 2nd April 1917. The points giving access to the siding were controlled by a ground frame, the key for which was kept at Middleton signalbox. The points were facing 'up' trains. The siding was dispensed with in 1922, but was reinstated in 1924, only to close again in World War II.

Lead mining was a much older activity in the hills on both sides of the Yorkshire/Durham border and, at one time, a siding in Middleton goods yard was set aside for use by the London Lead Company for handling timber; presumably pit props for their underground workings. The company also operated a sawmill adjacent to the siding but, around the turn of the century, both siding and sawmill were taken over by Messrs Pinkney & Harrison, and later by J. Harrison, who ceased trading about 1926.

The platform, with the goods shed and the wooden office.

On 25th May 1894, the Middleton-in-Teesdale Co-operative Society signed an Agreement with the NER for a private siding leading off one of the goods yard roads opposite the signal box at Middleton. Here the Society had its own coal cells (5) and warehouse but the entry in the NER 'Collieries, Works, Sidings & Depots' book was deleted (w.e.f. 1st July 1923) and replaced by a new entry naming the trader using the siding as Teesdale Workmen's Industrial Provident Society. A survey of the station, dated November 1930, shows the site to have been altered to accommodate a tarmacadam plant, with its own elevator and rail weighbridge, which remained in situ until the early 1950s.

On 25th April 1925, a train load of stone from Middleton overpowered the engine as it was descending the branch, mostly on a falling gradient of 1 in 78 and 1 in 86. The train was unusually worked by No. 1618, a Class N9 0-6-2T, instead of the usual 0-6-0 tender engine, and it transpired that the load was greater than that allowed for this class of engine on part of the journey, but within its load limit for the length of line where the accident actually occurred at Tees Valley Junction. It so happened that on the converging Kirkby Stephen line two trains were approaching the junction from opposite directions, as the train from Middleton over-ran the signals and fouled the junction. The runaway train was first in sidelong collision with the empty mineral train from Kirkby Stephen, and the ensuing wreckage was then run into by a mineral train bound for Kirkby. The engine of the westbound mineral train was overturned at the top of the embankment, and that of the goods from Middleton had the right side tank holed and the footplate damaged. Considerable damage was also done to the wagons of the three trains, twenty eight vehicles being derailed and thirty six damaged, of which six were totally wrecked.

*Locomotive and Train Working*
It is impossible to say what engines worked the branch when it first opened but, as it was part of the Central Division, it would most probably be an engine of Stockton & Darlington origin, most likely a 2-4-0 or 0-6-0 tender engine, as the S&DR did not build any tank engines for passenger trains. Eventually, a BTP 0-4-4T would be the most suitable engine, although subsequently tender engines were normally used as the Middleton engine was not restricted to working backwards and forwards between Middleton and Barnard Castle, but ran to Bishop Auckland, Durham, Sunderland, Darlington and Newcastle.

From official records it has been possible to list the various engines stationed at Middleton from 1923 onwards, starting with Class 901 2-4-0 No. 370 and, when this was withdrawn in the following year, it was replaced by 'Tennant' 2-4-0 No. 1468, but this engine was transferred to York in May 1925 in exchange for Class D23 4-4-0 No. 217. This useful engine remained at Middleton for five years, until being replaced in December 1930 by ex-Hull & Barnsley 0-6-0 No. 2514 (Class J23) from Darlington, with No. 217 moving to Barnard Castle Shed. However, in June 1931, No. 2514 returned to Darlington and No. 217 moved back to Middleton, only to be withdrawn on 8th August 1931. The replacement this time was one of the eight ex-Great Northern Class D3 4-4-0s, transferred to Darlington and its sub-sheds in 1930 and

1931 for working the services between Darlington, Kirkby Stephen, Penrith and Tebay. This turned out to be No. 4077, which was later replaced by No. 4354 of the same class, which remained at Middleton until it was transferred to Hull in July 1936 (on paper, at least). Actually, ex-Great Eastern 2-4-0 No. 7416 had been sent to Middleton in October 1935, and this 'foreigner' remained until July 1938 when it returned to Darlington.

In 1937, a new locomotive roster was introduced, and this meant that after leaving Middleton for Barnard Castle on the first train of the day at 6.31a.m., the engine worked through to Newcastle, via Bishop Auckland, Durham and Sunderland, arriving at 8.42a.m. The crew were then rostered to set off for home at 9.35a.m. using a fresh engine provided by Gateshead Shed, there being insufficient time for the Middleton crew to service their own engine. This meant that the early turn Middleton men set off from home with their own engine on Mondays, Wednesdays and Fridays, and with a Gateshead engine on Tuesdays, Thursdays and Saturdays. However, this arrangement was soon altered so that the Middleton men retained their own engine, and to give them more time, the first leg of their return working was the 10.47a.m. Newcastle to Sunderland train. They reached Middleton at 1.40p.m. and the late turn crew then took over and worked a similar duty to Barnard Castle, Bishop Auckland, Durham, Sunderland and Newcastle and return.

A Class V1 2-6-2T was sent on loan to Middleton for these duties and for a time Gateshead Shed had to provide a standby Class V1 engine each day in case the Middleton men required a fresh engine. Later, when Class A8 engines were allowed on the Middleton branch, the engine could be a Class A8 or a V1, and a fresh engine was provided weekly. Although Middleton was a sub-shed of Darlington, the engine did not actually visit Darlington, hence the need for the Middleton engine to be washed out and maintained at Gateshead.

Permission to use Class A8s to Middleton was granted in July 1938 and No. 1524 was transferred from Darlington on the 16th, on which date Class E4 No. 7416 was transferred back to Darlington, although it seems probable that, because of the two daily Newcastle trips, it had not been used by Middleton for some time. In fact, it was at Stratford Works from May to July 1938. Another Class A8, No. 1525, replaced No. 1524 in March 1939, and a newcomer in the shape of Class A5 No. 1766 moved in exchange in May 1939. Upon the outbreak of war in 1939, a reorganisation of rosters meant that the Middleton engine spent all its time working to and from Darlington and, as a large engine was no longer required, the Class A5 returned to Darlington and was replaced by Class G5 0-4-4T No. 1764, which remained at Middleton until June 1950 (latterly as No. 67309).

During the war, extra duties were found for the Middleton men during their stop overs at Darlington. In 1942, they worked through to Richmond at 8.15a.m., returning at 9.50a.m., and they also worked a 'Saturdays Excepted' workmen's train from Allens West to Darlington, leaving Darlington at 4.42p.m., and running out empty stock to Eaglescliffe to run round their train. On Saturdays they took over a Darlington Class A5 to work the 11.25a.m. Darlington to Richmond train and return.

From October 1946, the Middleton men took over a

*(Opposite):* Looking along the platform, past the 1888/9 extensions, to the goods shed and starting signal. The view is framed by the doorway of the new booking hall, which was fitted with two sliding doors, both sliding to the left as viewed here. The stationmaster and his wife, Mr & Mrs Archer, are seen admiring the flowers on the station, for which they were responsible. *Author's Collection*

The frontage in the 1980s.

*C. A. Kimber*

Class D23 4-4-0 No. 217, when it was the Middleton-in-Teesdale engine between May 1925 and December 1930. This photograph was taken in May 1930 by W. H. Whitworth after the engine had been turned prior to joining its train standing at the platform (right).

*W. H. Whitworth*

Darlington Class A5 for the 7.00p.m. to Middleton on Saturdays and, on the Sunday morning, they worked the same Class A5 on the 8.00a.m. to Darlington, but only as far as Barnard Castle, where they exchanged footplates and took over another Class A5 working a Darlington to Middleton train. This they stabled on their return to Middleton and it was next used on the 6.40a.m. Middleton to Darlington train on the Monday morning. On reaching Darlington they regained their own Class G5 for use throughout the week. The Sunday duty involved 42 minutes actual running time out of a duty covering 4 hours 39 minutes!

From June 1950, Middleton had no engine to call its own and was supplied with any of Darlington's Class G5s but, from June 1951, the Middleton to Darlington service went over to push-and-pull working, using Nos. 67273 or 67284. No. 67273 went to West Auckland in October 1952 and was replaced by No. 67305 from Stockton, leaving Nos. 67284 and 67305 to work the service for some years.

Diesel multiple unit railcars were introduced on 16th September 1957 and the shed was closed, but two drivers remained at Middleton for working the early and late turns. On Saturdays, the Middleton driver on the last train was accompanied by a Darlington driver, whose job it was to take the set back to Darlington for weekend maintenance. On Monday mornings, a Darlington driver took out an empty set at 5.10a.m. to form the first train from Middleton at 6.30a.m., which was worked by the Middleton driver, accompanied by the Darlington driver returning home.

In LNER days, the trains to and from Middleton were made up of three coach sets comprising one composite coach and two brake thirds, seating 24 first class passengers and 120 third class; the set weighing 65 tons. These sets worked a complicated roster and in Link B there were 33 sets, so that the coaches leaving Middleton as the first train on a Monday morning did not appear on the same train until the Wednesday five weeks and two days later!

The coaches were standard North Eastern bogie stock and could be clerestory, elliptical, or flat roofed stock, although the latter were uncommon.

At the same time (1932) Sentinel steam railcars from Shildon Shed worked to Middleton on the 10.25a.m. train from Barnard Castle, returning at 11.35a.m. The cars allocated to Shildon at that time were Nos. 263 *North Star*, 265 *Neptune*, 267 *Liberty*, and 272 *Hero*, all of the two cylinder variety. By 1937, Shildon Shed had been closed and the duties were taken over by West Auckland, which used one of its six cylinder railcars on the 8.40a.m. Darlington to Middleton train and the 10.10a.m. return journey, with another car on the 4.40p.m. Bishop Auckland to Middleton and the 6.06p.m. return. The cars at West Auckland Shed were Nos. 2136 *Hope*, 2144 *Traveller*, 2152 *Telegraph* and 2261 *Diligence*. Perhaps the most surprising visitor was a Tyne Dock-based car which worked the 4.06p.m. train from South Shields to Middleton (arrive 7.23p.m.) and returned on the 8.20p.m. from Middleton to Sunderland (arrive 10.25p.m.); this ran Mondays to Fridays. Tyne Dock cars were two cylinder, Nos. 237 *Rodney*, 244 *True Blue*, 254 *Phoenix*,, and six cylinder No. 2267 *Recovery*.

There was no engine shed at Middleton when the line opened in May 1868 but, on 2nd January 1869, a report was submitted estimating the cost of a shed at £194. 19s. 4d. However, the Secretary of the Tees Valley company reported that there was an old shed at Shildon which might answer the purpose, and he was instructed to ask Mr Bouch, the Engineer of the Stockton & Darlington section, what he would take for it. Estimates for the removal of the shed and its re-erection at Middleton were also called for, but it seems that nothing came of this suggestion as, on 31st March 1869, five tenders were considered for a new shed. These ranged from £190 to £230, but the Committee favoured the tender submitted by Mr Hepworth, which was not the lowest tender, so he was asked if he would accept the amount estimated by the

---

**Engines stationed at Middleton-in-Teesdale — 1923 to 1950**

| | | *Transferred to Middleton* | | | *Transferred from Middleton* | |
|---|---|---|---|---|---|---|
| *Engine* | *Class* | *From* | *Date* | *To* | *Date* | |
| 370 | 901 | — | — | Withdrawn | 10/24 | |
| 1468 | 1463 | Hull | 10/24 | York | 5/25 | |
| 217 | D23 | York | 5/25 | Barnard Castle | 12/30 | |
| 2514 | J23 | Darlington | 12/30 | Darlington | 6/31 | |
| 217 | D23 | Barnard Castle | 6/31 | Withdrawn | 8/31 | |
| 4077 | D3 | Darlington | 8/31 | Darlington | 10/33 | |
| 4354 | D3 | Darlington | 10/33 | Hull B.G. | 7/36 | |
| 7416 | E4 | Southern Area | 10/35 | Darlington | 7/38 | |
| ? | V1 | On loan | | | | |
| 1524 | A8 | Darlington | 7/38 | Saltburn | 3/39 | |
| 1525 | A8 | Darlington | 3/39 | Saltburn | 5/39 | |
| 1766 | A5 | Darlington | 5/39 | Darlington | 9/39 | |
| 1764 | G5 | Stockton | 9/39 | Darlington | 6/50* | |

*\* Class G5 No. 1764 was renumbered 7309 in May 1946.*
From June 1950, Middleton Shed had no allocation of its own, but used Darlington Class G5s
until steam working was replaced by diesel railcars in September 1957.

Another view of No. 217, ready to depart for Barnard Castle. The turntable and disused water tank are seen on the left.

*W. H. Whitworth*

In October 1933, Middleton Shed received Class D3 4-4-0 No. 4354, one of the Great Northern engines transferred to the area. In this view it is seen awaiting departure. The remains of one of the stone loading gantries can be seen in the left foreground.

*L. Ward Collection*

Company's engineer, and to this he agreed. The resulting single road dead end shed was situated in the station yard, and a 45ft. turntable was provided, although it was removed in the 1940s. The shed remained open until 16th September 1957, and it was demolished in the summer of 1961.

Although the Middleton branch usually saw only the smaller types of engines, there were times when large engines appeared; for instance, during World War II Class V2 2-6-2s worked in on troop specials and later appeared on excursions. On 14th May 1951, No. 60801 arrived on an excursion from South Shields and retired to West Auckland Shed until it was due to work its return train. Middleton's turntable had gone by then, but this would have been too small in any case, and West Auckland's only turntable was a 50 footer inside the roundhouse. Fortunately two triangles were available nearby, and there were no difficulties in turning the engine for its journey back to South Shields.

### Engine Working Middleton-in-Teesdale, Summer 1908

*Weekdays:*

|  | arr. | dep. |
|---|---|---|
|  |  | a.m. |
| Middleton-in-Teesdale | — | 6.45 |
| Sunderland | 9.40 | 10.22 |
| Barnard Castle | 1.00 | — |

*Driver and fireman passengers to Middleton-in-Teesdale*

*Second Set*
*Driver and fireman passengers to Barnard Castle*

|  |  | p.m. |
|---|---|---|
| Barnard Castle | — | 2.35 |
| Sunderland | 5.28 | 6.40 |
| Barnard Castle | 9.05 | 9.49 |
| Middleton-in-Teesdale | 10.12 | — |

### Engine Working Middleton-in-Teesdale, — Winter 1922-3

*Weekdays:*

|  |  | a.m. |
|---|---|---|
| Middleton-in-Teesdale | — | 6.46 |
| Sunderland | 9.40 | 10.30 |
| Barnard Castle | 1.04* | 1.36 |
| Middleton-in-Teesdale | 1.58 | — |

*Second Set*

|  |  | p.m. |
|---|---|---|
| Middleton-in-Teesdale | — | 2.10 |
| Barnard Castle | 2.30* | 4.22 |
| Bishop Auckland | 4.54 | 5.17 |
| Barnard Castle | 5.56 | 6.35 |
| Middleton-in-Teesdale | 6.57 | — |

*\* = Engine used for shunting at Barnard Castle*

### Passenger Engine Working Middleton-in-Teesdale, — Winter 1937/8

*Weekdays:*

|  | a.m. | a.m. |
|---|---|---|
| Middleton-in-Teesdale | — | 6.31 |
| Barnard Castle | 6.51 | 6.54 |
| Bishop Auckland | 7.14 | 7.25 |
| Durham | 7.59 | 8.05 |
| Newcastle | 8.42 | 10.47 (SX) |
| Sunderland | 11.19 | 11.33 (SX) |
| Durham | 12.12 | 12.14 |
| Bishop Auckland | 12.35 | 12.37 |
| Barnard Castle | 1.08 | 1.18 |
| Middleton-in-Teesdale | 1.40 | — |

*Second Set*

|  |  | p.m. |
|---|---|---|
| Middleton-in-Teesdale | — | 2.15 |
| Barnard Castle | 2.37 | 2.50 |
| Bishop Auckland | 3.20 | 3.24 |
| Durham | 3.45 | 3.50 |
| Newcastle | 4.32 | 7.23 |
| Durham | 8.03 * | 8.30 |
| Bishop Auckland | 8.57 | 9.10 |
| Barnard Castle | 9.43 | 9.45 |
| Middleton-in-Teesdale | 10.07 | — |

*\* = Assist 8p.m. ex-Newcastle (to King's Cross) to start from Durham Station at 8.26p.m.*

*Sundays:*

|  |  | p.m. |
|---|---|---|
| Middleton-in-Teesdale | — | 5.30 |
| Darlington | 6.47 | 8.25 |
| Middleton-in-Teesdale | 9.37 | — |

### *Closure*

Following the controversial closure of the Barnard Castle to Penrith line in January 1962, the Darlington-Barnard Castle—Middleton-in-Teesdale trains continued to operate, but as a purely local branch service, with seven trains daily from Darlington to Barnard Castle, five of which continued to Middleton. The 'Mondays Only' early morning train from Darlington to Middleton, and the 'Saturdays Only' late evening train from Middleton to Darlington conveyed passengers, but still their main purpose was to supply the weekly diesel multiple unit to Middleton on the Monday and to get it back to Darlington Diesel Depot on the Saturday.

A formal enquiry was held at Barnard Castle on 27th February 1964 to hear sixty five objections to the closure but, on 9th September, the Minister of Transport gave his consent, subject to the usual conditions regarding the provision of a modified bus service, including through buses from Middleton to Darlington at 6a.m. and 7.05 a.m. (replacing the 6.30a.m. and 7.34a.m. trains), and from Darlington at 4.35p.m. and 5.30p.m. (replacing the 4.35p.m. and 5.34p.m. trains). On 2nd November 1964, British Rail announced the forthcoming closure of the line under their standard reference to the 'Re-shaping of British Railways' and the last trains ran on 28th November 1964.

## Notes on the Drawings
## MIDDLETON-IN-TEESDALE

### General

The original single storey station buildings of 1868 are shown in the photograph and, by 1888, the house had been rebuilt with two storeys. The passenger accommodation was largely rebuilt in 1888/9, and the contractor for this work was W. & R. Blackett. A new booking hall was added about the turn of the century.

**Station buildings** *(Drawings 1 to 3)*
The additions to the house included the crenellated porch on the platform, the small porch on the opposite side of the house, and the extension of the front bay window from 9in. to a 3ft. 6in. projection. Other alterations were the provision of the room linking the stationmaster's office to the 1888/9 station buildings, and this became the new booking hall; the extension of the gentlemen's toilet, and a new coal house, both at the opposite end of the station buildings.

When the 1888 alterations were designed, it was intended that an 8ft. gap should be left between the stationmaster's office and the new buildings, and this is given on three of the original drawings. However, by mistake or design, the dimension was increased to 15ft. 2in., but no note of this was made on the drawings so that when the new booking hall was planned, it was assumed that, to get the required floor area, a 31ft. 1in. x 8ft. (internal) building would be required. This resulted in the awkward projection of this building on to the platform for 12ft. 2½in., as it was built to the specified 31ft. 1in. length, even though the builder must have discovered the error when he was 'setting out'; but it was completed to the increased width. This gave only an 8ft. clearance from the platform edge.

The track layout must have been remodelled in 1888, as the platform was widened to give nearly 30ft. from its edge to the stationmaster's house, which is considerably more than shown in the 1868 photograph.

*(Above):* A 1980s' view of the rear of the station buildings with the stationmaster's house on the right. The adjacent chimney breast and stack mark the remaining portion of the 1868 building, and between this and the 1888/9 extension (on the left) has been inserted a building running at right angles to the track, with the end of its roof-light visible in the photograph. This became the new booking hall, allowing the office accommodation in the north wing of the 1888/9 extension to be increased. The filled-in doorway was originally closed by sliding doors.

*C. A. Kimber*

*(Below):* Another view of the rear of the building, this time looking up the approach road, past the stationmaster's house to the 1888/9 block. The buildings in the previous view stand back out of sight in the gap.

*C. A. Kimber*

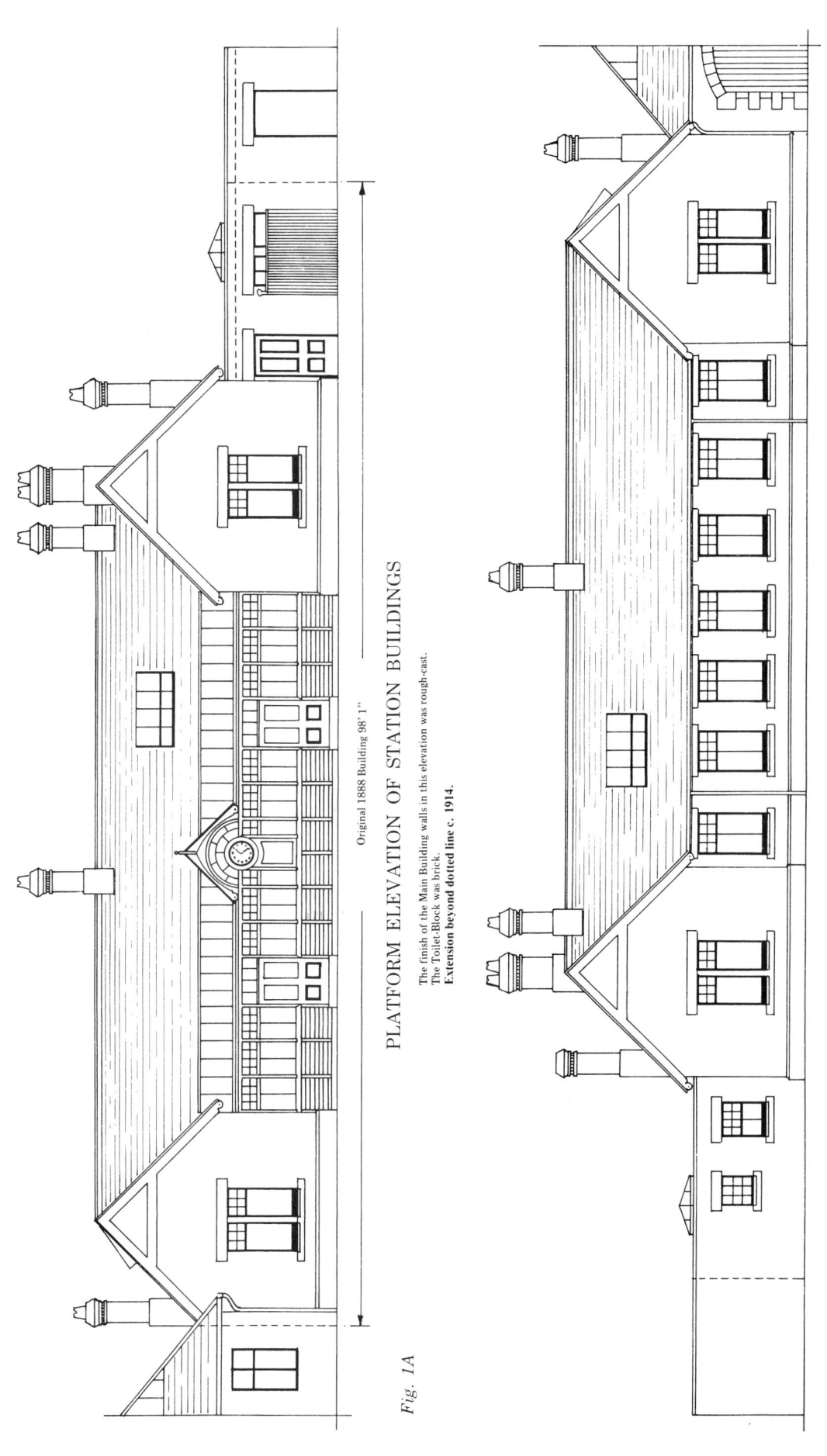

PLATFORM ELEVATION OF STATION BUILDINGS

Original 1888 Building 98' 1"

The finish of the Main Building walls in this elevation was rough-cast.
The Toilet-Block was brick.
**Extension beyond dotted line c. 1914.**

Fig. 1A

REAR ELEVATION OF STATION BUILDINGS (BRICK)

Fig. 1B

MIDDLETON-IN-TEESDALE

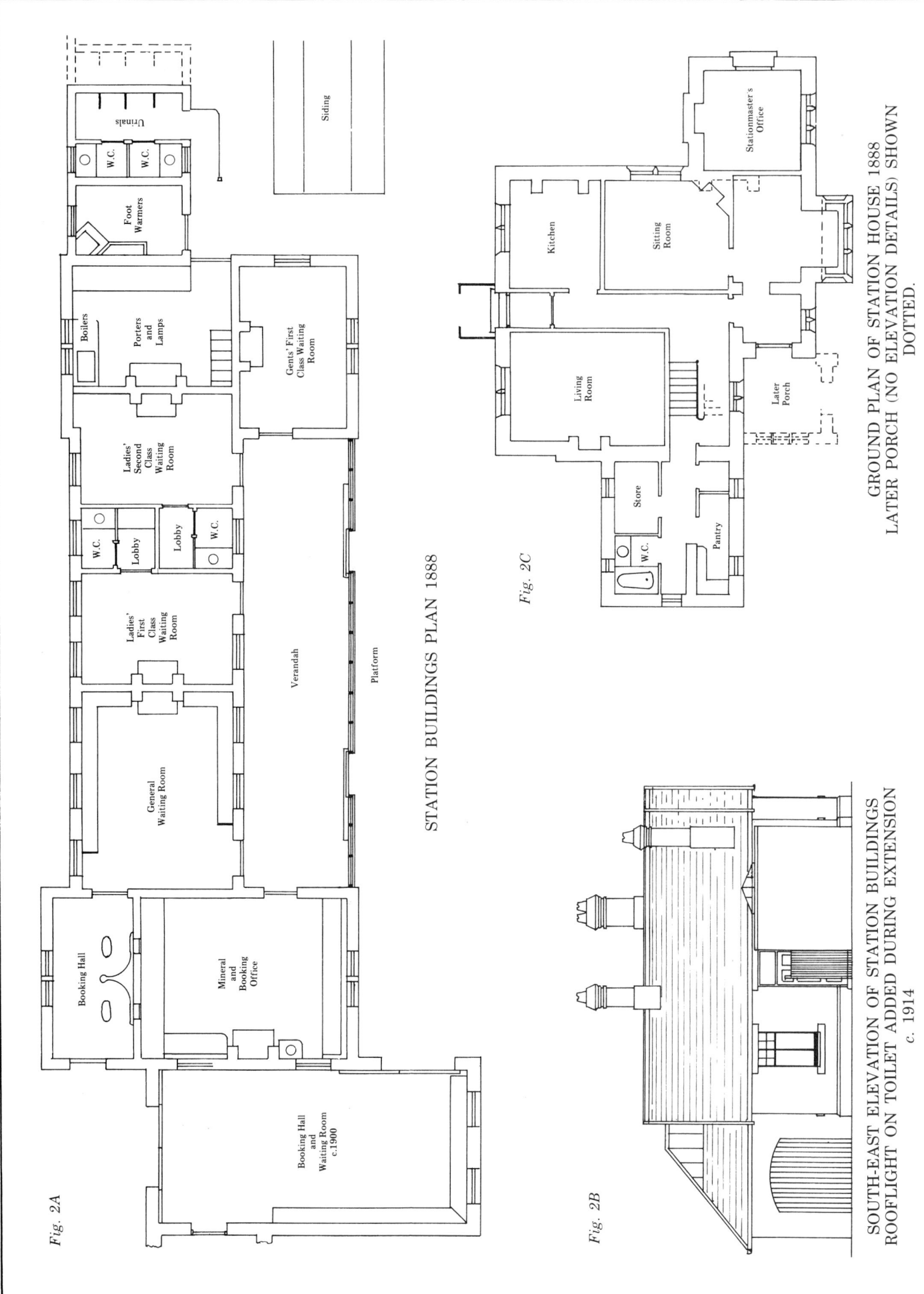

Siding

Urinals

W.C.

W.C.

Foot
Warmers

Boilers

Porters
and
Lamps

Gents' First
Class Waiting
Room

Ladies' Second
Class Waiting
Room

W.C.

Lobby

Lobby

W.C.

Ladies'
First
Class
Waiting
Room

General
Waiting Room

Verandah

Platform

Booking Hall

Mineral
and
Booking
Office

Booking Hall
and
Waiting Room
c.1900

Fig. 2A

STATION BUILDINGS PLAN 1888

Kitchen

Sitting
Room

Stationmaster's
Office

Living
Room

Store

W.C.

Pantry

Later
Porch

Fig. 2C

GROUND PLAN OF STATION HOUSE 1888
LATER PORCH (NO ELEVATION DETAILS) SHOWN
DOTTED.

Fig. 2B

SOUTH-EAST ELEVATION OF STATION BUILDINGS
ROOFLIGHT ON TOILET ADDED DURING EXTENSION
c. 1914

MIDDLETON-IN-TEESDALE STATION

The rear of the 1888/9 block, with the original booking office door on the right. A door has recently been made in the rear wall, taking the place of a window.

*C. A. Kimber*

A view looking along the rear of the extension towards the stationmaster's house.

*C. A. Kimber*

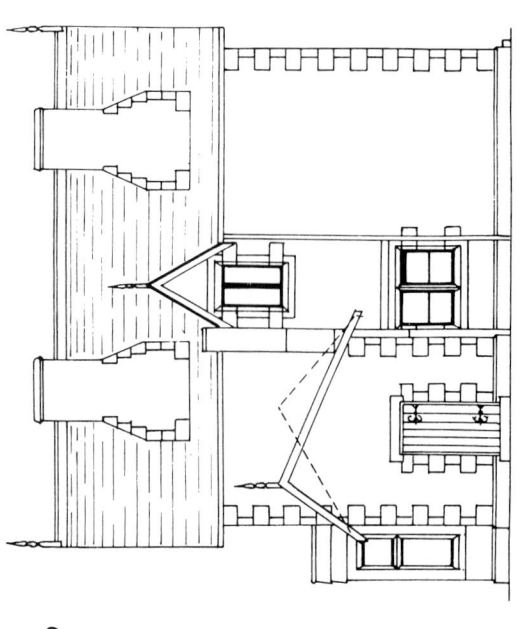

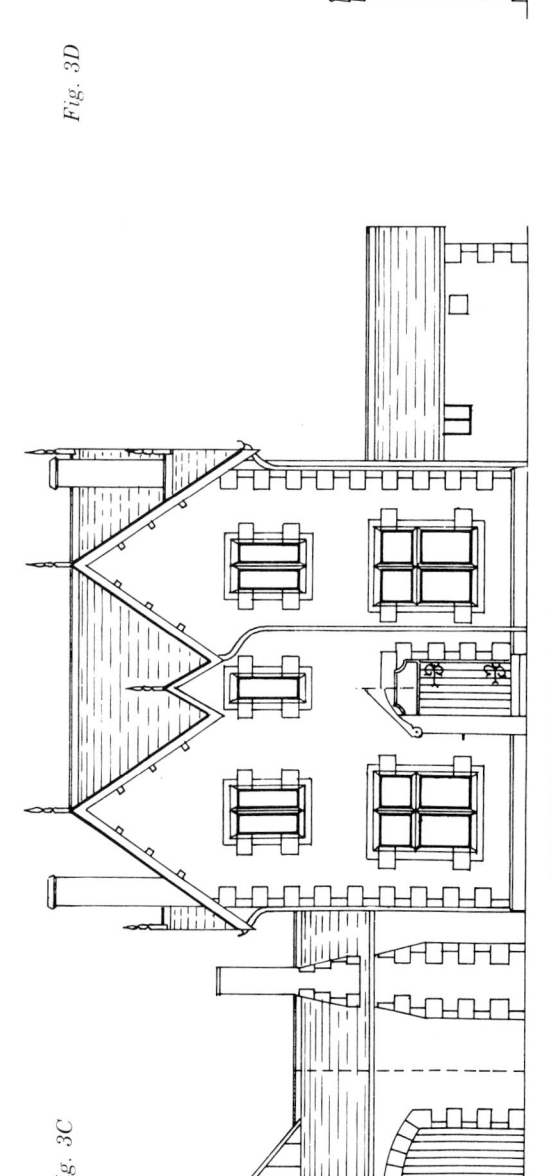

Fig. 3B

NORTH-WEST ELEVATION
ORIGINAL 9" PROTRUDING BAY SHOWN DOTTED.

Fig. 3D

SOUTH-EAST ELEVATION
SHOWING 1888 END TO STATIONMASTER'S
OFFICE. LATER ROOF LINE SHOWN DOTTED.

Fig. 3A

SOUTH-WEST (PLATFORM) ELEVATION
THE RIGHT HAND BUILDING SHOWN IN
HALF ELEVATION DATES FROM c. 1914

Fig. 3C

NORTH-EAST ELEVATION
ORIGINAL (1888) END OF STATIONMASTER'S OFFICE
SHOWN DOTTED. LATER PORCH SHOWN IN HALF
ELEVATION TO GIVE DOOR DETAIL.

MIDDLETON-IN-TEESDALE
STATION HOUSE 1888

The front of the house now that the site is used as a caravan park.

*C. A. Kimber*

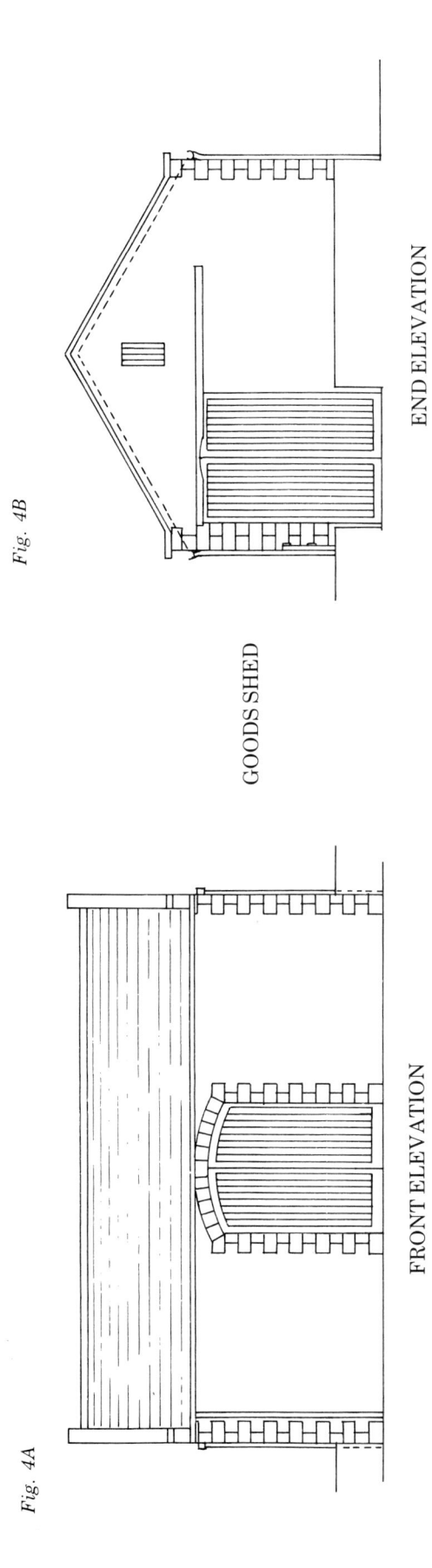

*Fig. 4B*

END ELEVATION

GOODS SHED

*Fig. 4A*

FRONT ELEVATION

**Goods shed**

The population of Middleton-in-Teesdale and Upper Teesdale may be smaller than Richmond and Swaledale, but surely not enough to justify the disparity in the goods warehouse facilities! The very small warehouse at Middleton was supplemented by a small wooden shed which served as an office. It is not known whether the shed dates from 1868 or from the 1888 rebuilding.

**Signal box**

No drawings survive for the box but it was of the standard Stockton & Darlington/North Eastern Central Division pattern shown in Figs. 4C, 4D and 4E. The right-hand elevation depicts the ornamental barge boards and cross bracings with which the boxes were built, and the opposite end shows the plain barge boards provided later on many boxes.

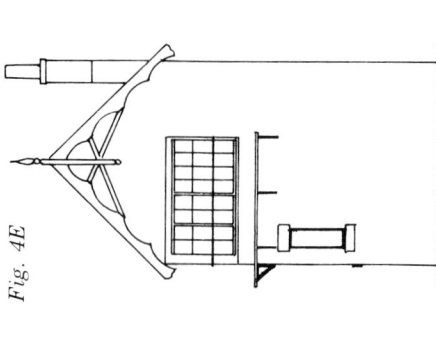

*Fig. 4E*

END ELEVATION (AS BUILT)

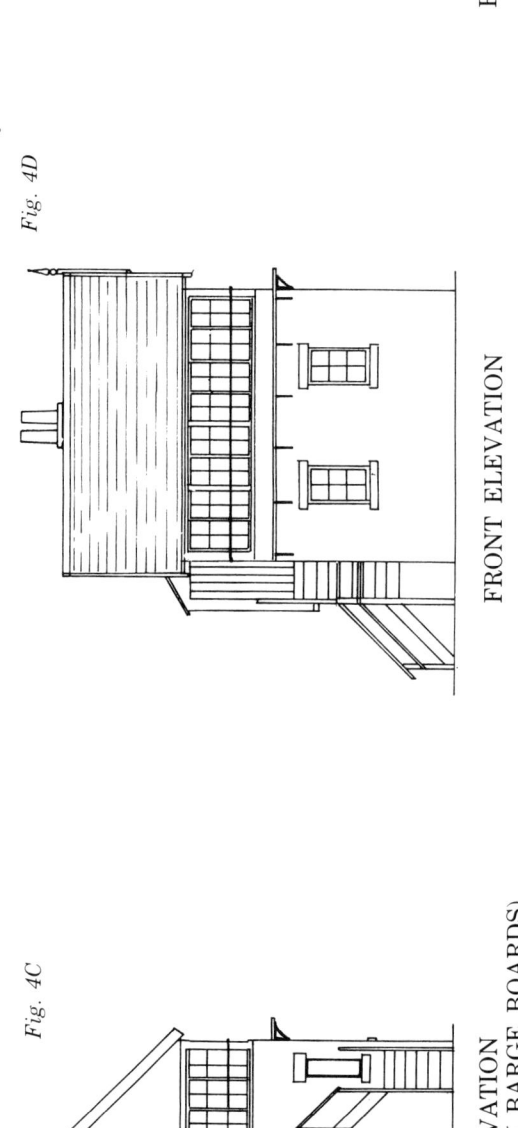

*Fig. 4D*

FRONT ELEVATION

*Fig. 4C*

END ELEVATION
(WITH LATER PLAIN BARGE BOARDS)

STANDARD STYLE OF CENTRAL DIVISION SIGNALBOX

**MIDDLETON-IN-TEESDALE**

In April 1964, a visit to Middleton was included in the itinerary of a RCTS railtour headed by 2-6-2T No. 67646 and 2-6-4T No. 42639. The ground frame for the run-round loop can be seen in the centre, and beyond it the out-of-use water tank, left in situ as the base was used as a platelayers' hut.

*Author*

Ord & Maddison's engines worked into the company's sidings at Middleton and here we see ex-NER Class H 0-4-0T No. 1302, purchased from the LNER in March 1930. The initials of the former owner have been obliterated from above the number. Middleton signal box is seen in the background.

*Author's Collection*

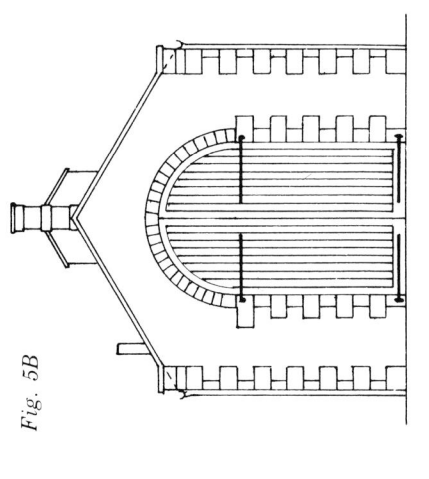

*Fig. 5B*

END ELEVATION

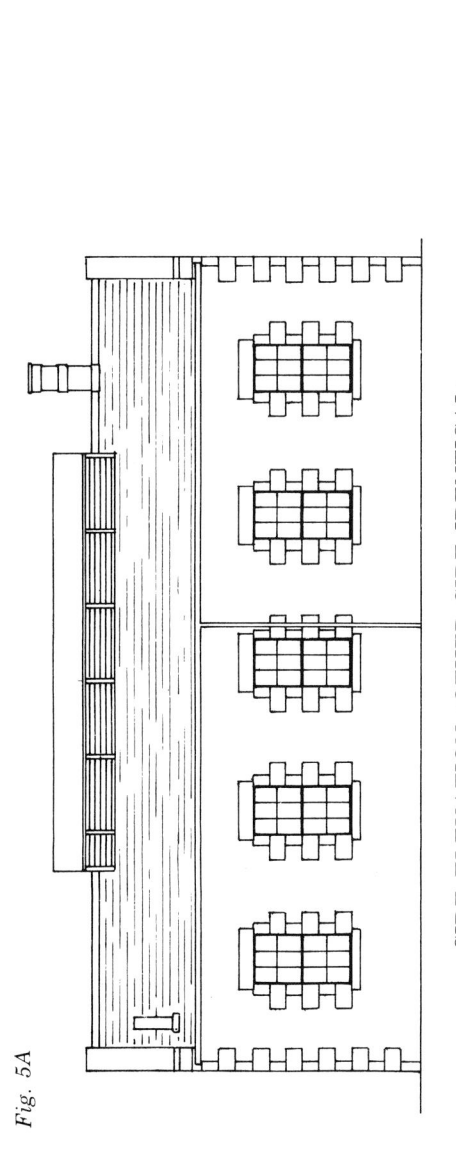

*Fig. 5A*

SIDE ELEVATION (OTHER SIDE IDENTICAL)

ENGINE SHED 1869

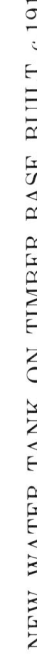

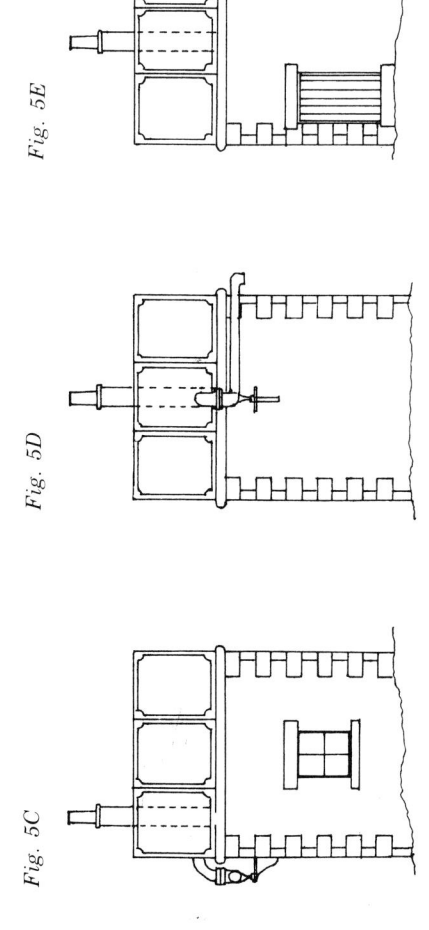

*Fig. 5F*

*Fig. 5G*

*Fig. 5C*

*Fig. 5D*

*Fig. 5E*

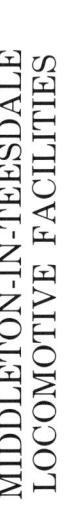

OLD TANK HOUSE, DISUSED FROM c.1910 AND
BASE USED BY PLATELAYERS

NEW WATER TANK ON TIMBER BASE BUILT c.1910

**Engine Shed and facilities**

The shed was built in 1869, or early 1870, and remained unaltered throughout its life.

Middleton was one of the few locations on the NER where the water delivery to the locomotive was straight from the tank, instead of via a water column. The original 6,000 gallon tank of 1869 was replaced, around 1910, by a 10,000 gallon tank on a timber base. The base of the old tank was used by the platelayers, which explains the position of the brick chimney passing through the inside of the tank.

MIDDLETON-IN-TEESDALE
LOCOMOTIVE FACILITIES

The stone sent down the branch originally came from Low Quarry, situated just across the Brough road from the station. This quarry has not been worked for many years and now stands overgrown, silent and deserted.

*Author*

A mile and a half north-west of Middleton, thousands of tons of stone were extracted from the hillside at Crossthwaite Scars and sent to Middleton behind Ord & Maddison's locomotives. These workings were abandoned in 1971.

*Author*

The engine involved in the runaway collision at Tees Valley Junction on 25th April 1925 was Class N9 0-6-2T No. 1618, here at Darlington in the following year, after being repaired and returned to traffic.

*Author's Collection*

Another 'foreigner' was former Hull & Barnsley Railway 0-6-0 locomotive, No. 2514, which was stationed at Middleton in 1930/1.

*Author's Collection*

However, many of the Middleton trains were worked by Class G5 0-4-4T engines, both in LNER and BR days. In this 1947 view, No. 7258, a Durham-based engine, prepares to leave Middleton for the cathedral city. The turntable has been removed and the pit filled in. Both water tanks are visible in this view.

*Author's Collection*

Between 1951 and 1957, the Darlington to Middleton service was worked by a Class G5 0-4-4T on a push-and-pull set, and pictured here is No. 67305 on the 5.30p.m. Darlington to Middleton train on 1st June 1957.

*J. F. Mallon*

The stationmaster's house appears to be the 1868 building considerably extended, with a bay window replacing the original window, using the original frames. At some time, probably by the turn of the century, an out-of-place square porch with castellations was added, but this has now been removed.

*Author's Collection*

A final view of Middleton as Class G5 0-4-4T No. 67284 leaves for Darlington. The 7½ milepost (from Tees Valley Junction) is seen in the foreground, with the gate to Ord & Maddison's sidings and Middleton-in-Teesdale signal box beyond. On the opposite side of the line is the disused tarmacadam plant.

*Author's Collection*

As can be seen in this view, the station is now used as a caravan park.

*C. B. Foster*

# CHAPTER FIVE

# Richmond

Not only had the railway company to construct a station at Richmond, but it also had to build an approach road and a bridge over the River Swale. For seventy years this road led only to the station and it was gated at the station end but, in World War I, a link road was put in between the south end of the bridge and the Richmond to Catterick Camp road.

*J. F. Mallon Collection*

Although authorised by the Great North of England Railway Act of 21st July 1845, the Richmond branch was actually opened in September 1846 by the York & Newcastle Railway, the name adopted when the GNER (York to Darlington) was formally leased by the Newcastle & Darlington Junction Railway (Darlington to Gateshead) from 27th July 1846.

The branch was planned to leave the GNER main line at Dalton, 5¼ miles south of Darlington, and run 9¾ miles to terminate at 'Back of Friars' at Richmond, and as the N&DJR had been in control of the GNER since August 1845 it was the former company that awarded the contracts for building the line and its stations. Thus, on 3rd June 1846, the tender of Roberts, Elwin & Jeffrey of Darlington was accepted for the construction of the coal depot, weigh house, engine house and warehouse at Richmond, the station and coal depot at Catterick, the gatehouse at Broken Brea (sic), stations and coal depots at Scorton and Moulton, and the station at Dalton. The price was £10,300.

Three days later, on 6th June 1846, the plans for Richmond Station and cottages were submitted and approved, but it was pointed out that the line would be ready for opening before the station could be completed,

and it was decided to build a temporary wooden passenger station, to be used until the permanent station was ready.

The branch was opened to the public on Thursday, 10th September 1846, with a service of three trains a day from Richmond to Darlington at 7.15a.m., 11.30a.m. and 3.45p.m., and from Darlington to Richmond at 7.20a.m., 1p.m. and 6p.m. All the trains were allowed 45 minutes for the journey, except for the first train from Richmond which was timed to reach Darlington in 35 minutes. The opening notice, dated 31st August 1846, was issued above the signature of James Allport, the General Manager, and included the times of connections to and from London, York and Newcastle. Within a year, the service had increased to four trains each way daily, with three each way on Sundays. Fares from Richmond to Darlington were 2s. 6d. (First Class) 1s. 6d. (Second Class) and 1s. 0d. (Third Class). By May 1849, the First and Second Class fares had been reduced to 2s. 0d. and 1s. 3d. respectively, but the Third Class remained at 1s. 0d., and there was a Fourth Class (1d. per mile) at 10d.

Although the actual station building was specially designed by the architect, G. T. Andrews, he used a standard design for the engine shed, following sheds to

A general view of Richmond Station and yard with the depot agent's house in the foreground. The stationmaster's house is seen to the right of the station.

*Author's Collection*

Richmond was at one time an important lead mining centre, and pigs of lead were weighed in the station yard before being loaded into railway wagons. Here the load is being carefully weighed and recorded, and alongside stands an NER porter in the uniform of the day, circa 1870.

*Author's Collection*

The frontage of Richmond Station, virtually indistinguishable from Andrews' water colour picture of the station prepared before it was built.

*C. B. Foster*

the same pattern at York, Darlington and Scarborough. The building had a hipped roof covering two tracks but, in June 1869, as the space in the shed was more than required, it was decided to convert part of the building into a stable for four horses at a cost of £445.

In April 1877, tenders were requested for a 45ft. engine turntable, to replace one reported as worn out. However, in the following month it was reported that all trains on the branch could be worked by tank engines, and it was recommended that a new turntable should not be provided. However, a few years later, the decision was reversed and a 45ft. turntable by Ianson of Darlington was provided, and this lasted for 70 years.

A smaller building in the yard, again to an Andrews design, is usually referred to as the pump house, but the LNER diagram of the shed layout dated 1929 shows it as 'Old Gas Works'. Inspection of the interior of the building reveals three firebrick-lined structures which were probably retorts for the production of gas, but further investigation is continuing.

Water was obtained from Sand Beck, about half a mile south-east of the station, where there was a pumping station. The pump had an 8in. diameter piston with a 10in. stroke, and it averaged 48 revolutions per minute. It was driven by a Carrick & Wardale vertical steam engine with a cylinder 10in. diameter by 10in. stroke (C&W 827/1892). Steam was supplied by a vertical boiler (Gateshead 781 of February 1909) which was 8ft. $4^{15}/_{16}$in. high and 3ft. 6in. diameter, working at a pressure of 70p.s.i., with one Friedman injector. The boiler was cut up

in October 1945 and it is presumed that, at that time, an automatically-controlled electric pump was installed. The installation was looked after by a NER pumping engineman who, in 1918, received 24s. 0d. per week of 53 hours, with no paid holidays.

The site chosen for the station had no road access and it was necessary to build a stone four arch bridge across the River Swale to enable the inhabitants of Richmond to reach the station. The bridge was known as Station Bridge for 129 years but, on 11th July 1975, it was renamed Mercury Bridge to mark the long connection between the town and the Royal Corps of Signals, the headquarters of which was at Catterick Camp.

About 1917, the road to the station was extended to join the older road from Richmond to Hipswell and Scotton, to make an easier route to Catterick Camp. Some three years later, the bridge was adopted by the local highway authority but, after 60 years, it still carried its NER bridge plate, No. 8, at the southern end.

Facing the station, across the River Swale, is Richmond School, which has connections with the railway going back many years. From 1796 to 1833, the Master of the school was James Tate, a noted classical scholar, and it was he who suggested the Stockton & Darlington Railway Company's motto for its seal *Periculum Privatum Utilitas Publica* (At Private Risk for Public Service). To mark his long and distinguished spell at Richmond, a new school was erected in 1850 by voluntary subscriptions, built to a design prepared by the York architect responsible for the station, namely G. T. Andrews. Both school

A view looking along the platform, with the signal box (left) and goods warehouse (right). The left-hand platform face, ending inside the train shed, was 268 yards long, and the right-hand face was made up of a platform of 186 yards long and a horse dock 42½ yards long. The raised section forming the horse dock can be seen opposite the far end of the goods shed.

*C. B. Foster*

A scene looking from the platform end, with a diesel multiple unit approaching. The NER pattern water column is seen beyond the signal gantry.

*C. B. Foster*

and station buildings remain, the former still used for its original purpose, but the station saw its last trains in 1969 and is now in use as a garden centre. A swimming pool has been built on the site of the goods yard, and plans have just been announced to turn the former engine shed into an arts centre.

Another part of Richmond's history is connected with the British Army, and this part of the former North Riding of Yorkshire (also known as Richmondshire) has, since 1782, provided men for the Green Howards, a regiment based at Richmond. The regiment was actually formed in 1688 and, to mark its 250th anniversary, it was decided to name a new Class V2 2-6-2 locomotive, fresh from Darlington Works. The engine chosen was No. 4806 and, on Saturday, 24th September 1938, it was named *The Green Howards, Alexandra, Princess of Wales's Own Yorkshire Regiment* by Major-General H. E. Franklyn DSO, MC, the General Officer Commanding the 5th Division and a former officer of the Green Howards. A guard of honour and a band were supplied by the 4th Battalion, and the driver and fireman in charge of the engine, both of whom had served with the regiment in World War I, were presented with a memento of the occasion in the form of a badge of the regiment. The locomotive worked in the North-East until June 1963 when it was transferred to Scotland, before being withdrawn in October 1965.

In April 1889, the tenancy of the refreshment rooms at Richmond was let at £4 a year; gas supplied at 4s. 6d. per 100cu. ft. and coal could be provided at £2 per ton. Amongst conditions imposed was one that service should be available from half an hour before the arrival of the first train to half an hour after the departure of the last train each day. A further condition was that 'in addition to the refreshments which are ordinarily sold at the counter, provisions such as joints, steaks, chops, tea, and coffee should be available at the stipulated rates':

| | First Class | Second Class |
|---|---|---|
| Hot dinner, in coffee room, joint, vegetables and cheese | 2s. 6d. | 1s. 3d. |
| Chop or steak with vegetables or cheese | 2s. 0d. | 1s. 3d. |
| Chop or steak | 1s. 0d. | 9d. |
| Soup with bread | 1s. 0d. | 6d. |
| Tea or coffee, with bread or butter, per cup | 4d. | 2d. |
| Tea or coffee, with bread or butter in coffee room | 6d. | — |
| Milk, per glass | 3d. | 2d. |
| Sandwiches (Plate of 4 — 6d.) | 2d. | 2d. |
| Buns, etc. | 1d. | 1d. |
| Port, sherry or claret, per glass | 6d. | 4d. |
| Brandy or whisky, per glass | 6d. | 4d. |
| Gin or rum, per glass | 4d. | 3d. |
| Bitter beer, per glass | 3d. | 2d. |
| Mild beer, per glass | 3d. | 2d. |
| Stout, per glass | 3d. | 2d. |
| Ginger beer, per bottle | 3d. | 2d. |
| Lemonade | 4d. | 3d. |
| Soda, seltzer, or potash, large bottle | 6d. | 3d. |
| Soda, seltzer, or potash, small bottle | 3d. | 2d. |

The fact that Richmond Station was in use until 1969, brought it into the period when some features of our declining railways were worthy of serious consideration for preservation. If the Great North of England Railway had been able to follow up the powers granted by Parliament in its 1845 Act, the station at Richmond would not have been designed by G. T. Andrews but, coming as it did under the control of George Hudson, he favoured the York architect who had designed stations for Hudson in Yorkshire and County Durham.

When work started, Andrews used standard designs for the ancillary buildings (goods shed, engine shed, etc.) but, because of the scenic riverside position chosen for the terminus, he had to take extra care to design a station building which would fit in with its surroundings, and not give offence. In any case, it seems probable that the station, as built, was not to the original design prepared by Andrews.

To show how the station would look when completed, Andrews prepared an excellent water colour of the building, depicting a busy scene with just a glimpse of a steam locomotive on the extreme edge of the picture, with the eye of the beholder taken up by the ruins of St. Martin's Priory in the background. Not shown in the painting is the row of six railway cottages to the south-east of the station, nor the Depot Agent's house to the north, guarding the entrance to the coal yard. This water colour came into the hands of a Scarborough dealer about twenty years ago and its existence was drawn to the attention of J. H. Scholes, then the Curator of Historical Relics for British Railways, who purchased it for the National collection; it is now held by the National Railway Museum at York. The painting does show the stationmaster's house, a detached residence now on the opposite side of the road from the station; no mere station house address for this building as it is shown on the ordnance survey maps as Station Villa!

A look at the 1in. Ordnance Survey map for the area west of Richmond will soon show that the hills on each side of the valley were dotted with lead mines and drifts,

The opposite view. The water column is dated 'LNER 1942'.

L. Ward

A view of the six railway cottages on the south-west side of the station.

*L. Ward*

all now disused, with only some ruined buildings to show where they once thrived. At one time these mines transported their products to the nearest railhead in the panniers of pack-horses but, later, horse-drawn carts were used as the roads were improved. From 1846, Richmond was the most convenient station for loading the lead into railway wagons and a siding was set aside for that purpose; each 'pig' was weighed before it was loaded. Records of lead and silver produced in Yorkshire exist in NER records from 1873 and show a continuous decrease, until the lead mining industry finally ceased during World War II:

| Year | Dressed Lead Ore tons | Lead tons | Silver ozs. |
|---|---|---|---|
| 1873/4 | 4,944 | 3,598 | 1,500 |
| 1900 | 885 | 609 | — |
| 1915 | 14 | 8 | — |

### What Might Have Been!

The valleys of the Rivers Swale and Ure acted as a magnet to various promoters planning railways from Newcastle to Liverpool because, as they ran from east to west, the valleys provided a suitable course for part of the route, and numerous schemes were floated from 1845. These proposed lines involved large expenditure and, as the financial support was not forthcoming, the schemes withered away. More likely to succeed was an extension from Richmond to Reeth which, although passing through a sparsely-populated area offering little in the way of passenger traffic, could serve the lead mines operating in the hills along the course of the line. Thus, on 26th July 1869, a Richmond & Reeth Railway Company obtained an Act to construct 10½ miles of line, but failed to gain the necessary support. The same fate befell a similar line in 1895, but, in 1911, another attempt was made to take advantage of the Light Railways Act of 1896, which allowed the stringent conditions for building and operating a standard line to be relaxed. This was known as the Swaledale Light Railway and was approved in November 1911. Three months later, the NER shareholders gave their approval to an agreement between the NER and the Swaledale Light Railway concerning the construction and operation by the NER of the proposed light railway. Support for the line was insufficient to make a start on the project before the outbreak of World War II in 1914, and the application to the Light Railway Commissioners was first suspended and later (1922) recorded as 'Removed from List'.

### Locomotive and Train Working

It is impossible to tell which engines worked the branch when it was opened in 1846 but, in the 1860s, a local photographer recorded at least two trains standing ready to depart for Darlington. The best-known picture shows 2-2-2 No. 69, one of a batch of seven ordered on 17th September 1839 by the Great North of England Railway from R. & W. Hawthorn & Co. at £1,500 per engine and

£235 per tender. It carried the name *Darlington* when received by the GNER in 1840, and later became NER No. 69. It was rebuilt in 1848, and replaced in December 1876. The other view shows only part of No. 60, also built for the GNER. It was ordered from Tayleur & Co. on 29th October 1839 as an 0-4-2 goods engine at £1,350 for the engine and £215 for the tender, and it was delivered in January 1841 with the name *Auckland*. It was replaced in March 1878. Both numbers, Nos. 60 and 69, were taken by Fletcher BTP 0-4-4T engines, and it seems probable that this was the class which worked the Richmond branch from the 1870s, followed by the Worsdell 2-4-2T Class A and 0-4-4T Class O. In LNER days, No. 2089 of Class O (LNER Class G5) was stationed at Richmond until December 1929, when it was replaced by Class A (LNER Class F8) No. 469.

In the summer of 1908, the Richmond engine started its day on the 6.10a.m. to Darlington, and the first shift men, on duty from 5a.m. to 3p.m., worked four return trips; the late shift crew worked from 2.40p.m. to 12.40a.m. and performed three return trips, the last being on the 10.58p.m. arrival from Darlington. In 1923, the eight hour day allowed the early turn crew to work only two return trips, with the late crew working two on Mondays to Fridays, and three on Saturdays, when they incurred 50 minutes overtime as the last train was not due in Richmond until 11.25p.m.

According to official records, 2-4-2T No. 469 remained at Richmond until the shed closed on 30th December 1933, but the engine appears to have moved to Darlington from 1st May 1933 when the workings from Richmond were taken over by a Sentinel steam railcar. Initially, this was the two cylinder car No. 272 *Hero*, but it was soon joined (on paper at least) by No. 2136 *Hope*, a six cylinder car (on 22nd May) and No. 265 *Neptune*, another two cylinder car (on 26th May); another six cylinder car, No. 2271 *Industry*, followed on 8th June. *Hero* left Richmond on 26th May and thus, from 8th June, there were three cars stationed at Richmond when only one was required for duty each day. In any case, from 17th July 1933, the service was worked from the Darlington end! Nevertheless, the three cars remained at Richmond; *Industry* until 30th December, the official date of closure of the shed, *Neptune* until 19th April 1934, and *Hope* until 7th July. These details, extracted from the LNER (North Eastern Area) Locomotive Transfers records maintained at York, are strange, to say the least!

In the 1923 Engine Diagram Book, all the passenger trains on the branch were worked by the Richmond engine, with one exception, the 7.55a.m. from Darlington and the 9.39a.m. return, but in the 1920s, Darlington Shed acquired further duties on which various classes appeared, such as D23 4-4-0, 398 and J21 0-6-0, E5 2-4-0, N9 0-6-2T and H1 4-4-4T. By 1937, the Sentinel railcars were little used on the branch on weekdays, although the 10.22p.m. Darlington to Richmond and return remained a railcar working, and the Sunday services were railcar-worked. Thus, the weekly turns were incorporated into the 'run of the mill' trains worked by Darlington engines and men, with a trip to Richmond sandwiched between a

The goods warehouse, for which the tender was let on 3rd June 1846, three months before the line was opened. The plan dimensions were exactly the same as those for the engine shed, erected at the same time by the same contractor. The goods office was an 1872/3 addition. The notice projecting from the wall of the warehouse at the far end reads 'Care to be exercised with corridor stock beyond this point', and the notice over the door on the goods office reads 'Steam engines not to pass this point'.

*C. B. Foster*

The north-west end of the train shed with one bay window.

*Author*

A general view of the station with the train shed (left), goods warehouse (centre left), engine shed (centre right) and gasworks (right) with the locomotive turntable. The nearest of the three grounded van bodies outside the warehouse carries a notice which reads 'Depot for Silcock's cattle foods'.

*W. A. Camwell*

trip to Crook and one to Saltburn with a Class A8 4-6-2T. In this way, many different engines appeared during the day. Also, engines from other sheds began working to Richmond, notably West Auckland, Saltburn, Middleton-in-Teesdale and Kirkby Stephen engines, filling in during their lay-over time at Darlington. For much of World War II, the branch was worked by large tank engines, necessary because of the wartime increase in military traffic, and Classes A5 and A8 4-6-2Ts were the most common, with Class V1 2-6-2Ts also in use. On troop specials, both during and after World War II, virtually any class of large engine could appear up to V2! In fact, leave specials ran for many years after the end of the war, taking two main line engines to Richmond every Friday. The 2.22p.m. empty stock train from Darlington to Richmond was booked for a Class V2, which left Richmond at 3.50p.m. for Eryholme, running tender first, and there it ran round its train and continued south, with the men working to York and the engine to Grantham. At 4.15p.m., another empty stock train left Darlington, rostered for a Class B1 4-6-0 running tender first; this then formed the 5.07p.m. from Richmond to Newcastle, running chimney first.

The building of Catterick Camp, in 1915, led to a large amount of additional traffic, not only at Catterick Bridge but also at Richmond. Some engines used on the construction work at the camp were based for a time at Richmond Shed, including WD No. 104, a former NER Class 1350 0-6-0ST, originally sold to the Darlington dealer J. F. Wake in 1911 for £300. This engine was actually repaired at Darlington Works for the War Department and it was returned to Richmond Shed on 19th October 1916. A NER Class H 0-4-0T is also believed to have been employed. To work these engines two drivers, W. Sharp and F. Sherris, were transferred from Newport to Richmond. The former had joined the NER in 1898, became a fireman in 1900 and a driver in 1914. Regular drivers and firemen stationed at Richmond about that time were W. M. Reed, A. Hunter, J. H. Stephenson, J. Render, J. Stabler and M. Callaghan.

Over the years, Richmond developed as a tourist centre and a notable annual event was the Athletic Sports and Bicycle Meet held on Whit Monday. This brought a number of excursions and specials to the town and, for instance, on 1st June 1903, there were excursions from Middlesbrough, Saltburn, Bishop Auckland (3), and two reliefs to ordinary trains from Darlington. The empty carriage sets were worked back to Darlington to stand, and ran out empty to Richmond in the evening for their return working. The return trains departed from the cattle dock sidings, which required hand points leading to the 'up' main line to be clamped, and the attendance of a flagman. Trains were restricted to 14 six wheel vehicles. During the day, tickets on all Richmond-bound trains were collected at Catterick Bridge. On the following day, 2nd June, there were six excursions, one each from Hartlepool, West Hartlepool, and Saltburn, and three from Newcastle.

Even before the large military camp at Catterick developed in World War I, the area around Richmond was the venue for summer camps, and the men attending them were invariably carried by rail. Thus, on 8th June 1903, some 530 militiamen from various towns in York-

### Engine Working Richmond, Summer 1908
Weekdays

| | | a.m. |
|---|---|---|
| Richmond | — | 6.10 |
| Darlington | 6.48 | 7.23 |
| Richmond | 8.01 | 8.11 |
| Darlington | 8.43 | 9.22 |
| Richmond | 9.58 | 10.12 |
| Darlington | 10.45 | 11.10 |
| Richmond | 11.44 | 11.55 |
| Darlington | 12.32 | 2.06 |
| Richmond | 2.44* | 3.05 |
| Darlington | 3.40 | 5.10 |
| Richmond | 5.47 | 6.18 |
| Darlington | 6.52 | 7.35 |
| Richmond | 8.13 | 8.30 |
| Darlington | 9.05 | 10.20 |
| Richmond | 10.58 | — |

*First Set 5a.m. to 3p.m.; Second Set 2.40p.m. to 12.40a.m.*
*\* = Change enginemen*

Sundays

| | | a.m. |
|---|---|---|
| Richmond | — | 7.23 |
| Darlington | 7.58 | 8.48 |
| Richmond | 9.23 | — |
| | | p.m. |
| Richmond | — | 6.55 |
| Darlington | 7.30 | 7.45 |
| Richmond | 8.23 | — |

*First Set 4.20a.m. to 11a.m.;
Second Set 6p.m. to
1a.m.*

### Engine Working Richmond, Winter 1922/3
Weekdays

| | | a.m. |
|---|---|---|
| Richmond | — | 7.45 |
| Darlington | 8.21 | 9.25 |
| Richmond | 10.07 | 11.44 |
| Darlington | 12.21 | 2.10 |
| Richmond | 2.49* | 3.42 |
| Darlington | 4.18 | 5.12 |
| Richmond | 5.51 | 6.10 |
| Darlington | 6.45** | 9.10 |
| Richmond | 9.49 | 10.10 (SO) |
| Darlington | 10.39 | 10.55 (SO) |
| Richmond | 11.25 | — |

*First Set 6.55a.m. to 3.10p.m. (6.55a.m. to
3.45p.m. (SO));
Second Set 2.45p.m. to 10.45p.m. (3.20p.m. to
12.10a.m. (SO))
\* = Change enginemen
\*\* = Engine used for piloting*

shire, ranging from Sheffield to Middlesbrough, travelled by ordinary trains to Darlington, and then by special train to Richmond. Later they were taken by a 15 coach special (sent out empty from York) to Strensall for training.

A mechanical cab-signalling system was developed on the NER in 1894, and it was in use until 1933. The original patent was in the names of Vincent Raven and S. L. Baister, and the apparatus consisted of a stop between the rails at distant signals. If the signal was 'on' the stop was raised, and it came into contact with a striker on the engine, partially applying the brakes and causing a whistle to blow in the cab. If the signal was 'off', then the stop was lowered and the driver received no indication. From this, Raven later developed a similar but more comprehensive system, operated electrically, with two metal brushes and a shoe on the engine coming into contact with 30ft. long metal ramps between the rails. With this system various indications could be given in the cab, such as:

1 Warning that a distant signal was being approached.
2 Indication displayed by distant signal.
3 Route to be taken if approaching a diverging junction or junctions.
4 Indication of home signal and route signalled.
5 Indication of starting signal after passing a junction.

These indications were given in the engine cab on a glass-fronted dial, which contained a miniature semaphore signal and a pointer indicating the left-hand or right-hand route, with a mid (warning) position. On 4th June 1910, authority was given to fit this apparatus at the distant signals between Eryholme and Richmond at a cost of £900 made up of:

| | |
|---|---|
| Permanent Way Dept. | £370 |
| Telegraph Dept. | £178 |
| Fitting 15 engines | £352 |
| | £900 |

The apparatus was brought into use on 14th August 1911 and, henceforward, only engines fitted with this type of gear were allowed on the branch. However, it appears to have fallen into disuse during, or soon after, World War I.

A siding for the use of Mr Jaques, Gentleman, was situated 68 chains from Richmond Station, just on the south-side of the bridge over the River Swale. It was also used by his tenants, mainly for coal and an occasional wagon of manure. It was unusual in that the original Agreement for the siding was dated 5th May 1845, some weeks prior to the Act authorising the line, and the probable reason for this is that the railway company agreed to provide a siding in return for some of the land owned by Mr Jaques, or the withdrawal of his objection to the railway. Futher Agreements were signed on 30th May 1894 and 3rd June 1919.

In January 1923, special instructions were issued for the working of the siding, which was connected with the 'up' line about 858 yards outside the Richmond 'up'

advance starting signal. The lever working the points at the ground frame was released and locked by the siding key, which was kept in the lock connected with the 'up' advance starting signal lever in Richmond box, so that when the key was withdrawn, the signal was locked in the danger position. Any train wishing to shunt the siding had to be accompanied by the porter, or other appointed person, who had to obtain the key from the signalman. The showing of the key to the driver authorised him to pass the advance starter at danger and to shunt the siding.

Before the train left Richmond, the signalman had to obtain acceptance of the train from the box in advance and, after shunting had been carried out, the train continued on its way. The porter restored and locked the points and returned the key to the signalman at Richmond, who could then resume normal working.

The instructions regarding the siding were withdrawn in March 1958.

*Closure and After*

On 10th October 1963, the North Eastern Region of British Railways gave statutory notice of their intention to withdraw all passenger services (except certain military trains) between Darlington and Richmond, but following objections to the proposals submitted to the North Eastern Area Transport Users' Consultative Committee (and forwarded to the Minister of Transport), the proposal was found unacceptable and the trains continued to run. On 26th January 1968, proposals for closure were again submitted, with a target date of 6th May 1968. The suggested replacement bus service listed one additional bus through from Darlington to Richmond, with two in the opposite direction. Other services from Darlington were extended to Richmond or gave connections. Once again objections were made but, on 11th November 1968, the Minister of Transport gave his consent to the closure, subject to the introduction of the revised bus service. On 10th January 1969, British Rail announced that passenger services to Richmond would cease from 3rd March 1969. Goods traffic had already been withdrawn from Richmond on 2nd October 1967.

Before the second closure application had been made, British Railways had taken steps to economise, by singling the line from a point 246 yards west of Catterick Bridge Station to Richmond. This section was then worked under the 'one engine in steam' arrangements, and Richmond signal box, together with all points worked therefrom, were abolished. All the points were secured out of use, in the normal position, pending removal. Before leaving Richmond Station the guard had to receive assurance from the signalman at Catterick Bridge box that the gates at Broken Brae and Parkgate Lane Level crossings were placed and secured across the roadway. On 26th August 1968, a contractor commenced to demolish Richmond signal box and the 1942 water column on the station platform, together with redundant track. The line between Catterick Bridge and Richmond closed completely on 3rd March 1969.

In October 1972, Richmond Rural District Council announced that Richmond Station site and buildings had been purchased from British Rail and that, in conjunction with adjacent Rural District Councils, it was proposed to develop the area as a recreation centre, with a swimming pool, learners' pool, restaurant, squash court and sports hall, and to utilise the old engine shed as a public hall. Suggestions were invited for naming the complex, with a prize for the most suitable. At the same time, the Rural District Council decided to purchase the three-quarters of a mile of trackbed as far as Easby, and to make it available for walking, horse-riding and cycling, and tenders for landscaping were sought.

During 1974, work went ahead on renovating the station building, at an estimated cost of £20,000, but when work on the roof was all but complete, the architects were instructed to restore the roof to its original condition as the result of an offer of an increased grant from the Historic Buildings Council. This involved putting in lead guttering and flashings throughout, instead of the synthetic materials already laid. Instead of the provisional sum of £5,000 allowed for repairs to the roof and guttering, the final figure was estimated to be £27,000!

In 1975, this building was opened as a farm and garden centre by a tenant of the council. This was followed by the completion of the swimming pool complex and, in November 1976, it was announced that the new building had been awarded a Structural Steel Design Award.

In April 1975, the Richmondshire District Council published a notice headed 'Conversion of engine shed into multi-purpose hall', and this announced a public meeting to be held to discuss possible uses of the old shed. The future of the shed came up again in September 1978, when a scheme to convert it into a prestige sports hall was turned down. It was revealed by the Council that only one person had requested such a hall when the public were consulted about Richmond's future developments.

In 1982, it was suggested that the old engine shed should become an arts centre and the local Amateur Dramatic Society offered to convert the building for this purpose, to carry out all the necessary repair work, and to maintain it. The Council's only commitment would be to agree a long term lease at a peppercorn rent and the District Council agreed to this scheme. However, in November 1982, the Amateur Dramatic Society pulled out because the restoration would cost at least £26,000 and this was beyond their resources. Next (March 1983) came a scheme from a Barnsley businessman to convert the building into a holiday hostel, and this is still under consideration at the time of writing.

The interior of the signal box. The frame carried a McKenzie & Holland plate behind levers 15 and 16.

*C. B. Foster*

*(Above):* The entrance to the station, looking across the platform to the west wall. The suspended sign reads 'Please show your tickets'.

*L. Ward*

*(Above right):* The door to the building after conversion to a garden centre.

*C. B. Foster*

# Notes on the Drawings — RICHMOND

**General**

The station was built in 1846 to the designs of G. T. Andrews of York in Gothic style, with an open port-cochère at the entrance and a two span train shed. The cast-iron arcades between the eight columns have ornate spandrels, cast by John Walker of York. It is possible that the design of the station allowed for a future railway extension up Swaledale, as it could easily have been modified to become a two platform through station. Had it been situated twenty or thirty yards further west, a far less cramped goods and locomotive yard would have resulted.

**Station buildings** *Drawings 1 to 5*

The drawings show the station as it existed in 1912, and

116

the only known alterations up to then were the provision of the water tank in 1854, and some alterations to the booking office in 1875. Apparently until 1912 the space occupied by the first class gentlemen's waiting-room, store, and stationmaster's office, had been the refreshment room. The first class waiting-room retained its status until 1916, when it became the general waiting room, to take the place of the general room taken over when the parcel office was extended. The booking office was altered in 1913, and it is possible that the window in the centre of the porte-cochère was replaced by a door at this time.

In the platform elevation, some of the windows became doors and other minor alterations took place, including the provision of a W. H. Smith's bookstall on the platform outside the store-room, and a ticket collectors' cabin at the entrance. Unlike Whitby, any alterations to the building have been carried out carefully so as not to detract from its appearance.

As with all the older stations, the platform was built low, but in this case it was wide enough for the height of the platform edge to be increased by back-sloping the platform toward the buildings. The platform was extended between 1860 and 1892, and the extension was later rebuilt with a facing of standard concrete platform units.

PART EAST ELEVATION

Cut
Line

PART EAST ELEVATION 1854–1912

Cut Line

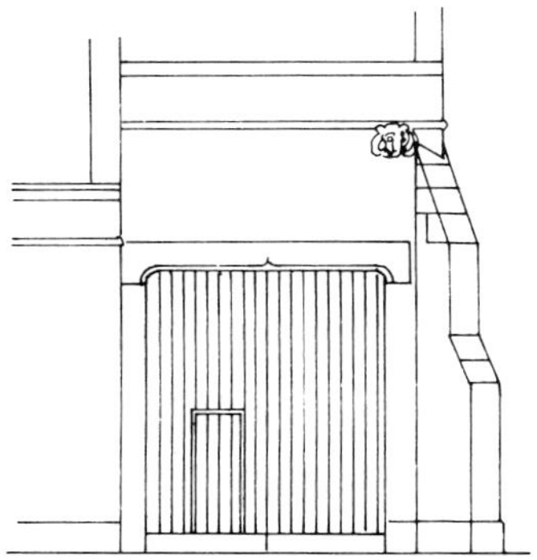

LATER DOORWAY AT EAST END

RICHMOND STATION

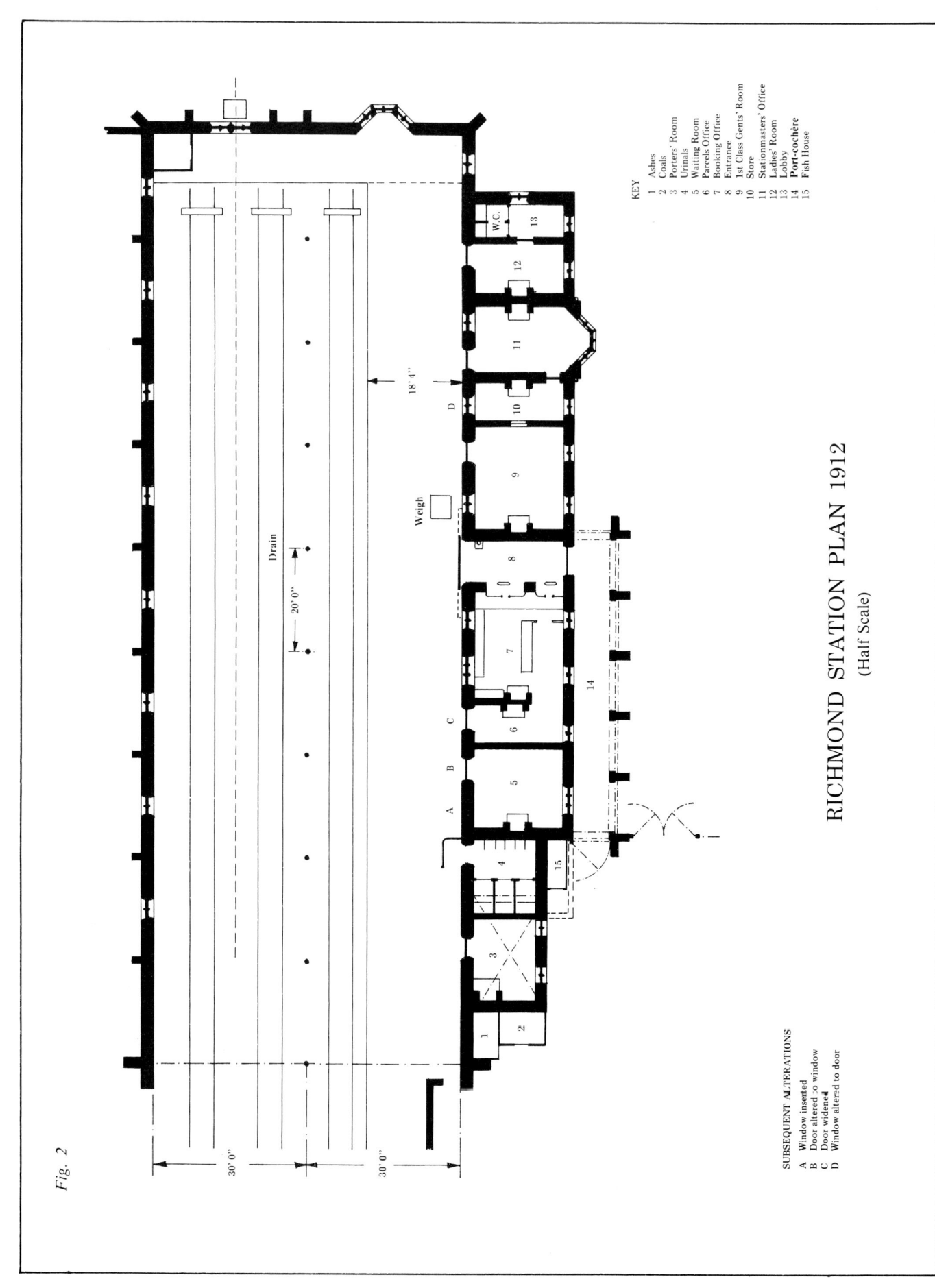

*Fig. 2*

30' 0"

Drain

20' 0"

30' 0"

Weigh

18' 4"

A    B    C    D

W.C.

1    2    3    4    15    5    6    7    8    9    10    11    12    13    14

RICHMOND STATION PLAN 1912

(Half Scale)

KEY

1    Ashes
2    Coals
3    Porters' Room
4    Urinals
5    Waiting Room
6    Parcels Office
7    Booking Office
8    Entrance
9    1st Class Gents' Room
10    Store
11    Stationmasters' Office
12    Ladies' Room
13    Lobby
14    **Port-cochère**
15    Fish House

SUBSEQUENT ALTERATIONS

A    Window inserted
B    Door altered to window
C    Door widened
D    Window altered to door

The train shed roof appears in numerous photographs taken over the last 120 years, perhaps the earliest being this view also showing 2-2-2 locomotive No. 69, photographed in the 1860s. Note the short length of the main platform.

*Author's Collection*

In 1937, Class G5 0-4-4T No. 1334 leaves for Darlington. Note the rise in the level of the platform as it emerges from the train shed, and compare this with the previous view. The siding outside the station wall on the left is being used for unloading petrol, with a chock (open) on the line to prevent wagons from running out of the siding.

*W. Potter*

The eastern corner of Richmond Station in 1966, with the water tank on top of the porters' room. Some of the plates forming the tank are lettered 'E. Thompson, York 1854'. The mouldings on the barge boards are clearly visible in this photograph.

*C. B. Foster*

Ten years later the tank was still in place, but the porters' room had been converted into an electricity sub-station.

*C. B. Foster*

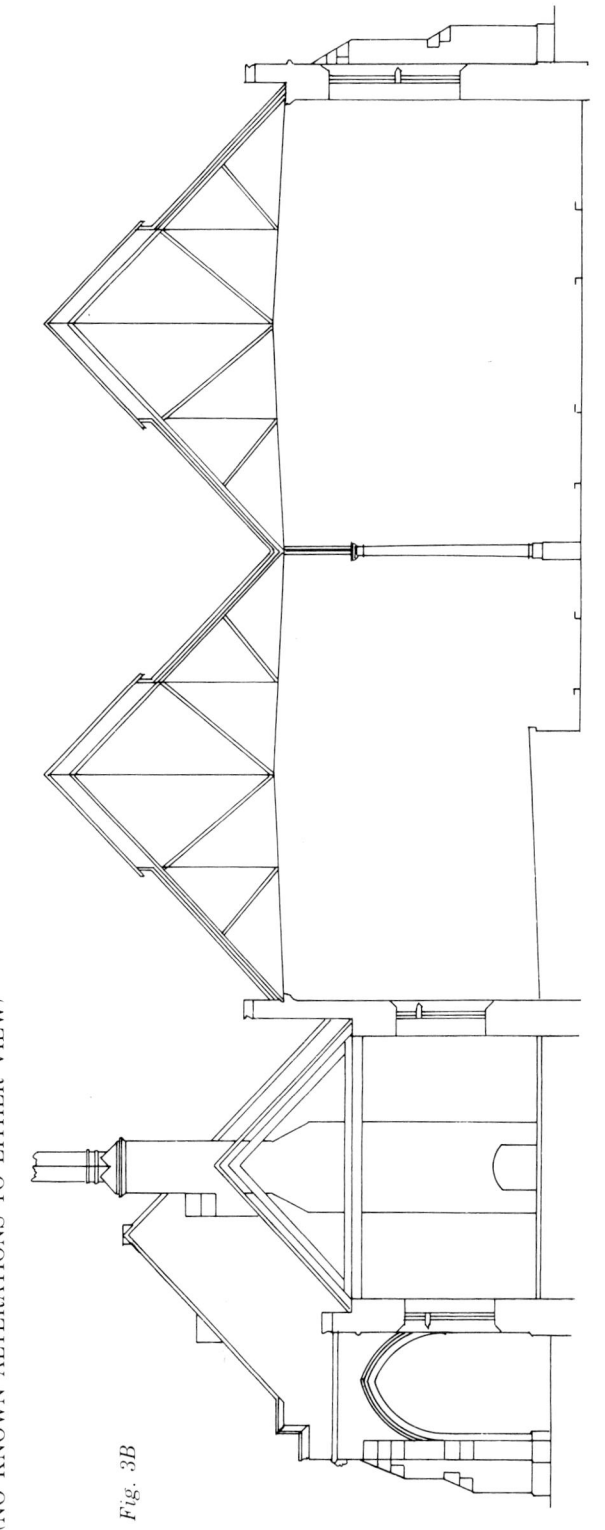

Fig. 3A

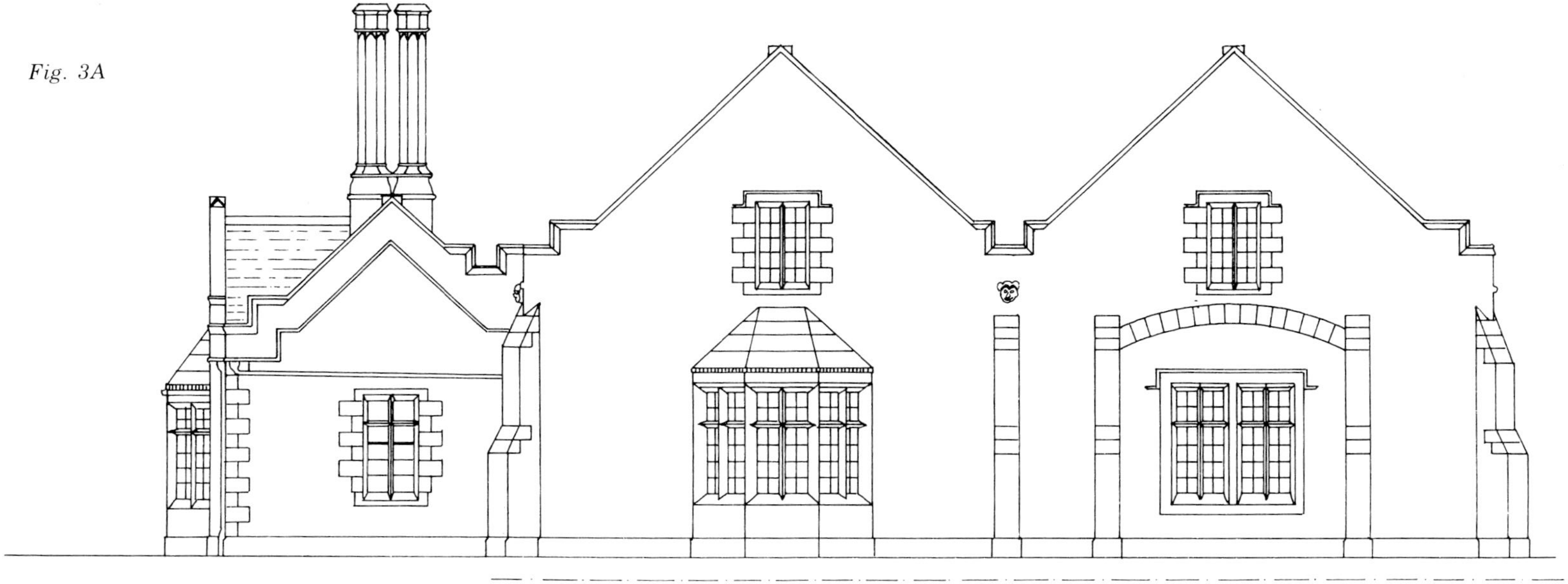

NORTH END ELEVATION

(NO KNOWN ALTERATIONS TO EITHER VIEW)

Fig. 3B

SECTION

RICHMOND STATION

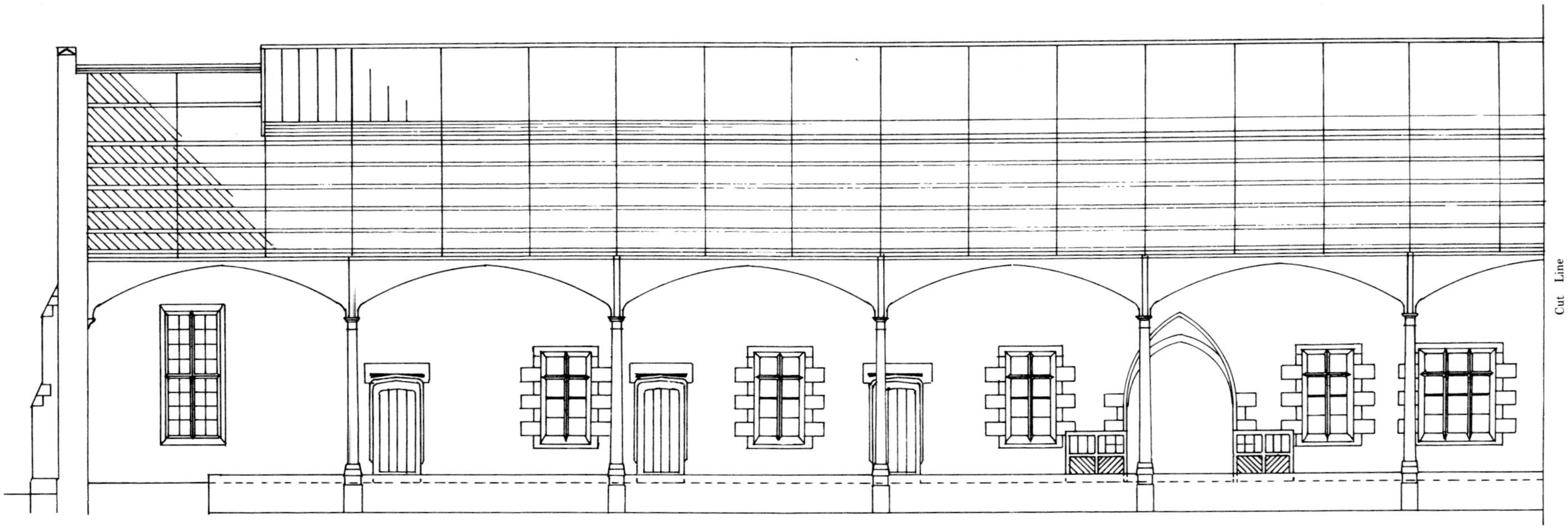
Cut Line

*Fig. 4A*

PART PLATFORM ELEVATION 1912

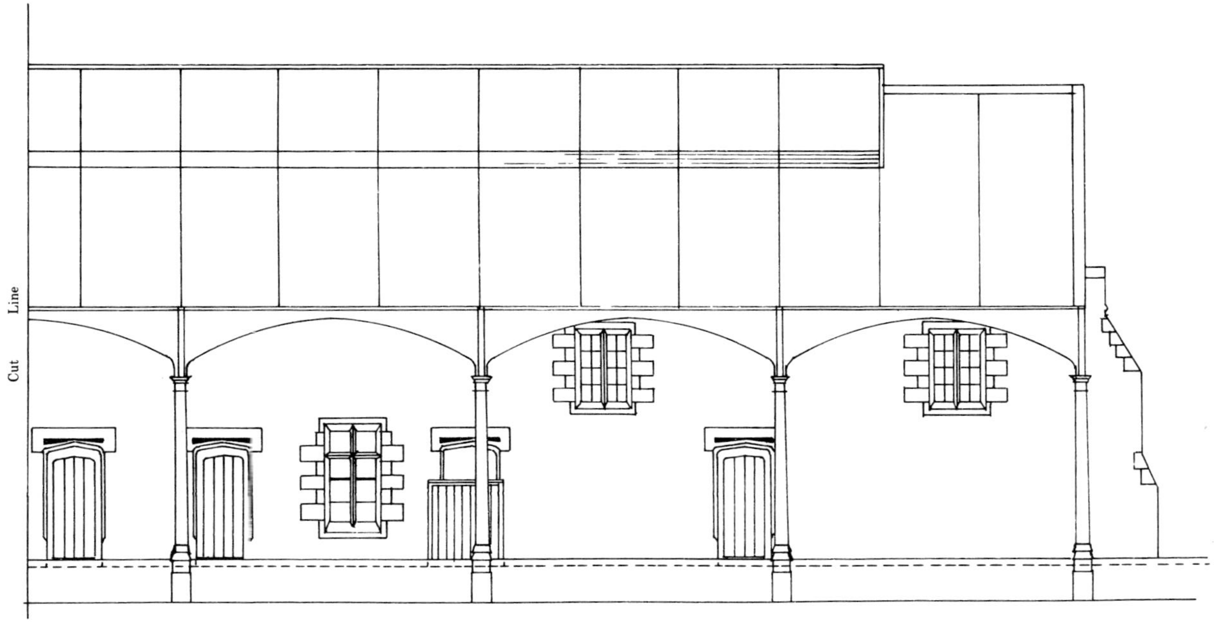
Cut Line

*Fig. 4B*

PART PLATFORM ELEVATION 1912

*Fig. 4C*

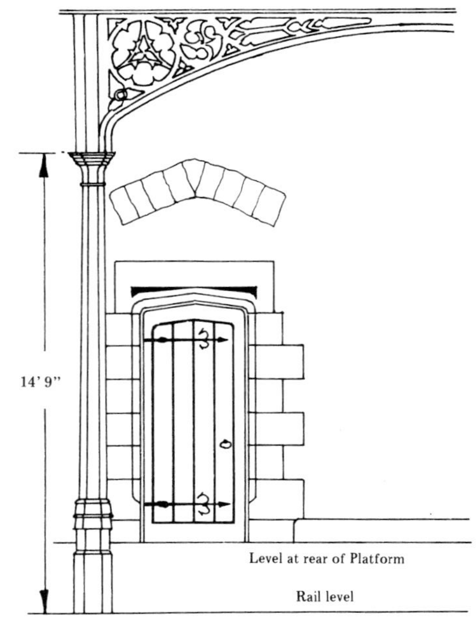
14' 9"
Level at rear of Platform
Rail level

DETAIL OF COLUMN, SPANDREL, AND DOOR, WITH RANDOM STONE RELIEVING ARCH
2× *SCALE*

RICHMOND STATION

The year is 1947 and another Class G5, No. 7309, is ready to leave for Darlington. The siding on the left has the chock closed.

*W. A. Camwell*

In its final days the Richmond branch was worked by diesel multiple units.

*C. B. Foster*

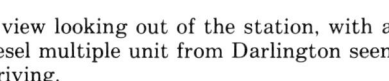

A view looking out of the station, with a diesel multiple unit from Darlington seen arriving.

*C. B. Foster*

Detail of the cast ironwork in the roof spandrels. For many years a loading gauge hung just inside the roof over the platform line.

*L. Ward*

The interior of the train shed looking towards the buffer sto[p] The arch of the entrance can be seen through the second bay fr[om] the right and, at ground level in the next bay, is a 'dolly' for t[he] engine release road, the points for which were immediately o[ut]side the roof.

*L. Wa[rd]*

The glass screen, which was erected when the train shed became a farm and garden centre in 1974.

*Author*

The north-east span of the train shed and platform, with t[he] engine release road points in the foreground.

*L. Wa[rd]*

*Fig. 5A*

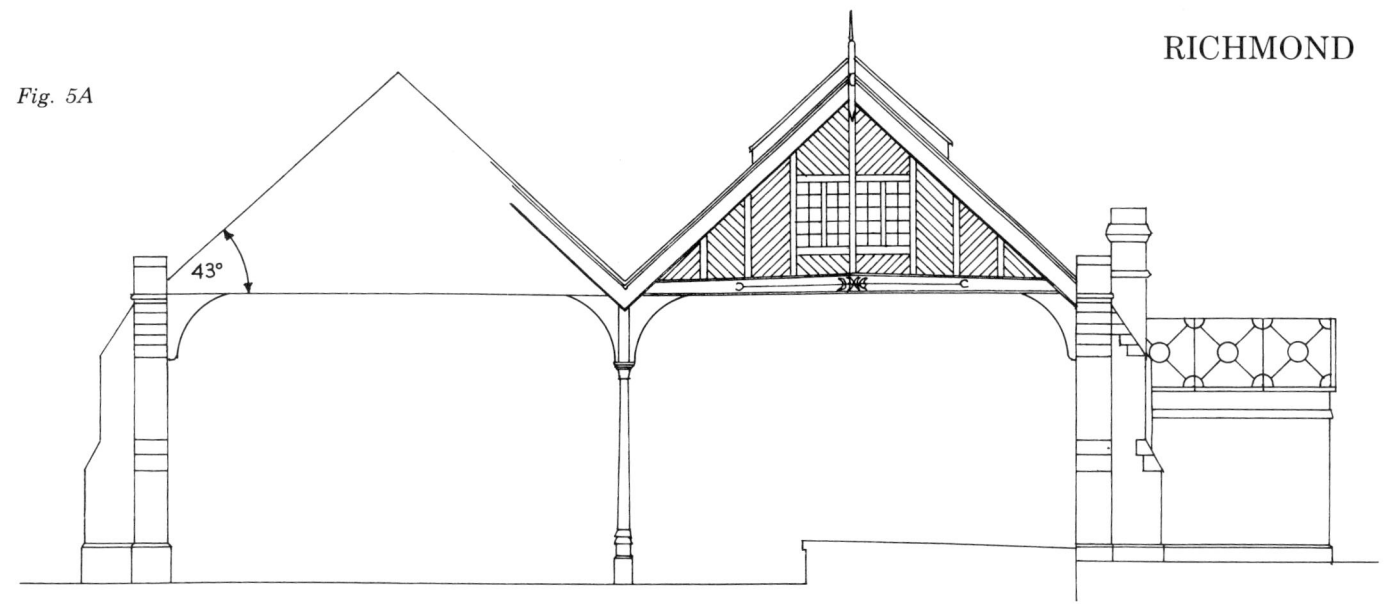

43°

SOUTH END ELEVATION SHOWING GABLE END DETAIL
THE BARGE BOARDS CARRIED A FOLIATED
ORNAMENTATION (SEE PHOTOGRAPHS)

*Fig. 5B*

WEST ELEVATION

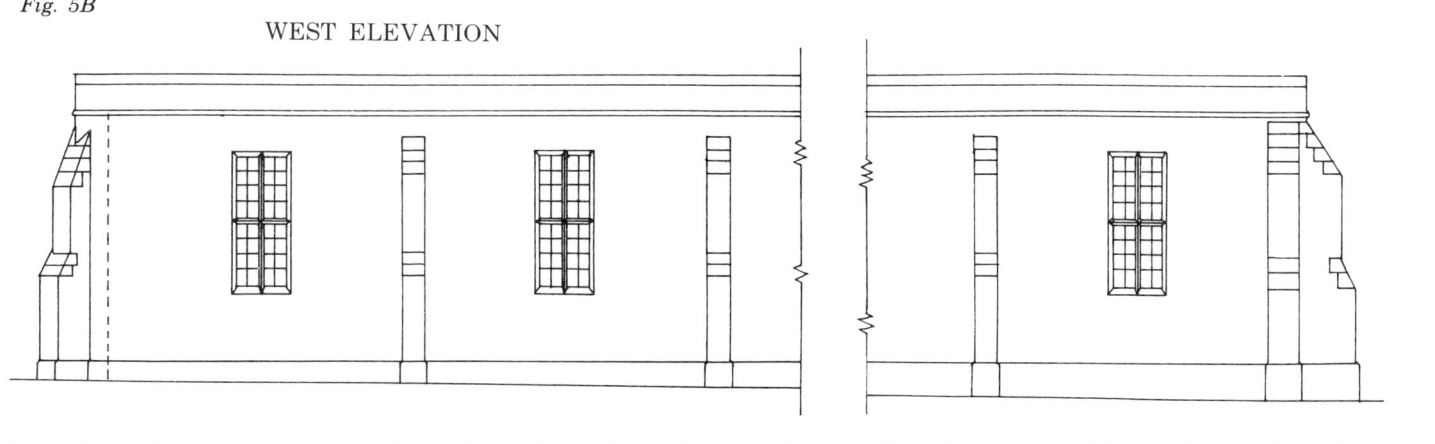

**Goods warehouses** *(Drawings 6 to 8)*
The goods shed of 1846 was to a fairly standard
G. T. Andrews design, except that the doors in the east
elevation were 8ft. wide instead of the more usual 10ft.
The dates of the various extensions are given on the
drawings. The cramped spacing of the yard made the
1872 grain warehouse difficult to position, and it was
placed with its centre line at an angle of approximately 17
degrees to the original shed. The radius of the siding past
the new shed was only 150ft. (2¼ chains), and therefore
unworkable by any NER locomotive. The plan allowed for
access to the line adjacent to the new warehouse via a
trailing connection off this siding, but this arrangement
survived for only two years, when the turnout and siding
were removed and a loading platform was provided to the
original siding.

Two sets of coal cells were built, but access to one could
only be gained through the engine shed.

**Engine shed and facilities**
The engine shed of 1846 is almost identical to the
original building at Whitby (see Whitby drawings,
Drawings 10 and 11), and it still stands at the time of
writing, although its future is uncertain. As early as 1869,
the north-west corner of the shed was converted to a
stable, and much later the remains of the western track
were removed and the space converted to a trader's store
for Messrs Bibby. The final alteration, not long before the
closure of the branch, was the widening of the doorways
over the eastern track to 15ft., and the replacement of the
arches by lintel beams to make safer access to the coal
cells.

The engine shed at Richmond. Until about 1950, both doorways at each end were arched and there was a triple chimney stack in the centre of each end of the building. At the time of writing, discussions are proceeding regarding the use that can be made of the building, which is in urgent need of repair if it is to be retained.

*C. B. Foster*

A view through the former engine shed to the coal depots, which could be reached only through the shed. This was an unusual feature for the NER and was, presumably, made necessary by the restricted space available. The former gasworks building is on the right, with a modern pre-fabricated warehouse beyond. The gasworks originally had a handsome square chimney at the far end.

*L. Ward*

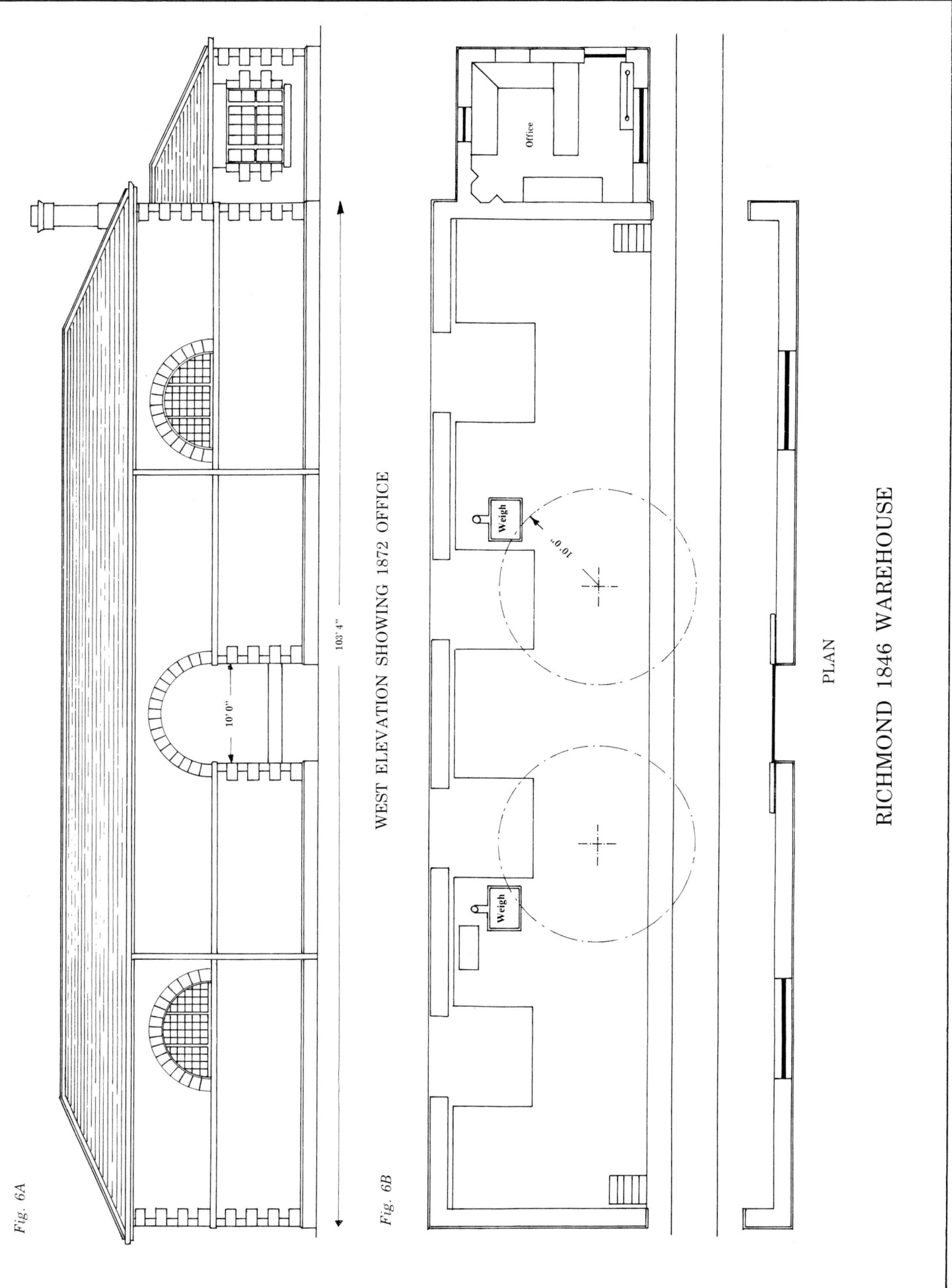

Fig. 6A

WEST ELEVATION SHOWING 1872 OFFICE

103' 4"

10' 0"

Fig. 6B

Office

Weigh

Weigh

10' 0"

PLAN

RICHMOND 1846 WAREHOUSE

Fig. 7A

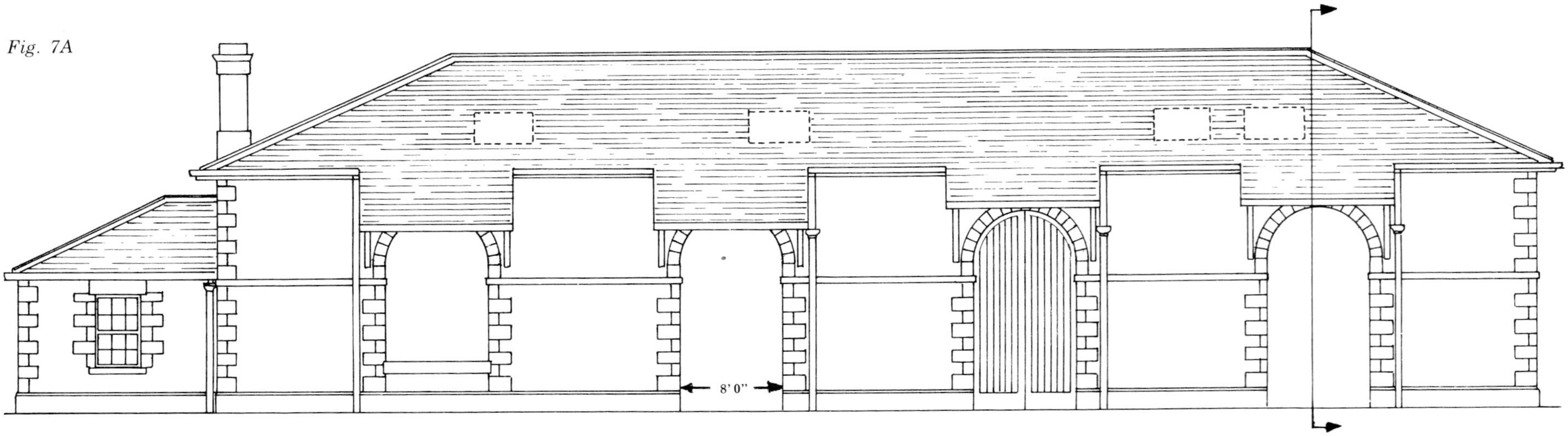

EAST ELEVATION OF 1846 WAREHOUSE
SHOWING 1872 OFFICE AND EARLIER AWNINGS (LEFT
HAND DOORS) WITH LATER AWNINGS (RIGHT HAND
DOORS), ALSO APPROXIMATE POSITION OF SKYLIGHTS

8' 0"

Fig. 7C

SOUTH END ELEVATION OF 1846 WAREHOUSE WITH 1872
OFFICE AND LATER AWNING STYLE

8' 0"

Fig. 7B

11' 9"

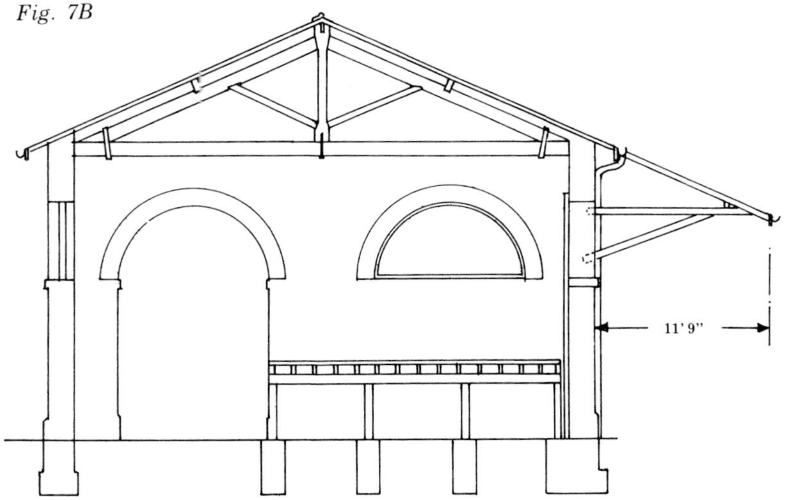

SECTION THROUGH 1846 WAREHOUSE
SHOWING EARLIER AWNING STYLE

RICHMOND WAREHOUSE

The north side of the original warehouse, and beyond is the grain warehouse which was added in 1872. Note the raised office in the angle between the two buildings.

*C. B. Foster*

A view looking across from the coal cells to the grain warehouse.

*L. Ward*

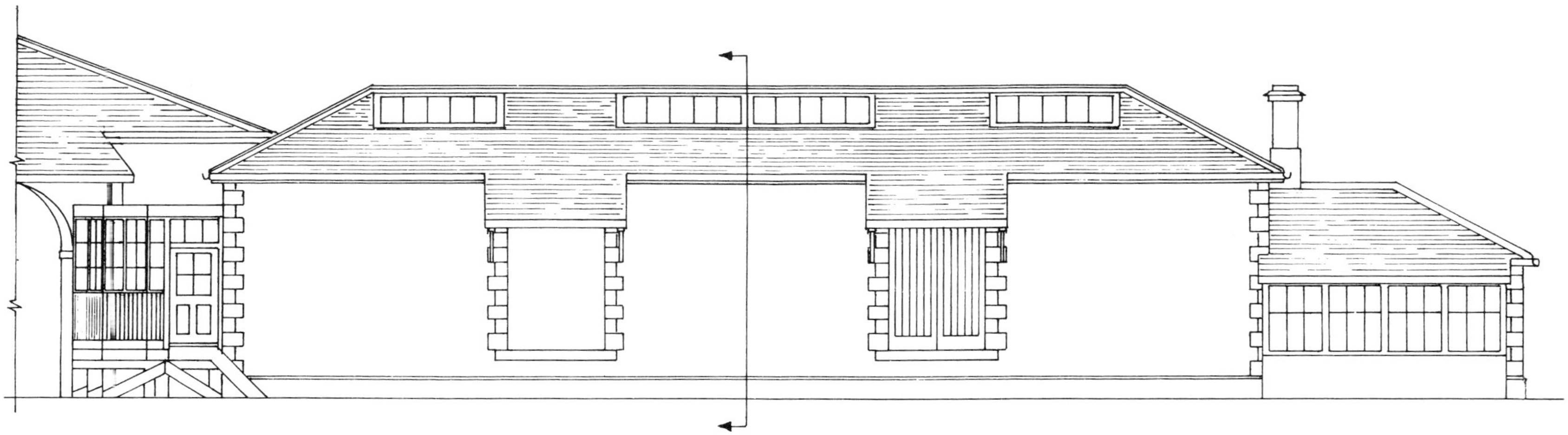

Fig. 8A

EAST ELEVATION OF 1872 WAREHOUSE
SHOWING 1874 OFFICE WITH 1909 PORCH AT RIGHT
HAND END AND UNDATED OFFICE AT LEFT HAND END

Fig. 8D

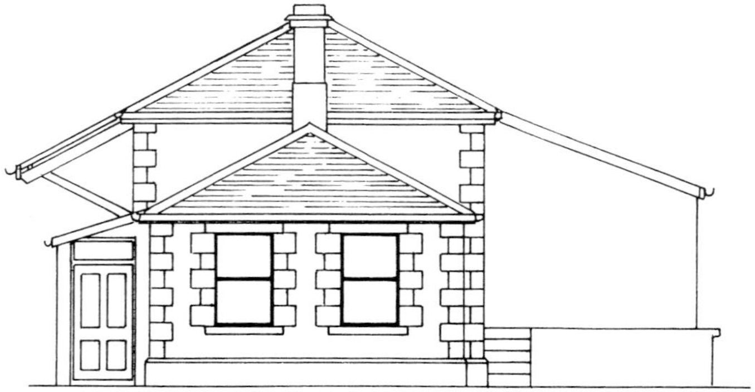

NORTH ELEVATION OF 1872 WAREHOUSE
SHOWING MODIFICATIONS OF 1874 AND 1909

Fig. 8C

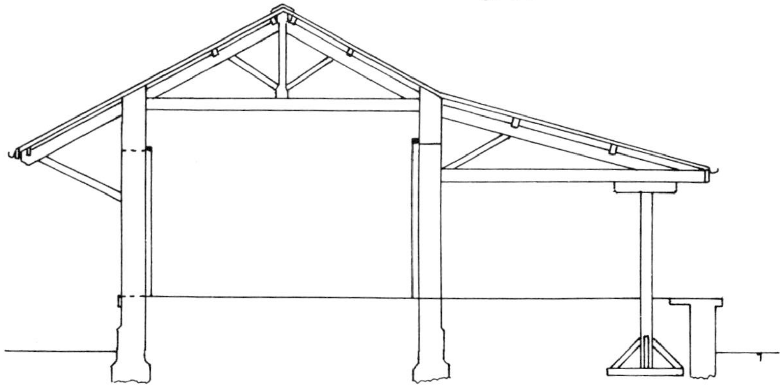

SECTION THROUGH 1872 WAREHOUSE
WITH 1874 AWNING AND PLATFORM

Fig. 8B

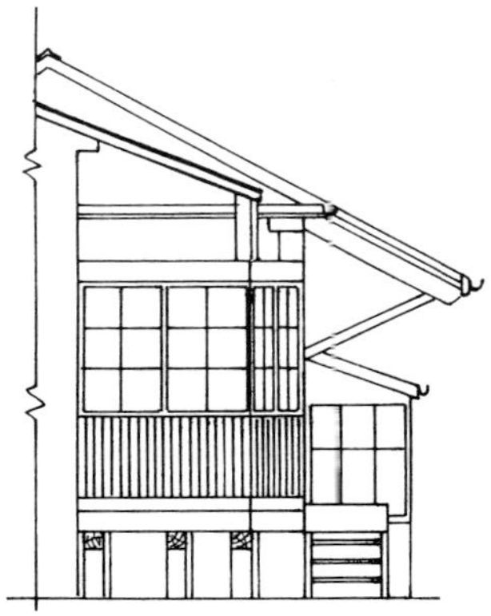

SOUTH END ELEVATION
SHOWING OFFICE (UNDATED)

RICHMOND

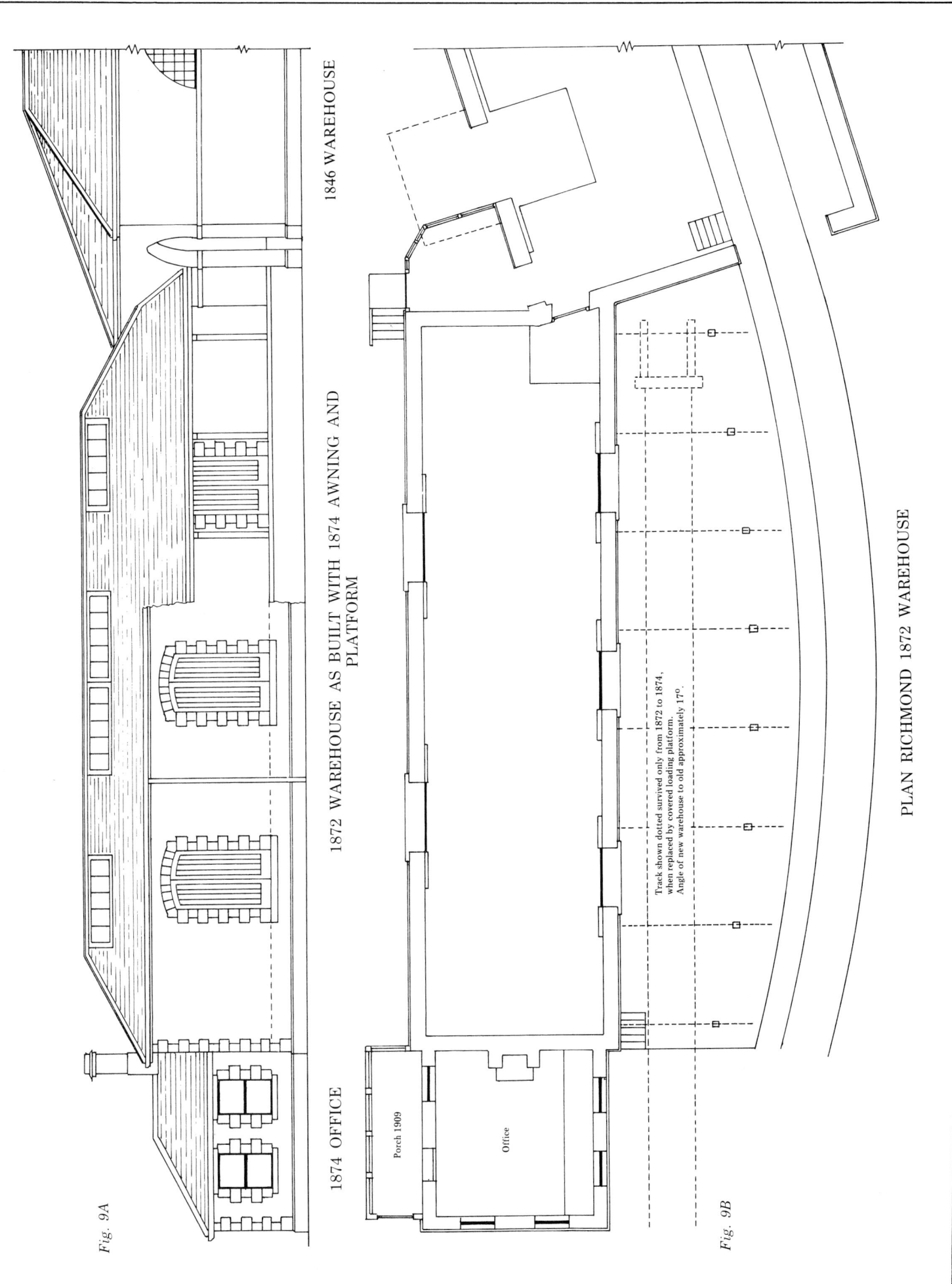

1846 WAREHOUSE

1872 WAREHOUSE AS BUILT WITH 1874 AWNING AND PLATFORM

1874 OFFICE

Fig. 9A

PLAN RICHMOND 1872 WAREHOUSE

Track shown dotted survived only from 1872 to 1874, when replaced by covered loading platform. Angle of new warehouse to old approximately 17°.

Porch 1909

Office

Fig. 9B

RICHMOND SIGNAL BOX

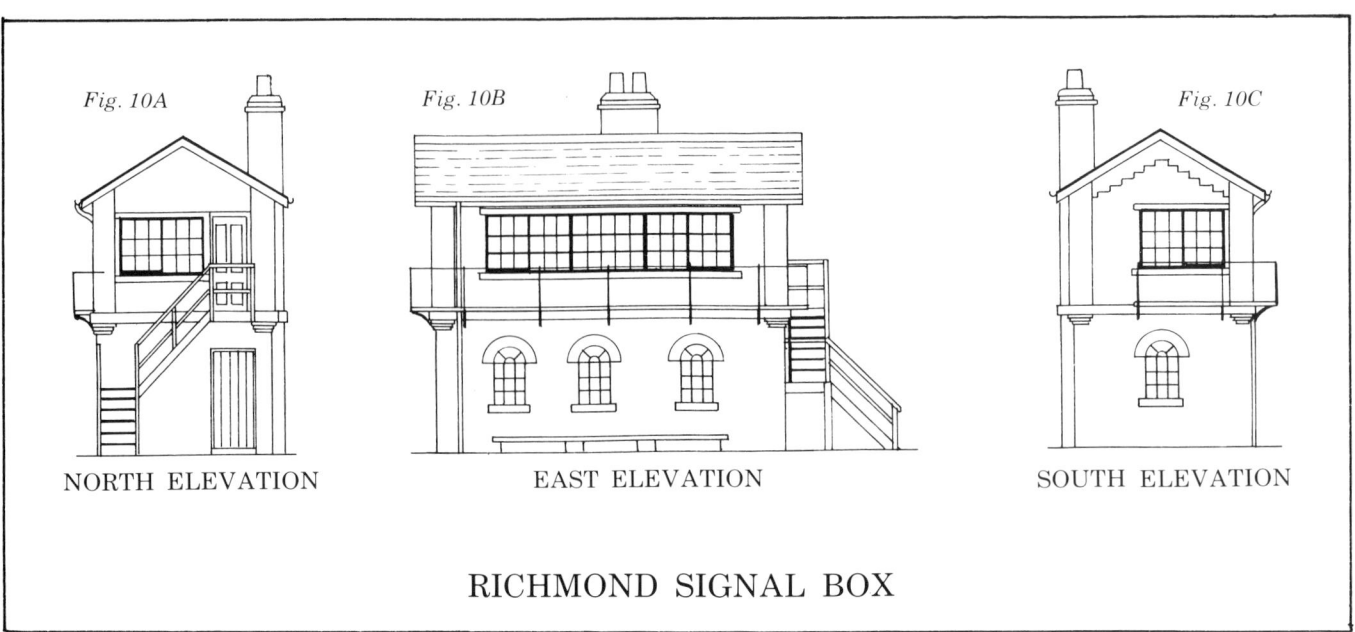

**Signal box**

The box was a variation on the old standard type of NER Southern Division. The standard design had two 7ft. windows separated by an 18in. brick pier in the front elevation, a 5ft. 6in. window in the door elevation, and another 7ft. wide, centrally-placed, at the opposite end.

Richmond box was extended about the turn of the century and, as it was an intermediate length which did not allow for another pier plus a 7ft. window, the practice of providing a continuous front window was followed.

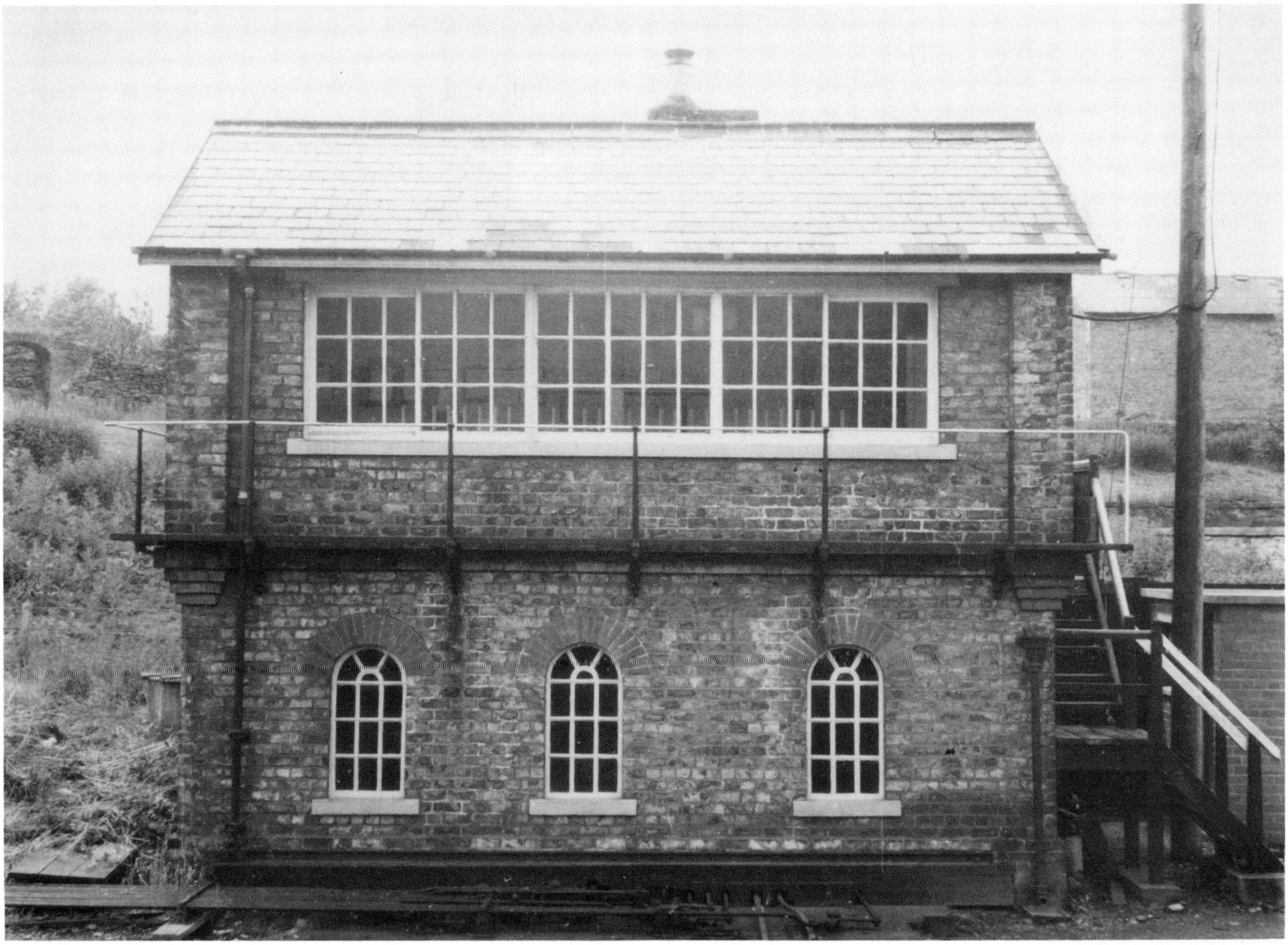

Three views of the signal box.

*L. Ward & C. B. Foster*

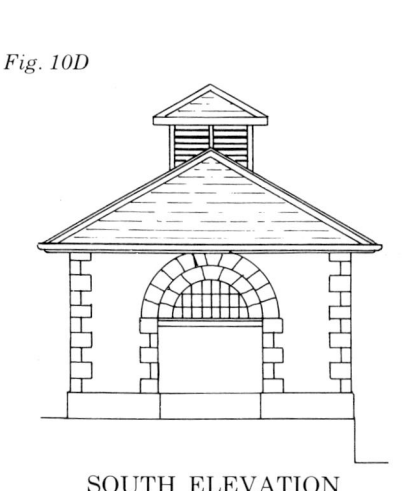

*Fig. 10D*

SOUTH ELEVATION

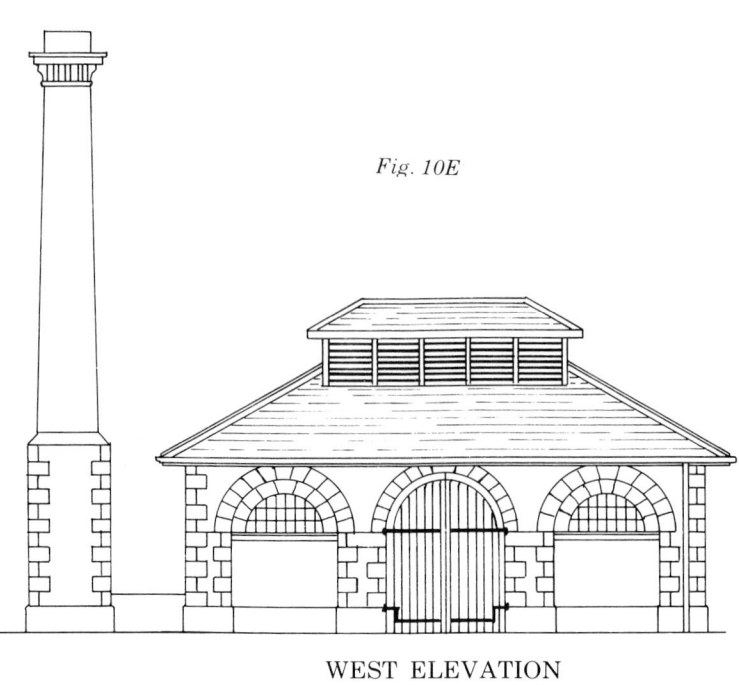

*Fig. 10E*

WEST ELEVATION

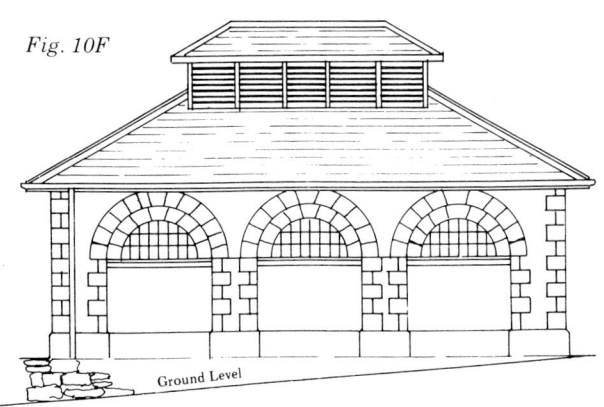

*Fig. 10F*

Ground Level

EAST ELEVATION
OF GAS HOUSE

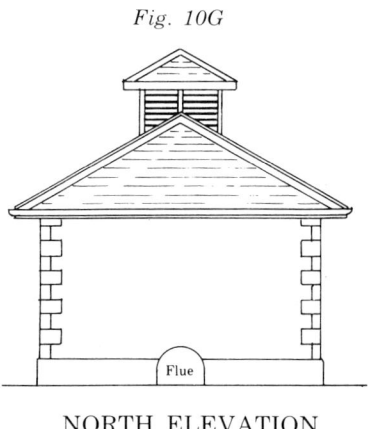

*Fig. 10G*

Flue

NORTH ELEVATION

# RICHMOND GAS HOUSE 1846

**Other buildings**

A separate stationmaster's house and a Goods Agent's house were provided and these survive, also a row of cottages for other railway staff. The gasworks building, which dates back to the building of the station, also survives, but the chimney has been demolished.

The gasworks building, which is still standing, retains signs of its former use as inside there are some firebrick structures which appear to have been retorts.

*C. B. Foster*

The stationmaster's house.

*C. B. Foster*

The depot agent's house.

*Author*

Bound for Richmond in NER days, with 0-4-4T Class O No. 468 seen in green livery. Behind the front coupling the engine carries a bracket for the Raven electric cab signalling apparatus once used on the branch.

*W. Rogerson*

Bound for Richmond in LNER days, with Class G5 0-4-4T No. 2089 in black livery. The engine retains the NER class letter on the front buffer beam. No. 2089, photographed at Croft Spa, was stationed at Richmond throughout the 1920s, until it was transferred to Northallerton on 19th December 1929 and replaced by Class F8 2-4-2T No. 469 from Hawes Junction.

*W. Rogerson*

Class F8 No. 469 leaves Croft Spa for Richmond on 26th July 1930. It is at the head of a three coach set of NER elliptical roof vehicles.
*W. Rogerson*

Sentinel steam railcar *Industry* and four wheel trailer leave Darlington for Richmond on 28th July 1934.
*W. Rogerson*

Class V2 No. 4806 *The Green Howards, Alexandra, Princess of Wales's Own Yorkshire Regiment* was named at Richmond on 24th September 1938. This was probably the first visit of this class of locomotive to Richmond, but, in later days, engines of this type worked in frequently.

*Author's Collection*

A last look at Richmond. A view taken about 1912 to illustrate the ramps of the Raven electric cab signalling apparatus, which was brought into use on the branch in 1911. The view was taken looking towards the terminus, and the station roof, signal box, engine shed and gasworks are all visible. The signal in the foreground is lit by gas, fed from the raised main running alongside the 'down' track.

*Author's Collection*

# CHAPTER SIX
# Whitby

The main entrance to Whitby Town Station in 1963, with the portico designed by G. T. Andrews.

*Author*

The station at Whitby can trace its history back to the days before the North Eastern Railway was even thought of and, in fact, to George Hudson, the so-called 'Railway King'. Even then, Hudson was not the first to appreciate the value of a railway serving this ancient port, as the horse-worked Whitby & Pickering Railway had opened its line throughout in 1836.

The Whitby & Pickering Railway was formed in 1832 in an attempt to provide an outlet for the goods brought into Whitby by sea and, in the long discussions leading to the formation of the company, there were conflicting views; should the line be built to the north-west to join the expanding Stockton & Darlington Railway, or to the south-west in the hope that, eventually, lines would be built linking Pickering to West and South Yorkshire. Eventually, it was decided to run along the Esk Valley to Grosmont, and then to tunnel through and surmount the hills barring the way to Pickering.

Following the opening of the York & North Midland Railway from York to Altofts Junction (Normanton) in 1840, thoughts turned to a line from York to Scarborough and, in March 1841, the Y&NMR announced its intention

of applying to Parliament for powers to build the line, with a branch from Rillington to Pickering to join the Whitby & Pickering line. However, Hudson was closely watching the piecemeal development of an East Coast line from London to Edinburgh and, when he saw the possibility of linking lines in Yorkshire and County Durham, to form a route under his control from Normanton to Gateshead, the Scarborough and Pickering branches were postponed, so that he could devote his resources to the completion of the East Coast line. As the Darlington to Gateshead section neared completion, it was considered appropriate to resuscitate the Scarborough line scheme, and it was approved in August 1843, and the necessary Bill submitted to Parliament. The first through train from London to Gateshead ran in June 1844 and, in the same month, the revised Scarborough branch bill received Parliamentary approval; formal Royal Assent being given on 4th July 1844.

Tenders were quickly obtained and contracts awarded, so that the whole of the Scarborough line, together with the branch to Pickering, was ready for opening in July

The north end of Whitby Station, with the two bays of the portico occupied by a tobacconist's shop, with matching shops on each side. These shops were erected in 1927 and are illustrated with post-war modifications.

*Author*

The interior of the train shed looking towards the buffer stops. For increased clearances, the first column has been replaced to the right, and the second has been altered by cutting out the lower portion and placing the new support, also to the right. Note the loading gauge suspended from the roof (right).

*British Rail*

1845. However, the steam-hauled trains could work only as far as Pickering, where passengers for Whitby had to change into the horse-drawn coaches of the Whitby & Pickering company. Hudson soon purchased the Whitby & Pickering Railway (at an inflated price), and immediately put in hand a scheme for rebuilding the line so that York & North Midland trains could run through to Whitby. The first steam locomotive reached Whitby on Friday, 6th June 1847. However, locomotives could not work the branch throughout because of the notable Goathland (or Beck Hole) incline, and one engine worked the train between Rillington and the top of the incline, and another from the foot of the incline to Whitby.

The new Whitby Station was designed by the York architect, G. T. Andrews, who received most of the commissions for stations on Hudson's lines, and it was situated nearer the town than the W&PR terminus, on the site of a shipyard owned by Messrs Barry & Barwick.

On 20th August 1846, the contract for building the station was awarded to Messrs Bellerby & Shaftoe, at a price of £10,640 and, on 29th April 1847, the York & North Midland Railway gave notice to the Board of Trade that the Raindale to Whitby section was ready for inspection. After permission to open had been granted, the updated line was re-opened throughout on 1st July 1847.

The layout of the station was typical of its period, with the arrival platform (later platform 1) down the inside of the west wall, and the departure platform (later platform 2) down the inside of the east wall, with a cross platform joining the two, inside the end wall. There was a centre road for carriage storage and the whole was covered by a typical Andrews-designed train shed, 64ft. wide, in two spans, supported on a row of columns between the arrival track and the carriage siding. The station was built on a curve and the two spans were of unequal width, disguised at each end by an apron span across the roof. At the outer end of the station this cross span was supported by one of the girders designed by Andrews and used at many of his roofed stations in Yorkshire.

With his roofed through stations, Andrews had to provide the main entrance, and the office and waiting accommodation on one side of the station, and he followed the same practice for his terminal stations; no doubt due to the insufficient space across the ends. However, Whitby was unique in having a portico at the end as well as at one side. The main entrance to the station was through a five bay portico on the departure (east) side of the station, with a similar portico, but of only two bays, placed centrally on the end wall. Although the main portico remained uncluttered, the end portico was disfigured by having three shops built in and around it, in 1927, one in the portico itself and one or either side. Thus the north end of the building is largely obscured by these lock-up shops, except for the portion above them. A clock is mounted centrally between the arches of the end portico.

Andrews' Whitby Station was very inadequately supplied with offices, and there was not even the hotel or refreshment room usually provided at Y&NMR stations of any importance. Another unusual feature was that the main entrance on the east side did not give direct access to the booking hall, but led passengers along a passage on to the departure platform, from which the various offices, including the booking office, were entered. When the inconvenience of this arrangement was realised, the south wall of the passage was breached to allow direct access to the ticket windows, forming a booking hall with an entrance at both ends.

Over the years, the actual offices have changed their usage. For instance, in 1900, when extensions to the telegraph office and the parcels office were necessary, it involved taking over the stationmaster's office and providing him with a new office along the platform, in what, until then, had been the ladies' room. This, in turn, was replaced by a new ladies' room, in a wooden building, in the angle between the north end of the station office block and the projecting section of the east wall of the train shed. The extensions to the telegraph office and parcels office were provided by another wooden annexe, built out from the existing offices to the south end of the main entrance portico, from which there was a public entrance to a counter.

Until the turn of the century, carriage storage accommodation was almost non-existent and, at busy times, empty trains had to be stored during the day at Ruswarp, Sleights and Grosmont, and in the goods yard. The difficulties were caused by the shipyard and wharfage in the Bog Hall area, which also included a dry dock. However, by the 1890s, space had been found for a through siding and two short dead-end sidings south of the shipyard; incidentally the dry dock extended from the river bank to the through siding, and directly opposite was the old Bog Hall signal box, some 60 yards south of the present box.

In 1901, the NER was able to acquire the site of Bog Hall Dockyard. The dry dock was filled in and carriage sidings laid, together with the new engine turntable on the former wharf at the north end of the site. The relevant Act contained a proviso that the NER 'shall provide for persons on foot . . . a means of access or regress from any vessels lying in the River Esk or harbour of Whitby adjoining the Company's premises between Station Square or Victoria Square and Bog Hall signal cabin'. The old Bog Hall box continued in use until about 1911, when it was replaced by the present box adjacent to the right of way across the lines which, at one time, led to a ford across the river.

With only the sparse Pickering and Rillington service to cater for at first, there were only three 'up' trains and four 'down' each day, even in 1864. The two original platforms were sufficient, but the opening of the Goathland deviation line in July 1865, and the Esk Valley line to Castleton (completing a link with Battersby and Stockton) in October of the same year, brought a greatly-increased service. Thus, it seems probable that the two short bay platforms (Nos. 3 and 4), on the east side of the station, date from that period, and this is supported by the fact that under the NER (Pelaw & Other Branches) Act of 1865, the company was authorised to acquire land adjoining the station. At some time between 1939 and 1947, (the exact date has not been located because of wartime conditions) an instruction was issued stating that only one of these platforms at a time could be used for coaching stock. 'If standing in No. 3 platform line, No. 4 to be clear; if standing in No. 4 platform line, No. 3 to be clear'. However, No. 3 platform line was removed in the 1960s. Bradshaw's Guide for July 1847 merely quotes:

The exterior of the train shed, photographed on 6th March 1952. Nine months later a start was made on removing the roof after 106 years. of service.

*British Rail*

*Whitby branch, 24 miles in length*

From Whitby to Pickering at 7.45 and 10.30a.m.
and 4.30p.m.
From Pickering to Whitby at 8.45a.m. and 1.45 and 7p.m.
No times were quoted for intermediate stations, nor were
arrival times given.

By 1861, there were three trains a day from Whitby to Rillington, where connections were made with Scarborough to York trains; these were at 8.10a.m. (passenger), 12.40p.m. (passenger express), and 5.25p.m. (passenger and mail). Journey time to Rillington was 1hr. 40mins. for the first and last train, but the express accomplished the 30 miles or so in two minutes less, by omitting the Marishes Road stop. In the opposite direction, trains left Rillington at 7.25a.m., 10.55a.m., 4.05p.m. and 7.55p.m. On Sundays, there was a 7.18a.m. mail from Rillington to Whitby and a 5.25p.m. mail in the opposite direction. To provide engines for these trains there was a 6.45a.m. Pickering to Rillington and a 7.30a.m. Whitby to Beck Hole train.

Following the opening of the deviation line on 1st July 1865, which allowed locomotives to work throughout, the service was accelerated and the trains from Whitby ran through from Rillington to Malton, where connections were given with Scarborough to York trains. In addition, an express service between Whitby and Scarborough was introduced, leaving Whitby at 8a.m. and 4.45p.m., arriving at Scarborough at 9.30a.m. and 6.15p.m., with a stop at Pickering only. At that time, there was no direct line between Whitby and Scarborough and it was thought that these trains would fill a need. They used a short-lived curve at Rillington, which allowed trains from the Whitby direction to run to Scarborough without entering Rillington Station, and without the need for reversing. However, the service was not a success and it was withdrawn in 1866.

Later, in 1865 (2nd October), the route along the Esk Valley was at last completed with the opening of the Castleton to Grosmont section. This had originally been authorised in 1846 under the Whitby & Pickering Extension Act, but Hudson overreaching himself led to the abandonment of the scheme.

The awnings erected to replace the overall roof, photographed in September 1964, with a new overall roof over the link platform at the north end.

*Author*

A view of the goods warehouse staff outside the goods office at Whitby in 1888. The signal box is on the right and this picture reveals that the entrance was originally at first floor level, with an interior flight of stairs to reach the working floor. The goods office was later extended to cover the space occupied by the group. The notice-board to the right of the door is headed 'North Eastern Railway' and specifies the 'Table of Charges made by the North Eastern Railway Company upon goods passing over their Quay at Whitby'. The notice is dated York, 14th May 18XX (unfortunately the last two figures are obscured by the man's arm).

*Author's Collection*

This new length of line led to the introduction of a Whitby to Stockton service, via Battersby, Picton and Eaglescliffe, so that Whitby Station now became the terminus for two services. First class, second class, and Government trains left Whitby at 7.15a.m., 3.15p.m. and 6.15p.m., and a first and second class passenger train at 10.30a.m., arriving at Stockton at 9.20a.m., 5.20p.m., 8.20p.m. and 12.35p.m. respectively. Trains from Stockton arrived at 9.53a.m., 12.54p.m., 5.39p.m., and 10.45p.m.

Schemes for lines along the coast, north and south of Whitby, were mooted in the 1860s and, although two companies were actually formed, they were both independently sponsored, and shortage of cash postponed their openings until the 1880s. First to open was the Whitby, Redcar & Middlesbrough Union Railway from Whitby to Loftus. This had been taken over by the North Eastern Railway in 1875 but, because of extensive engineering works, it was not ready for opening until 3rd December 1883.

South of Whitby, the Scarborough & Whitby Railway struggled on to complete its line, which was finally opened on 16th July 1885, with trains from Whitby to Scarborough at 7.30a.m., 11.15a.m., 3p.m. and 6.35p.m. However, this service did not prove satisfactory, and in the following month, the timetable was recast, with five trains in each direction. Connections were given to and from Saltburn, Middlesbrough, West Hartlepool and Newcastle. The Scarborough & Whitby Railway was worked by the NER from the outset, and taken over in 1895.

Thus, from 1885, Whitby had four services radiating from the town, with a minor increase from 1st July 1908 when an 'autocar' service started running between Whitby and Beck Hole. When Goathland Incline went out of use in 1865, with the opening of the deviation line, the section from the top of the incline to the junction with the new line, near Summit box, was abandoned, but the section from the foot of the incline to the junction with the new line at Deviation Junction was left in and used for goods and mineral traffic to the goods depot and ironworks at Beck Hole. With the introduction of the push-and-pull 'autocar' services in 1905, short journey workings from Whitby to Kettleness, Robin Hood's Bay etc. were run during the summer months for the benefit of holiday-makers, and the Beck Hole service was an addition to this facility with five trains in each direction daily.

When the WRMU line, north of Whitby, was opened in December 1883, a station was opened at West Cliff, the newer part of the town, situated high above the old town clustered on both sides of the River Esk. A contemporary account of the opening of the line refers to West Cliff as 'the well-built station which has been erected specially for the residents and visitors in that fashionable locality'. West Cliff was, at first, served only by the trains between Whitby (Town) and Saltburn, although when the Scarborough & Whitby Railway came along in 1885, trains from Scarborough could only reach the Town Station by reversing at West Cliff. This event led to the introduction of a Scarborough to Saltburn service calling at West Cliff, with a shuttle service providing connections to and from Whitby Town, and this method of working continued

until the line north of Whitby (West Cliff) closed in 1958. The main change was in the southbound direction where, prior to World War I, the first train of the day from Saltburn to Scarborough ran down from West Cliff to Town. The engine then ran round its train and set off back to West Cliff, where it again ran round its train and departed for Scarborough.

In 1955, a similar working was introduced. After running down to Town Station, the engine propelled its train back to Prospect Hill Junction, where it reversed and set off for Scarborough. This was allowed only during the winter months when the Middlesbrough to Scarborough trains were formed of only two coaches. It was not allowed in the summer months because the trains then consisted of five coaches, too many for a train conveying passengers up a 1 in 54 gradient with the engine at the rear! However, as the shuttle service between the two Whitby stations required only two coaches, this operated in the summer months also, with a Class A8 4-6-2T engine attached at the lower end of the train, so that it propelled its train to West Cliff, and headed the coaches on the descent.

The greatest change affecting rail traffic at Whitby occurred in 1933 when, after 48 years, the northern terminus of the service from Scarborough and Whitby was changed from Saltburn to Middlesbrough. The passenger traffic increased beyond all expectations and, for the summer of 1934, additional facilities were provided, including a short bay platform (converted from a loading dock) at West Cliff to accommodate the shuttle service to and from Whitby Town. It had been suggested that the northbound platform at West Cliff should be converted to an island platform (at an estimated cost of £3,183) to handle the increased traffic, but the bay platform was found to be a cheaper alternative. In the 1930s, the shuttle service between the two Whitby stations was often worked by a Sentinel steam railcar and, from 1935, railcars were allowed to work in pairs under special instructions contained in the Appendix to the Working Timetable.

Whitby's busiest time was in the summer months of the 1930s, when there was an intensive service on all the lines radiating from the town. The first departures were to Scarborough at 6.45a.m., to Stockton and Ferryhill at 6.54a.m., to Malton at 7.07a.m., and to Middlesbrough at 7.15a.m. In the opposite direction the Scarborough line was open until late to cater for holiday-makers spending the day or evening in 'The Queen of Watering Places', with the last train from Scarborough at 10.51p.m. arriving at Whitby at 12.03a.m. On summer Saturday nights the departure from Scarborough was not until 11.45p.m., arriving Whitby 12.50a.m. on the Sunday morning.

The passenger trains were so frequent that on the Scarborough and Loftus routes, which were mostly single line, the Carlin How pick-up goods had to leave Whitby at 3.45a.m., getting back to Whitby before the start of the day's passenger traffic, and the Scarborough to Whitby goods had to leave Gallows Close at 11.55p.m., arriving at Whitby at 3.25a.m., and it set off on its return trip at 4.15a.m., getting back to Scarborough at 7.06a.m. During the winter months both trains ran during the day.

The North Eastern Railway used motor buses for feeder

The North Eastern Locomotive Preservation Group's Class K1 locomotive No. 2005 stands at No. 1 platform in August 1975. The signal box and goods warehouse are seen in the background.

*J. M. Boyes*

The Bog Hall area about the turn of the century, with the old Bog Hall signal cabin. The cabin faced a dry dock directly across the tracks where there was a fixed crane on its northern quay. The signal box was later replaced by a new box nearer the station, at the site of a footpath which crossed the tracks at the near end of the set of empty coaches seen standing in the goods yard. The cleared site to the northern end of the dry dock was used for the new locomotive turntable which was installed in 1903.

*Author's Collection*

services from September 1903 and, in August 1905, commenced running charabanc tours from Bridlington Station yard to the surrounding beauty spots. Similar tours followed at Scarborough in 1906, Harrogate in 1907, and eventually from Whitby, commencing in the summer of 1912. These started from the station yard and ran during July, August and September only, although it seems probable that the services did not run their full course in 1914 because of the outbreak of war. Some of the shorter tours ran both morning and afternoon, but the longer tours took all day, such as those to Scarborough (fare 7s. 0d.), and Saltburn (fare 6s. 0d.). The vehicles used were Durkopp, Fiat, Saurer, and Hallford, with the bodies built by the NER at York Carriage Works.

Many of the NER road vehicles were commandeered on the outbreak of World War I, and the Company never did resume its tours which, after the war, were operated by Robinson's Motors Ltd. of Scarborough, until eventually taken over by United Automobile Services.

*Locomotive and Train Working*
The severity of the curves on the Pickering line severely restricted the locomotives that could be used, and for many years, only four-coupled and short wheelbase six-coupled types could be seen. In the very early days, it seems that some 0-4-0 tender engines were retained for the line, but there were, from 1864, the ten 'Whitby Bogies'; a type of 4-4-0 specially designed for the line by Edward Fletcher, the North Eastern's Locomotive Superintendent

On the goods trains, the Class 93 and Class 1001 short-coupled engines put in a great deal of work from both Whitby and Malton sheds and, in fact, the last engine of both classes ended their days working to Whitby from Malton Shed; No. 1766 of Class 93 in September 1909, and No. 1275 of Class 1001 in February 1923.

In the 1890s, the passenger traffic around Whitby was handled by the Fletcher BTP 0-4-4T engines which had proved so useful all over the system, together with T. W. Worsdell's Class A 2-4-2T introduced in 1886, with McDonnell 4-4-0 engines on the longer workings. In 1903, it was decided to use Worsdell Class G1 4-4-0 engines for the summer service between Whitby and Malton and, at the same time, the Whitby turntable was replaced on a new site and increased in diameter to 50ft. Previously, the turntable had been in the shed yard, west of the running lines (which hereabouts run north and south), but the new turntable was sited on the opposite (east) side, closer to the river and on the south side of Bog Hall level crossing.

With a Whitby to Malton train stopping at Grosmont, the Class G1 engines were allowed to take up to five 45ft. bogie coaches, plus one six wheel coach or two four wheel horse-boxes, totalling 125 tons, but above that load an engine had to assist in the rear from Grosmont to Summit box. A train not stopping at Grosmont was allowed to take six 45ft. bogie coaches plus one six wheel coach or one four wheel horse-box. The Class G1 engines put in a large amount of work between Whitby and Malton and did not finally disappear from the route until May 1930, when No. 214 was withdrawn from Malton Shed. Other North Eastern 4-4-0s noted at Whitby included Classes F (LNER D22), M (D17/1), Q (D17/2), R (D20) and R1 (D21), although none of these were actually stationed at Whitby Shed.

When the LNER was formed in 1923, the types of six-coupled tender engines allowed over the line were still severely restricted and Classes J21, J24, J25, J26, and J27 were prohibited between Pickering and Whitby and, even more surprising, the ubiquitous Class 398 engines were also banned. Thus, at that time, apart from the sole remaining Class 1001 engine already mentioned, the only six-coupled tender engines allowed were the McDonnell Class 59 0-6-0s, for which permission was given in 1917.

Over the ensuing forty years, the 0-6-0s working over the line gradually increased in size. As the Class 59 engines went for scrap, the Class J24 engines were allowed, and similarly as the J24 engines went for scrap the J25 engines were permitted. Eventually, in 1964, Class Q6 0-8-0 and WD 2-8-0 engines were allowed, although it is doubtful if any of these ever did appear although, of course, the North York Moors Railway's Class Q6 has worked frequently between Grosmont and Pickering since then. Also Class Q6 engines worked the Tees Yard to Whitby pick-up goods and thus used the Whitby to Grosmont section of the Whitby & Pickering line.

In an attempt to achieve more economical branch and suburban services, the North Eastern Railway devised a push-and-pull unit using a BTP 0-4-4T, and a coach with a driving compartment. At first, only one coach could be attached (at the bunker end of the engine), but later modifications allowed a similar coach to be attached at the chimney end, and the driver of one of these two-car units spent the whole of his shift driving from one end or the other, with only the fireman on the engine. The regulator, reversing gear, brake and whistle could be operated from the driving compartment at each end, with the controls of the regulator and reverser connected to the engine by rodding and universal joints. However, unofficially, the fireman often used to work these two controls on the engine in response to 'pops' on the whistle from the driver.

In the summer of 1908, when the Beck Hole service was introduced, Whitby Shed operated two single coach auto-cars. No. 11 turn left the station at 9.50a.m. for Beck Hole and, during the day, operated three further return trips to Beck Hole, also to Sleights, Robin Hood's Bay, Kettleness and West Cliff, getting back to Whitby at 7.50p.m. As this engine was prepared for them, the crew booked on at 8.35a.m., fifteen minutes before the first departure, but they had to stable their engine at the end of the day and thus did not book off until 8.50p.m., giving them a day of 11¼ hours.

Whitby No. 12 turn's crew prepared their own BTP engine, and also a similar engine for No. 11 turn (above), booking on at 7.50a.m. and off at 7p.m. Their tour of duty included working return trips to West Cliff, Robin Hood's Bay and Middlesbrough (via Battersby), ending their day with the 4.40p.m. Whitby to Beck Hole and 5.20p.m. return working.

With the decrease of summer visitors to the coast in World War I, the autocar services were not required but, after the war, they were reintroduced on services similar to those before the war, without the Beck Hole services, but with a working through to Scarborough.

The BTP 0-4-4T and the Class A 2-4-2T were eventually joined by the Class O (LNER Class G5) 0-4-4T engines, working not only from Whitby Shed but also from

In September 1940, a German plane dropped bombs on Whitby, obviously aiming for the railway, and hit the goods warehouse and extension. Within a few hours trains were running again and the warehouse was patched up and continued in use.

*British Rail*

Malton, Scarborough, Stockton and Saltburn, and these engines worked on the line until the 1950s and BR days. During 1907/8, Wilson Worsdell built ten Class W 4-6-0Ts, especially for the lines radiating from Whitby, but initially they were not a great success, partly because of the small bunker which restricted their coal capacity, and they were, at first, stationed at Leeds and Starbeck. Commencing with No. 688 in 1914, they were rebuilt as 4-6-2T, allowing a larger bunker to be fitted and, at the same time, the cab side sheets were extended backwards to give better protection to the crews on the exposed coast lines. However, one engine that was used in its original condition was No. 690 of Saltburn, which daily worked to Scarborough and back, and it returned to Saltburn Shed after rebuilding. In 1920, No. 692 was stationed at Whitby but the others were still at Leeds and Starbeck. However, by 1924, Whitby housed Nos. 686/8/9/91/2/5, Saltburn had Nos. 687 and 690, and Scarborough used Nos. 693 and 694. Their distribution remained constant for ten years until their age began to tell, and they began to be replaced by larger engines, particularly on the workings to Saltburn and Scarborough. However, Whitby Shed retained five Class A6 engines until February 1940, when Nos. 686, 688 and 691 moved to

Malton to allow three Class J24 0-6-0s to be used elsewhere, and No. 692 also went to Malton in May as part of the Evacuation Scheme whereby any engines, which could be spared from coastal sheds, were moved to a shed further from the coast. No. 695 remained at Whitby until March 1945, when it was transferred to Starbeck, and its departure left Whitby without a Class A6 after many years with them, although Nos. 688, 695 (as No. 9799) and 690 (as No. 69794) all spent some months there during 1947-9, when extra engine power was required.

Saltburn Shed had nine Class D 4-4-4T locomotives in 1923 (Nos. 2144/5/6/8/9/50/1/2/62) and one of the class frequently worked the 7.09a.m. to Scarborough (the turn formerly worked by No. 690) which called at West Cliff from 8.24a.m. to 8.31a.m. on its outward journey, and at 1p.m. to 1.17p.m. on the return. In 1931, No. 2162 was rebuilt as a 4-6-2T (Class A8) and tried out working from Middlesbrough to Scarborough, and from Scarborough to Hull. Results were very satisfactory; so much so that it was decided to alter the other 44 engines in the class, and all were rebuilt during 1933-6. The change of terminus from Saltburn to Middlesbrough, in 1933, brought numerous extra passengers in the summer, all wanting to go to Whitby or Scarborough. There were not enough

Bog Hall signal box and level crossing, with a Class A8 4-6-2T locomotive shunting the goods yard in August 1957.
*Author's Collection*

The 42ft. turntable in the shed yard, replaced on the opposite side of the running lines in 1903, with Class A 2-4-2T locomotive No. 674.
*Author's Collection*

The 60ft. turntable on the 'up' side of the line at Bog Hall, with Class K4 No. 3442 *The Great Marquess* on 13th April 1964. The engine had worked a special train from Leeds for the BBC.

*Author*

trains and not enough suitable engines for the difficult route and the trains sometimes ran up to five hours late!

The Class A6 engines found themselves in difficulties and the Class A8 engines were the answer; but there was not enough of them! As a palliative, the Engineer allowed Class J39 0-6-0s from Teesside sheds to work to Whitby and Scarborough, but after No. 1449 spread the track and derailed itself near Prospect Hill on 9th August 1937, they were banned. By this time, fifteen Class A8s were available from the three sheds working the line; three at Whitby (Nos. 1523/7, 2155), three at Scarborough and nine at Middlesbrough. Except for a period in World War II, when loads on the coast line were light, and the Class A8 engines could be better employed elsewhere, Whitby Shed had Class A8 engines on its strength until October 1958.

With the purchase of 273 GCR-designed 2-8-0s from the Government in the period 1924-9, the LNER was able to draft some of these engines to the former Hull & Barnsley section, where they displaced many of the native Stirling Class J23 0-6-0s. These superfluous engines were transferred to many sheds throughout the North Eastern area, and Whitby Shed received Nos. 2440 and 2476 in 1930, followed by Nos. 2459 and 2522 in 1931. Whitby usually had four or five of the class and, over the years, accommodated seven different engines. The last were Nos. 2477 and 2522 (withdrawn in 1937), and Nos. 2460 and 2476 ( the last Hull & Barnsley tender engines to remain in service, both withdrawn on 5th November 1938).

These engines were not popular and they were used only when nothing else was available. Some could usually be found at Whitby, standing out of use, although occasionally they were sent on loan to the Southern Area, such as Nos. 2460, 2469 and 2476, at Doncaster for some months during 1937/8.

The engines at Whitby were:

| Engine No. | At Whitby | Disposal |
|---|---|---|
| 2440 | July 1930 to June 1933 | Withdrawn |
| 2459 | July 1931 to September 1933 | Withdrawn |
| 2460 | June 1934 to November 1938 | Withdrawn |
| 2469 | July 1933 to July 1936 | Transferred to Hull |
| 2476 | July 1930 to November 1938 | Withdrawn |
| 2477 | July 1934 to May 1937 | Withdrawn |
| 2522 | July 1931 to May 1937 | Withdrawn |

In March 1938, the LNER reintroduced push-and-pulll working in the North Eastern Area, this time using Class G5 0-4-4T engines, but this method of working was not allowed on any of the lines radiating from Whitby. However, as mentioned earlier, in 1955 special regulations were issued which permitted engines to propel two coaches from Town to West Cliff stations without the need for a driving compartment in the leading coach. This method of working was allowed for Middlesbrough to Scarborough trains, (but not for Scarborough to Middlesbrough trains) and for the Town to West Cliff shuttle service. The introduction of BR diesel multiple unit railcars, in 1958, greatly simplified the reversing problems in the area.

The last through train from Middlesbrough to Scarborough, on 3rd May 1958, consisted of 4MT tank No. 80116, hauling five coaches, and it ran down to Whitby Town in the usual way. There it was necessary to attach Class A8 No. 69861 at the opposite end of the train to work it back up to West Cliff, with No. 80116 still attached at the rear. With a two coach train, reversal could have been carried out at Prospect Hill signal box but, because of the length of the train, and to dispose of the

Class F8 2-4-2T No. 1581 and Class A6 4-6-2T No. 693 are seen outside the shed in 1934, when the stationmaster and locomotive shed master positions were combined in one post and were occupied at the time by G. C. Gold, later Works Manager at Darlington and Mechanical Engineer at Gorton.

*Author's Collection*

Tank engines were favoured for the coast lines and to Malton, and used for many years were the Great Central-designed Class A5 engines, built for the North Eastern Area during 1925/6. Although not stationed at Whitby, No. 1719 was photographed outside the shed there.

*Author's Collection*

## Locomotive Allocation-Whitby

*Nos.*

**1923**

| | | |
|---|---|---|
| Class A6 4-6-2T | (5) | 686/9/91/2/5 |
| Class F8 2-4-2T | (5) | 490, 537, 1577/9/83 |
| Class G5 0-4-4T | (3) | 1319, 1739, 1914 |
| Class J22 0-6-0 | (3) | 142, 208, 1485 |
| Class J24 0-6-0 | (1) | 1952 |
| Class J25 0-6-0 | (1) | 2060 |

**1932**

| | | |
|---|---|---|
| Class A6 4-6-2T | (6) | 686/8/9/91/2/5 |
| Class G5 0-4-4T | (4) | 1319, 1739, 1865, 1914 |
| Class J23 0-6-0 | (4) | 2440/59/76, 2522 |
| Class J24 0-6-0 | (2) | 1947/58 |

Sentinel steam railcars (six cylinder) 2136 *Hope*,
2257 *Defiance*

**1939**

| | | |
|---|---|---|
| Class A6 4-6-2T | (5) | 686/8/91/2/5 |
| Class A8 4-6-2T | (3) | 1523/7, 2155 |
| Class G5 0-4-4T | (3) | 1319, 1739, 1865 |
| Class J24 0-6-0 | (2) | 1850, 1947 |
| Class J27 0-6-0 | (1) | 1231 |

Sentinel steam railcars (six cylinder) 2219 *New Fly*
(twelve cylinder) 246 *Royal Sovereign* and 248 *Tantivy*

**1947**

| | | |
|---|---|---|
| Class A8 4-6-2T | (1) | 9852 |
| Class G5 0-4-4T | (5) | 7262/93, 7302/8/35 |
| Class J24 0-6-0 | (3) | 5609/12/29 |

Sentinel steam railcar (six cylinder) 2136 *Hope*

**1954**

| | | |
|---|---|---|
| Class A8 4-6-2T | (6) | 69860/1/4/5/88/90 |
| Class G5 0-4-4T | (2) | 67240, 67302 |
| Class J25 0-6-0 | (3) | 65647/63/90 |

**1959**

At closure, on 6th April 1959, the engines stationed
at Whitby were distributed as follows:

Nos. 42083/5 transferred to York
No. 42084 transferred to Low Moor
Nos. 77004/13 transferred to Neville Hill

## WHITBY — Summary of Engine Workings, Winter 1908/9

*Weekdays*

*1*
7.00a.m. Whitby to Ferryhill
9.45a.m. Ferryhill to Whitby
3.08p.m. Whitby to West Hartlepool
7.05p.m. West Hartlepool to Whitby

*2*
8.35a.m. Whitby to Malton
10.48a.m. Malton to Whitby
1.30p.m. Whitby to Stockton
4.15p.m. Stockton to Whitby

*3*
8.10a.m. Whitby to Scarborough
10.23a.m. Scarborough to Whitby
12.10p.m. Whitby to Malton
2.15p.m. Malton to Whitby

*4*
3.50p.m. Whitby to Malton
5.46p.m. Malton to Gilling
6.35p.m. Gilling to Malton
7.45p.m. Malton to Whitby

*5*
11.15a.m. Whitby to West Cliff
11.50a.m. West Cliff to Whitby (Empty)
12.55p.m. Whitby to West Cliff
1.17p.m. West Cliff to Whitby
2.07p.m. Whitby to Scarborough
4.02p.m. Scarborough to Saltburn
7.32p.m. Saltburn to Whitby

*6*
4.20p.m. Whitby to Scarborough
6.10p.m. Scarborough to Filey
6.43p.m. Filey to Scarborough
7.28p.m. Scarborough to West Cliff
8.54p.m. West Cliff to Whitby (Empty)
9.10p.m. Whitby to Grosmont (Saturdays only)
9.35p.m. Grosmont to Whitby (Saturdays only — Empty)

## WHITBY — Summary of Engine Workings, Winter 1937-8

*Mondays to Fridays*

*1 — Class A8 or Class A6 engine*
7.10a.m. Whitby to Malton
10.42a.m. Malton to Whitby
3.55p.m. Whitby to Malton
5.55p.m. Malton to Whitby

*2 — Class G5*
6.54a.m. Whitby to Stockton (via Middlesbrough)
10.10a.m. Stockton to Whitby (via Picton)

*3 — Not applicable*

*4 — Class A6 or Class G5 engine*
10.10a.m. Whitby to Grosmont (light engine)
10.25a.m. to. 4.40p.m. Grosmont Pilot
4.46p.m. Grosmont to Castleton (School term only)
5.22p.m. Castleton to Grosmont (Empty; school term only)
5.43p.m. Grosmont to Whitby (light engine)

*Carriage Roster 437 (Sentinel steam railcar)*
7.15a.m. Whitby to Middlesbrough (via Loftus)
10.03a.m. Middlesbrough to Scarborough (via Loftus)
2.17p.m. Scarborough to Whitby
4.07p.m. Whitby to Middlesbrough (via Loftus)
6.20p.m. Middlesbrough to Whitby (via Battersby)
9.05p.m. Whitby to Goathland (Wednesday and Thursday only)
9.41p.m. Goathland to Whitby (Wednesday and Thursday only)

*Carriage Roster 446 (Sentinel steam railcar)*
11.30a.m. Whitby to West Cliff
11.46a.m. West Cliff to Whitby
12.04p.m. Whitby to West Cliff
12.23p.m. West Cliff to Whitby
1.20p.m. Whitby to Stockton (via Picton)
3.41p.m. Stockton to Ferryhill
4.45p.m. Ferryhill to Stockton
5.42p.m. Stockton to Middlesbrough
6.04p.m. Middlesbrough to Whitby (via Loftus)

Steam railcars were a familiar sight in the area until 1948. On a trial run from York on 6th April 1927 was 2 cylinder car No. 22, later named *Brilliant* after an earlier stage coach, preparing for the next stage of its journey from Whitby to Scarborough. The railcar is in the LNER standard teak livery originally adopted for railcars.

*H. G. W. Household*

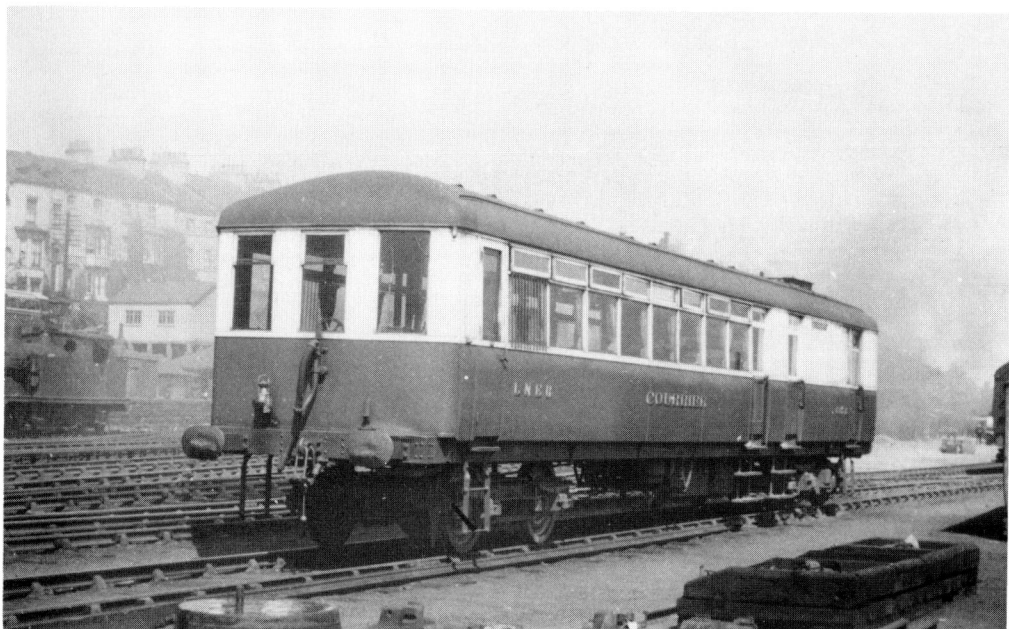

In the more familiar green and cream livery is 6 cylinder car *Courrier*, standing in the goods yard at Whitby.

*Author's Collection*

The most powerful cars were those with 12 cylinders and Woolnough water tube boilers, which worked the winter service between Scarborough and Middlesbrough. No. 248 *Tantivy* was standing out of use at Whitby when photographed.

*Author's Collection*

leading engine, it was necessary to run as far as West Cliff and reverse there.

A similar method of working was used for the scenic excursions, introduced in the 1930s, using tourist or open coaches. These usually ran only on Sundays, and were made up of eight coaches, making them too long to use the passing loops, and they could only operate when there was no traffic in the opposite direction. Starting from various inland towns, they ran via Malton and Pickering to Whitby, where the passengers were able to stretch their legs and spend part of the afternoon, before leaving for Scarborough around 4p.m. From Whitby Town to West Cliff these trains were worked by two or three engines. If two engines were used, a tank engine, preferably running bunker first, would head the train up the 1 in 50 gradient, with the train engine (a Class D49 4-4-0 pre-war and a Class B1 4-6-0 post-war) attached in the rear. At West Cliff, the tank would change ends and couple up in front of the train engine to give assistance as far as Ravenscar (if a Whitby engine) or through to Scarborough (if a Malton engine). When three engines were used, the Whitby pilot would head the train to West Cliff, with the train engine and assisting engine attached at the rear. All that was necessary, at West Cliff, was for the pilot to be uncoupled, and the train was ready to depart for Scarborough with two engines at the head.

Special regulations also governed the working of two Sentinel steam railcars coupled on the Town to West Cliff service, but this was more for technical reasons rather than for operating considerations. Only cars of the same type could be used in pairs, and both cars could be the same way round, so that a boiler compartment was next to a driving compartment, or with the boiler compartments adjacent, or with the boiler compartments at the outer ends of the unit.

*Railcars at Whitby*
In the 1920s, the Sentinel Waggon Works of Shrewsbury, a company already well-known for its steam road vehicles, was attempting to gain a foothold in the railway field, and the company would lend a demonstration vehicle to any prospective customer. Some of its products were on display at the 1924 British Empire Exhibition and, following this, the LNER expressed an interest, and tried out various railcars. One of these cars (exact identity unknown) was tried out in the autumn of 1924 on a route which became a regular testing run for new cars, namely York—Malton—Whitby—Scarborough—York. This involved the long climb to Goathland Summit, between Pickering and Whitby, and an even more severe climb to Ravenscar, between Whitby and Scarborough. There was an opportunity to try out the speed capabilities of the vehicle on the Scarborough to Malton leg as it headed back to York.

As a result of the 1924 test, the LNER purchased two cars but these were used in East Anglia, and it was not until 1927 that two cars were obtained for the North Eastern Area, followed by a further twenty in 1928. One of the 1927 cars, No. 22, then un-named but later named *Brilliant* was tried on the circular route and fortunately Humphrey Household, assistant to the Editor of the *LNER Magazine* (then produced at York) was able to travel on the car and take photographs, including a fine view at Whitby.

The LNER also ordered a Clayton steam railcar, for comparative purposes, and this was delivered to the Southern Area (GNR Section) and allocated the number 41 in the carriage stock list. It was subsequently transferred to the North Eastern Area, where it was renumbered 2121 and named *Pilot*. This was tried on the usual route on 26th July 1927, followed on 7th May 1928 by the first Sentinel six cylinder car *Nettle*, continuing the practice of naming the cars after stage-coaches. The next railcar to cover the course was the Armstrong Whitworth diesel-electric car, *Lady Hamilton*, on 21st January 1932, with the LNER Chairman, Sir William Whitelaw, and the Chief Mechanical Engineer, H. N. Gresley on board, as well as representatives of the makers. On all the trial runs the cars ran into Whitby from the Ruswarp direction and, after reversing, climbed to Prospect Hill, where they reversed again to cross Larpool Viaduct, and so to Scarborough.

In the 1930s, three cars were regularly stationed at Whitby, but other cars appeared at times, usually when one of Whitby's cars was laid off for repairs, or was undergoing a complete overhaul at Darlington Works. The position in 1934, was six cylinder car No. 2219 *New Fly* (ex-Middlesbrough in April 1934) and two twelve cylinder cars Nos. 246 *Royal Sovereign* and 248 *Tantivy*. One car worked all day between Town and West Cliff stations and, on Mondays and Thursdays, worked a late trip to Scarborough at 10.15p.m., getting back at 12.45a.m. on Tuesdays and Fridays. This was to bring home those holiday-makers who had visited the magnificent open air theatre at Scarborough, where productions did not start until 8.45p.m. and finished about 10.30p.m. Another car worked all day (from 7.25a.m. to 10.07p.m.) between Whitby and Glaisdale or Goathland, and the third car made an afternoon trip to Ferryhill, via Battersby, Picton and Stockton, returning via Stockton, Middlesbrough and Battersby, ending the day with a trip to Glaisdale and back.

In the winter months, two cars were used daily, one being a Whitby—Middlesbrough—Scarborough—Middlesbrough—Whitby turn, and the other on the afternoon Ferryhill turn and various Town to West Cliff trips.

Railcar *Tantivy* was withdrawn in November 1939 and *Royal Sovereign* in August 1941; *Telegraph* and *Defiance* were at Whitby in 1942, and *New Fly* was transferred to Malton in October 1944 after ten years at Whitby. Railcar *Times* was withdrawn from Whitby in October 1944 and was replaced by No. 2136 *Hope* from Selby, which lasted until February 1948, and was the last LNER Sentinel railcar to remain in traffic.

*Coaching Stock — and Restrictions imposed*
The severity of the curves on the lines radiating from Whitby restricted the coaches just as they did the locomotives, and four wheel vehicles lasted on these lines longer than they did on any other parts of the North Eastern Railway, although the NER did not cease building four wheelers until December 1885. Quantity production of six wheel coaches started in 1883, although odd vehicles had been built from about 1870, and clerestory-roofed bogie vehicles were built from 1895. The 1892 Appendix to the Working Timetable stated that four wheel coaches with a wheelbase of more than 19ft.

The site of the carriage sidings and turntable at Bog Hall in 1981, originally occupied by Bog Hall dockyard. The signal box can be seen in the distance. The photograph was taken from the new road bridge spanning the River Esk, which was opened on 21st March 1980.

*Author*

The confluence of the former Whitby & Pickering and Whitby, Redcar & Middlesbrough Union lines looking towards Whitby. The line on the left is dropping down from West Cliff Station and was opened in 1883, and that on the right is from Ruswarp, opened in 1835. The carriage sidings are seen on the right.

*Author*

Fortunately the Whitby photographer F. M. Sutcliffe took some photographs of railways under construction in the Whitby area, including Larpool Viaduct, built for the Scarborough & Whitby Railway, which was opened in 1885. The siding passing through the gateway led into the local gasworks.

*Author's Collection*

and six wheel coaches, were not allowed on the Whitby to Pickering, Loftus and Scarborough lines.

Although bogie vehicles measuring 45ft. over head-stocks (compared with the usual 52ft.) were introduced in 1898 specially for the Whitby lines, it soon became obvious that all types of NER bogie stock could traverse the lines, and restrictions on the 52ft. vehicles were lifted in 1901, although for years it was still laid down that no 'foreign' six wheel stock could be used, and that 'foreign' four wheel vehicles should not exceed 19ft. wheelbase. From 1st January 1909, East Coast Joint Stock vehicles were allowed, and by 1922 coaches up to 65ft. 6in. long could be worked over the branches, although six wheel coaches were still prohibited. In 1924, it was stated that all LNER coaches were to be accepted.

It was this severe restriction on coaching stock that forced the Great Northern Railway to use four wheel coaches on the summer King's Cross to Whitby service, known as 'the Whitby bathing machines'! Two four wheel vehicles for this service were built as late as 1886/7, with a first class saloon seating nine, and a third class compartment. The saloon and the compartment both had access to the same lavatory which extended across the full width of the coach, and there was also a luggage compartment. The bodies were 26ft. long and the wheelbase was 16ft. 8in. *(see From Stirling to Gresley, 1882-1922 published by Oxford Publishing Co. 1974).*

On the Whitby—Grosmont—Picton—Stockton service, six wheel coaches with 21ft. wheelbase were allowed, but only thirty specially-modified vehicles could be used and these had extra side-play in the centre axles. These coaches were made up into five sets, each comprising a brake third—third—third—first—third—brake third. These restrictions were withdrawn by 1909.

*The Engine Shed at Whitby*
The first engine shed at Whitby was provided by the York & North Midland Railway when the present station was built in 1847, and it is certain that this would be designed by G. T. Andrews. By 1865, the accommodation was proving insufficient and a new shed to hold eight engines was proposed, but no action was taken until January 1867 when Mr Harrison (Engineer) and Mr Fletcher (Locomotive Superintendent) were asked to report on the extent of the extra accommodation required. On 1st February 1867, Mr Harrison reported that the erection of a new shed could be avoided by extending the existing shed to take another four engines, and the outline plan he submitted was approved. A fortnight later detailed plans of the extension (which included a fitting shop) were approved at an estimated cost of £1,500 and the advertising for tenders was authorised.

A tender of £1,570 3s. 0d. was accepted on 15th March 1867, and work soon started. However, on 10th May, the

Coaling at Whitby was by steam crane and small 4 wheel tubs, of which one end was hinged. A BR Class 3MT 2-6-0 is seen being coaled in August 1957.

*Author's Collection*

Whitby was a shed with an adjacent public road and thus the engines could easily be photographed, making an attractive scene with the River Esk and the Abbey in the background. Also visible in this view is a 6 cylinder Sentinel steam railcar behind Class A6 No. 692 and Class J24 No. 1958.

*Author's Collection*

Larpool Viaduct from the east side of the river. The entrance to the gasworks is on the right, with Foundry Siding signal box visible through one of the centre arches. The actual foundry is seen in the distance through the left-hand arches.

*Author's Collection*

NER received an objection regarding the height of the extension, drawing its attention to a restrictive convenant. Mr Prosser, the NER Architect, was instructed to stop work and to modify the plans so that the building could be brought within the specified height. This delayed the work and the extension was not completed until 1868, when an excess expenditure of £181 19s. 2d. was authorised.

Since then, few changes have been made to the building, except for the roof, and it is not difficult to distinguish the original part of the shed, and the extension. In 1903, it was reported that the building required repairs and renewals, and it was decided to re-roof the shed and to remove a dividing wall left in place during the 1867 alterations.

The original roof was of the pattern favoured by G. T. Andrews, with a flattish hipped roof and a large central ventilator, as used on sheds at York, Scarborough, Market Weighton, Richmond, Darlington etc., and the undated print in Tomlinson (*Plate XXIV*) appears to show a building of this type. The roof of the extension dating from 1867 had a span over each track to reduce the height, and there was a row of columns down the centre of the building. Thus the south elevation had two gables.

This was changed to a single span roof under the 1903 scheme, and the building remains in this form to this day, although no longer used for locomotive purposes.

Coaling was, for many years, by means of a hand crane on the west side of the tracks, outside the south end of the shed but, in 1910, as a result of the grievances brought to light by a strike, Mr Raven, Chief Mechanical Engineer, agreed to look into the matter. The men contended that because of the delays caused by this slow method of coaling, they were entitled to more than the standard time allowance for stabling engines. Eventually, a steam crane was provided and this method was used until the shed closed. A spare crane based at York was available for the sheds at Malton and Whitby and this was used when the normal crane was away for overhaul.

A 42ft. turntable was situated in the shed yard, but in July 1902, the Locomotive & Stores Committee decided that it should be replaced by a 45ft. turntable from Church Fenton, to be sited adjoining Bog Hall Dock. However, a 50ft. turntable was actually provided, so that the largest NER 4-4-0 then running (Class R) could be turned, even though the largest 4-4-0 working to Whitby at the time was a Class G1. This turntable was replaced by a 60ft. version on the same site in 1936.

A view on 21st June 1957, with Class A8 No. 69864 propelling its two coach train to West Cliff, and the Whitby & Pickering line following the river. Larpool Viaduct, carrying the Scarborough & Whitby line across the river, is just out of sight round the bend of the river.

Author

The Whitby & Pickering weigh house on the lineside approaching Whitby. It is now, unfortunately, only a pile of stones due to lack of interest and cash by the local authority and British Rail.

*Author's Collection*

The viaduct out of use, after the Scarborough line had been closed in 1965.

*Author*

The reroofed engine shed, south end, circa 1919, with two Class A 2-4-2T locomotives, Nos. 1579 and 35. The local tool vans stand in a siding on the far side of the running lines.

*Author's Collection*

Because of the limited space at the shed, engines out of use and not required were often stored in a siding between the 'up' main line and the goods yard. During the summer months, the engines off excursions etc. stood on their trains in the goods yard.

A plan, dated 29th September 1900, showed a proposed single roundhouse to be built at Ruswarp, replacing the building at Whitby, which was incapable of further extension. The scheme was not proceeded with and the cramped shed at Whitby continued in use until the end.

*Services Reduced*
The first service to be withdrawn was that to Beck Hole, which normally ran from 1st July to 30th September each summer, from 1908. However, because of the outbreak of World War I, it closed prematurely on 21st September in 1914, never to reappear. On two occasions, in 1930 and 1931, a bridge over the River Esk, east of Glaisdale was destroyed by floods, caused by an exceptionally heavy rainfall, and the service between Whitby and Stockton

had to be suspended. As a stopgap measure, trains ran from Whitby to Egton and from Glaisdale to Stockton. On 14th June 1954, the Whitby to Stockton service ceased for good with the closure of the line between Battersby and Picton, but trains continued to run between Whitby and Middlesbrough by reversing at Battersby, and Stockton could easily be reached by changing at Middlesbrough.

The next closure to affect Whitby was on 5th May 1958, when the former Whitby, Redcar & Middlesbrough Union line was closed between West Cliff and Loftus, thus cutting the Whitby—Guisborough—Middlesbrough service. However, the simultaneous introduction of diesel railcars meant that reversals were easier, and an improved service was provided between Scarborough—Whitby—Middlesbrough, via Battersby, although this also meant reversing at Whitby Town and West Cliff.

The hardest blow for Whitby was undoubtedly the withdrawal from 8th March 1965 of the services to Malton and Scarborough, in spite of long and vigorous protests. Crowds turned out to travel over the doomed lines on the last day, Saturday, 6th March. A railtour starting from Manchester was headed from Market Weighton by Class K4 *The Great Marquess* and Class K1 No. 62005, arriving at Whitby (via Scarborough) at 4.53p.m., 72 minutes late, and departing for York at 5.55p.m., 85 minutes late. The last regular trains over the historic Whitby & Pickering line were the 6.54p.m. Whitby to York train, headed by Class 40 diesel No. D259, and the 5.55p.m. York to Whitby diesel multiple unit.

I am sure that as the Class K4 and the K1 blasted their way up the deviation line on that March evening, not a

The Class J24 0-6-0s were followed by the slightly larger Class J25 engines, such as No. 65663, seen here with a snowplough when photographed at Whitby in April 1956.

*Author*

Next came the considerably larger Class J2 and J27 engines, such as No. 65849 photographed after working the Malton to Whitb goods in 1958.

*Autho*

The last steam locomotives to work the Malton goods were the Class B1 4-6-0s from York. Here No. 61319 is being turned on the Bog Hall turntable prior to working back to Malton in August 1964, a few months before the line was closed.

*B. Webb*

On the same day as No. 61319 was on the Malton goods, English Electric Type 3 diesel No. D6770 was on the pick-up goods along the Esk Valley, working from Thornaby Shed. The largest class of diesel locomotives to work into Whitby were the English Electric Type 4s from York, although more recently, in August 1981, a special train was worked by a Class 55 'Deltic' locomotive.

*B. Webb*

single passenger on the train ever thought the line would reopen but, thanks to the great efforts of a small band of people, the section between Grosmont and Pickering is now operated by the North York Moors Railway, with a large variety of steam and diesel power, including the two natives, Class J27 No. 5894 and Class Q6 No. 2238. Who would have ever imagined that a regular performer on the line would be a former Southern Railway 4-6-0 locomotive? Unfortunately the NYMR trains do not (as yet!) run through to Whitby, but, on occasions, NYMR locomotives have been allowed to work trains over the BR section, notably the Class K1, now in green livery and carrying the number 2005.

Approaching Whitby, on the remaining route from Middlesbrough, the line crossed the River Esk for the last time at Ruswarp, on a girder bridge which at one time carried a public footpath, but this has now been dismantled. This was followed by a level crossing as the train runs into Ruswarp Station, with its attractive buildings designed by G. T. Andrews. Half a mile beyond Ruswarp was Hutton's Siding, serving an iron foundry and, in fact, the signal box controlling the points into the siding was named Foundry Siding. It was a wooden box on the river side of the line, with the foundry buildings on the opposite side. Even by 1908, the box opened only when the Whitby pilot engine required to shunt Foundry Siding or the nearby Gas Works Siding. In 1930, after the foundry had disappeared, the box was reclassified as a ground frame and renamed Gas Works; the box itself remaining standing until destroyed by fire on 11th May 1949.

The local gasworks was situated on the Esk side of the line, just on the Whitby side of the tall Larpool Viaduct which was opened by the Scarborough & Whitby Railway in 1885, but since the introduction of natural gas, no gas has been made at Whitby, and the siding has been removed.

Next, still on the river side of the line, was a house once owned by the railway, in the garden of which was a large canvas-covered shed. The framework of the shed con-

sisted of seven pairs of whales' jawbones some 9ft. in length, arranged in pairs to form arches. This interesting relic of Whitby's connection with the whaling industry, was dismantled in April 1930.

A short distance nearer Whitby was the weigh house used for stone travelling on the W&PR from the Whitby Stone Company's quarries in the Grosmont area. Unfortunately, no steps have been taken to preserve this old and interesting building which is now little more than a pile of squared stones.

On the opposite side of the running lines is the overgrown course of the Whitby, Redcar & Middlesbrough Union line, coming down from Prospect Hill on its 1 in 50 gradient, which joined the Whitby & Pickering route at Bog Hall Junction. On the river bank, a large derelict area once housed the carriage sidings, with the turntable pit adjacent to the level crossing at Bog Hall box. The box controlled the outlets from the engine shed and the goods yard, on the west and east sides of the running lines respectively.

Beyond Bog Hall box, the engine shed remains. After closure, it was at first used as a fish packing warehouse but it is now occupied by a ships' chandler serving the many small craft moored in the river. Across the running lines is the truncated goods shed, damaged by German bombing in September 1940. Because of the restricted space between the goods shed and engine shed there are only two running lines up to the entrance to the platforms, but both-way working is permitted between Bog Hall and Station boxes. The tracks, fanning out to the various platforms, are controlled by the tall signal box situated at the station end of the goods shed. It is of typical NER Southern Division design; brick built, with an extra storey to give the signalman a view over the roof of the goods shed. The box has been disfigured by the insertion of a door in the front wall, at working level.

Goods traffic was withdrawn from Whitby in May 1983 and it is expected that this lead to the closure of Bog Hall signal box.

Working at the station was controlled by a signal box, built with an extra storey to look over the earlier goods shed. The goods office behind the steps of the box is the extended version.

L. Ward

A front view of the box in 1969.

*C. B. Foster*

## Notes on the Drawings — WHITBY

### General

The station was built in 1847 to the designs of G. T. Andrews. The main (east) elevation consisted of a five arch portico flanked by two identical single storey wings. A two arch portico was provided at the north end of the building. The train shed had two unequal spans. The west platform appears to have been incorrectly built, as it gradually widens from the buffer stops, from 14ft. 8½in. to 14ft. 11in., then at 40ft. from the south end of the roof it widens relatively quickly to 16ft. 1½in. This made the clearance between the track and the roof support columns extremely tight and, with the introduction of bogie stock, intolerable. In 1900, alternatives were considered but the obvious solution to reduce the platform width to a quoted dimension of 14ft. 11in. was rejected. Instead, the first and second support columns were replaced by rolled-steel joists, giving increased clearances to the platform line of 1ft. 5½in. and 7½in. respectively, with corresponding reductions to the less important centre siding.

The available details of the construction of the roof are extremely limited and sometimes contradictory, the most obvious being the height of the wing roofs. By 1914, the lower roof was in existence *(Fig. 1b)* and therefore, if improbably, the higher roof *(Fig. 1a)* was built in 1847, it must have been altered between 1900 and 1914.

In plan, the geometry of the station is incompatible. Taking the radius of the east platform at 630ft., the radial lines from the extremities of the covered platform intersect more than 200ft. different from the intersection of similar lines from the north and south ends of the roof.

Fig. 1A

4' 3"

Wing Roof (dimension as on 1900 drawing)

NORTH ELEVATION AS BUILT

Fig. 1B

2' 6"

Low Wing Roof (as existing 1914)

NORTH ELEVATION 1927
SHOWING 1900 LADIES' ROOM AND 1927 SHOPS
SOME DETAIL MODIFICATIONS HAVE BEEN CARRIED
OUT TO THE SHOPS IN RECENT YEARS

## WHITBY STATION

**Station** *(Drawings 1 to 5)*
From 1890, the appearance of the station was progressively ruined by the addition of timber buildings. The year 1891 saw the porters' room built fairly unobtrusively at the south-east corner, but within the next nine years, the only brick extension was the boiler room for the foot warmers. In 1900, the real rot set in with prominent additions to the booking/parcels/telegraph offices, and also to the ladies' room in the north-east corner. Four years later the gentlemen's toilet was extended to make the whole southern wing a vision of timber planking. In 1906, the first real assault on the north elevation occurred with the provision of the timber-built stationmaster's office within the portico and, in 1927, the whole of the north face was covered with shops, both inside and outside the portico. These changes meant that the

stationmaster's office moved from No. 18 *(see Key, drawing 3)* to No. 21, then to No. 23, and back to No. 18!

Other alterations included the replacement of the north window in the entrance portico by a 6ft. wide door (between 1905 and 1914), the alteration of doors to windows, and vice versa on the platform elevation *(Fig. 5d)*, the removal of the wall between the booking hall and the entrance, and the shortening of the tracks to increase the width of the link platform (all before 1927). A canopy over the northern door of the west elevation was added in 1900 and, at some later date, the window immediately south of it was replaced by a sliding door *(Fig. 5b)*. The last major disfigurement was the removal of the overall roof and cornice, in 1953. The low cantilevered awning, erected in place, necessitated blocking off the upper part of the three large arched doorways leading on to the platform.

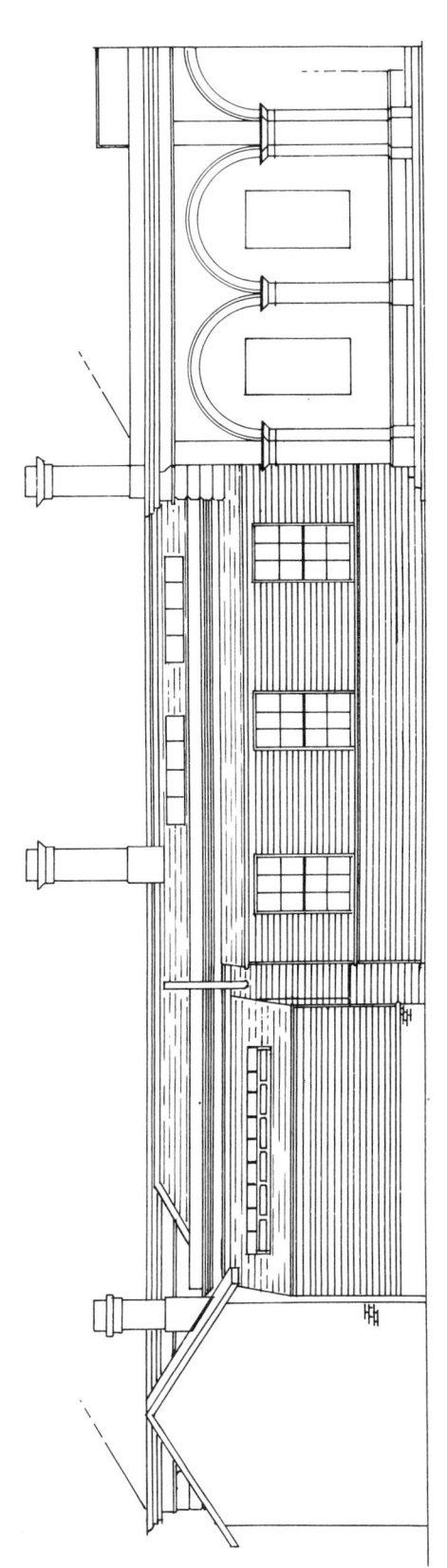

NORTHERN HALF OF EAST ELEVATION, AS BUILT

Fig. 2A

SOUTHERN HALF OF EAST ELEVATION,
AS MODIFIED BETWEEN 1890 AND 1904

Fig. 2B

WHITBY STATION

ROOF CRESTS AND VALLEYS SHOWN ————————

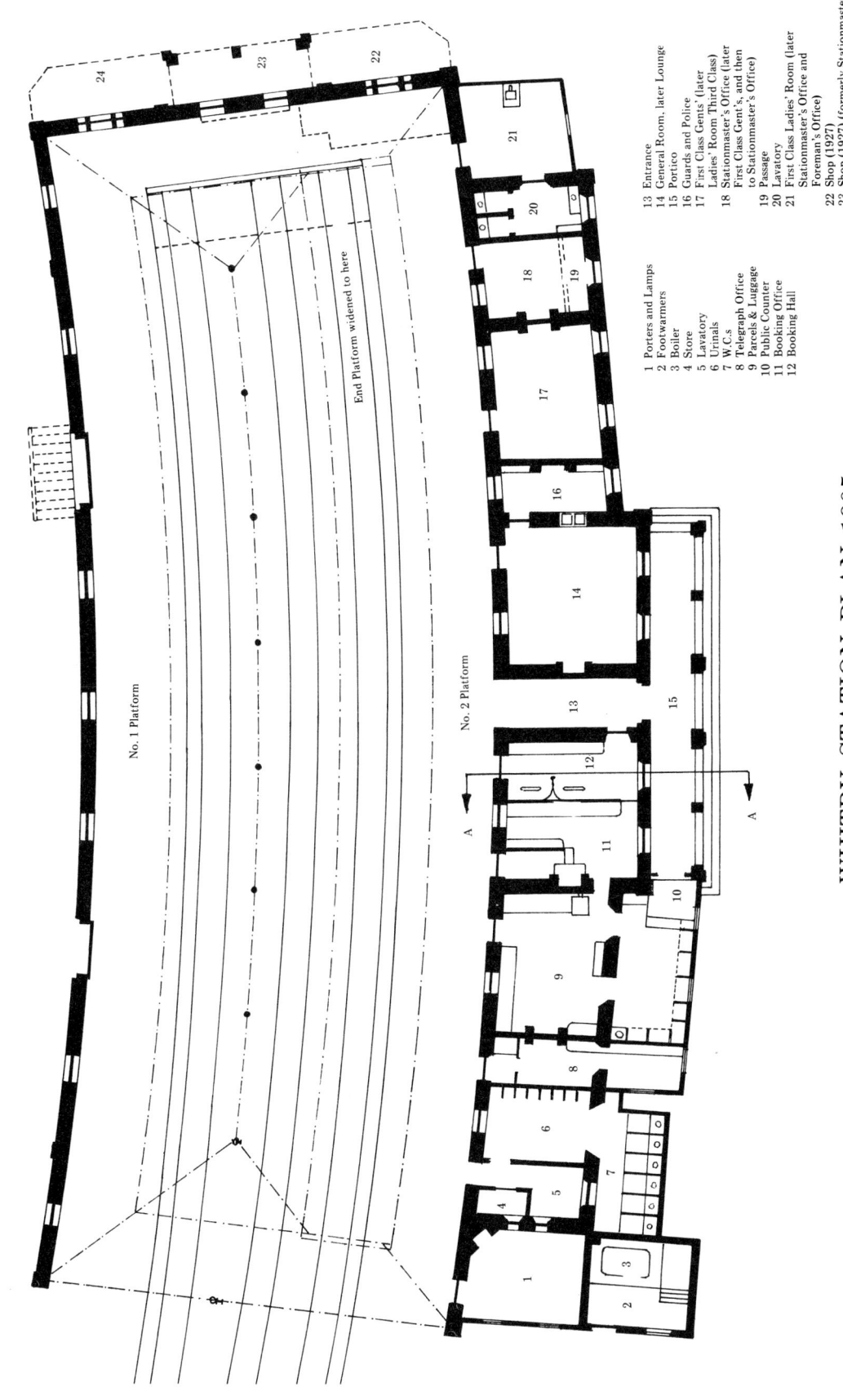

No. 1 Platform

End Platform widened to here

No. 2 Platform

A

A

1  Porters and Lamps
2  Footwarmers
3  Boiler
4  Store
5  Lavatory
6  Urinals
7  W.C.s
8  Telegraph Office
9  Parcels & Luggage
10 Public Counter
11 Booking Office
12 Booking Hall

13 Entrance
14 General Room, later Lounge
15 Portico
16 Guards and Police
17 First Class Gents' (later
   Ladies' Room Third Class)
18 Stationmaster's Office (later
   First Class Gent's, and then
   to Stationmaster's Office)
19 Passage
20 Lavatory
21 First Class Ladies' Room (later
   Stationmaster's Office and
   Foreman's Office)
22 Shop (1927)
23 Shop (1927) (formerly Stationmaster's Office)
24 Shop (1927)

WHITBY STATION PLAN 1905
HALF SCALE

Fig. 3A

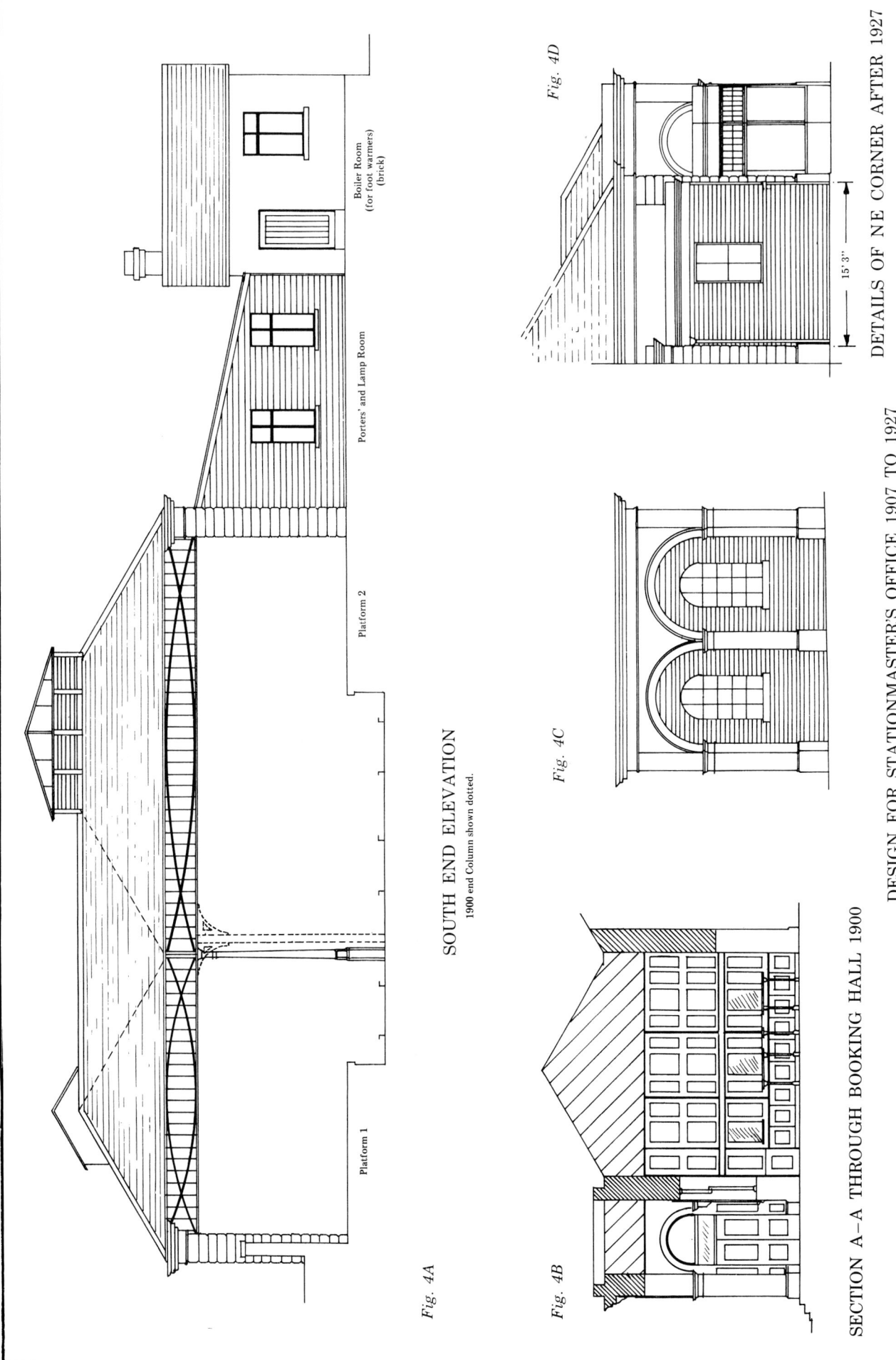

Boiler Room
(for foot warmers)
(brick)

Porters' and Lamp Room

Platform 2

Platform 1

SOUTH END ELEVATION

1900 end Column shown dotted.

Fig. 4A

Fig. 4D

DETAILS OF NE CORNER AFTER 1927

15' 3"

Fig. 4C

Fig. 4B

SECTION A–A THROUGH BOOKING HALL 1900

DESIGN FOR STATIONMASTER'S OFFICE 1907 TO 1927

Left-hand original Window was made into Doorway to platform.

WHITBY STATION

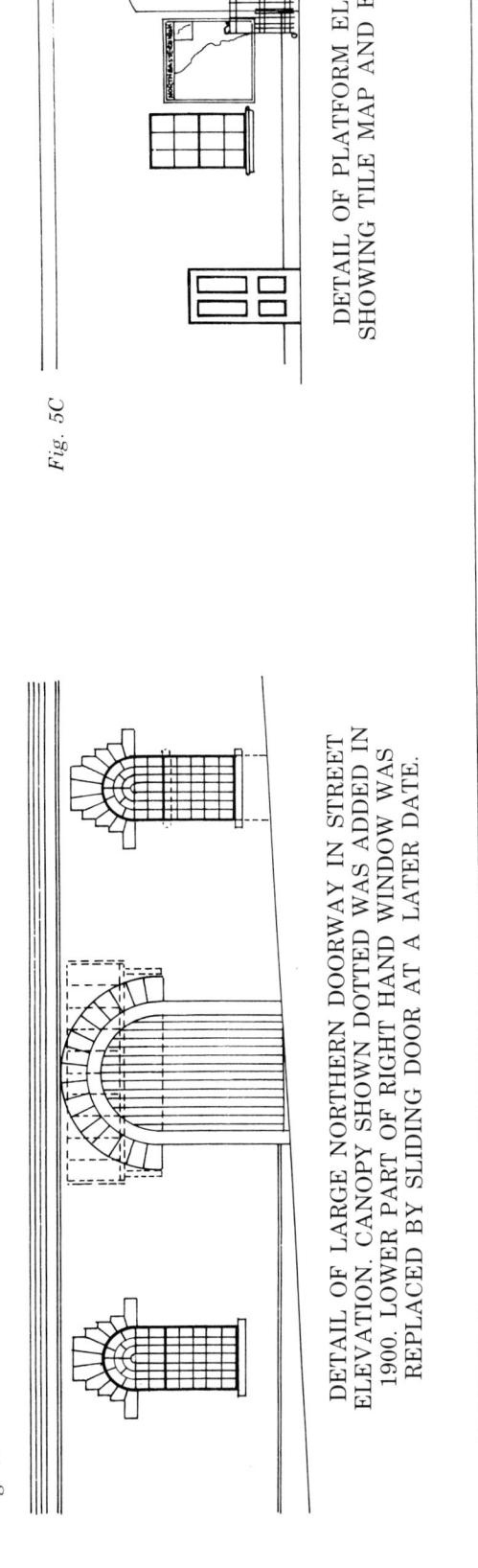

Fig. 5A

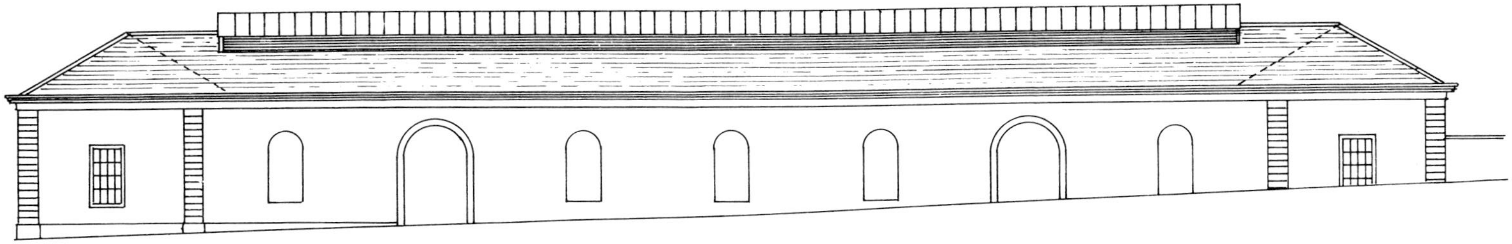

STREET (WEST) ELEVATION
(Half Scale)

Fig. 5B

DETAIL OF LARGE NORTHERN DOORWAY IN STREET
ELEVATION. CANOPY SHOWN DOTTED WAS ADDED IN
1900. LOWER PART OF RIGHT HAND WINDOW WAS
REPLACED BY SLIDING DOOR AT A LATER DATE.

Fig. 5C

DETAIL OF PLATFORM ELEVATION
SHOWING TILE MAP AND ENTRANCE

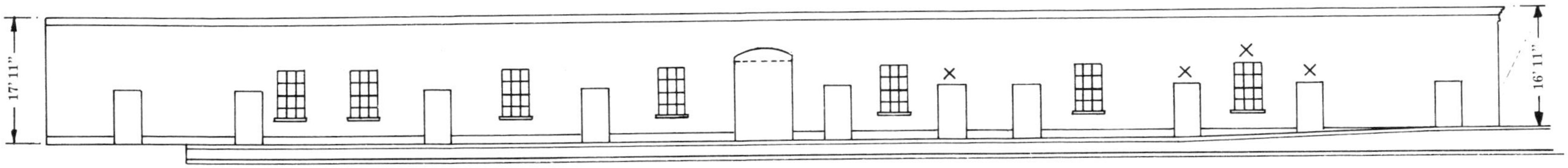

Fig. 5D

1900 PLATFORM ELEVATION.
DOORS MARKED X REPLACED BY WINDOWS AND
WINDOW MARKED X REPLACED BY DOOR.
(HALF SCALE)

WHITBY STATION

16' 11"

17' 11"

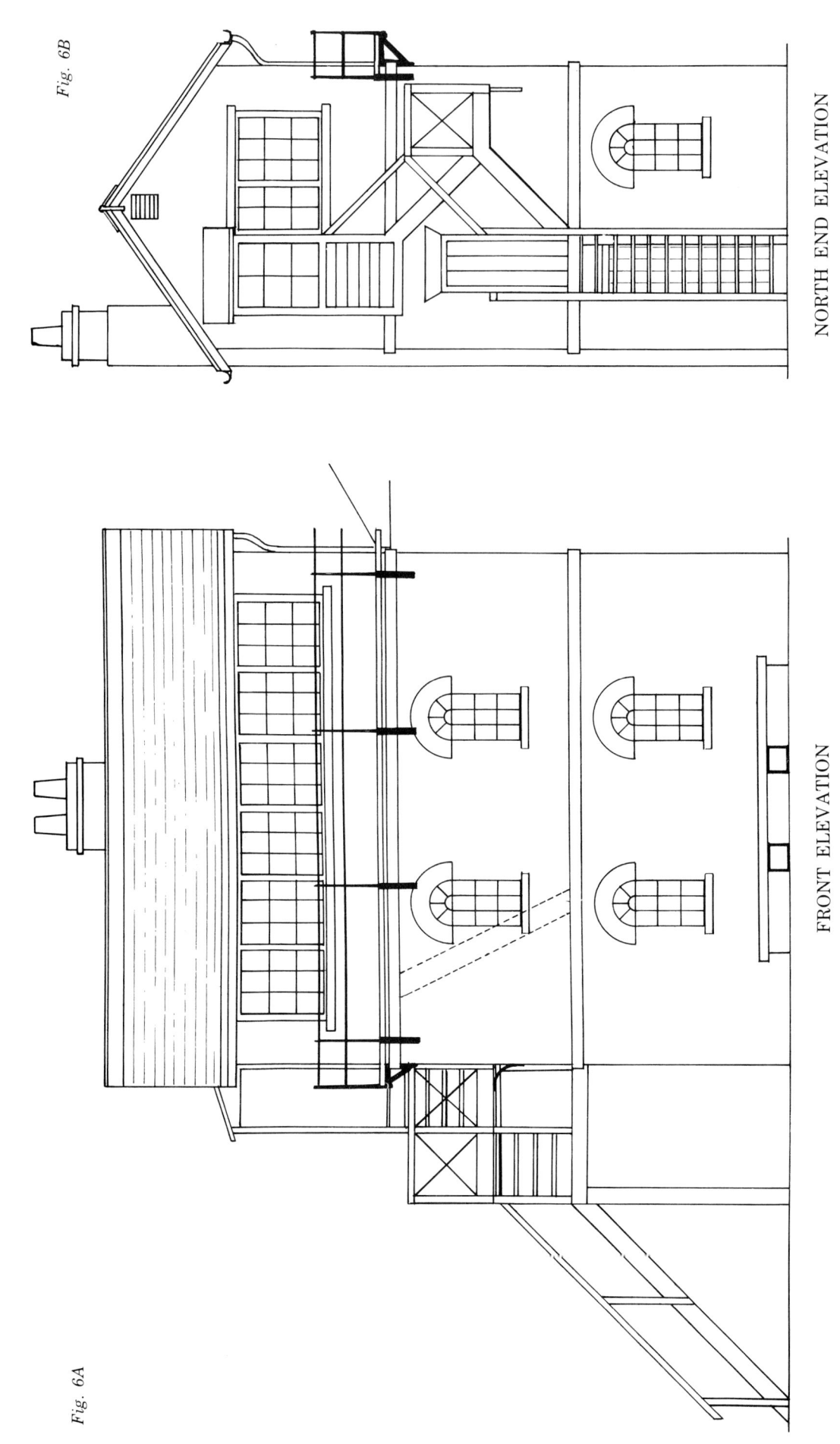

*Fig. 6B*

NORTH END ELEVATION

FRONT ELEVATION

*Fig. 6A*

SHOWING FINAL STAIR ARRANGEMENT; THE ORIGINAL
STAIRS BETWEEN THE FIRST AND SECOND FLOORS
WERE INSIDE (SHOWN DOTTED)

WHITBY SIGNALBOX (LATER CONDITION)
(Twice Scale)

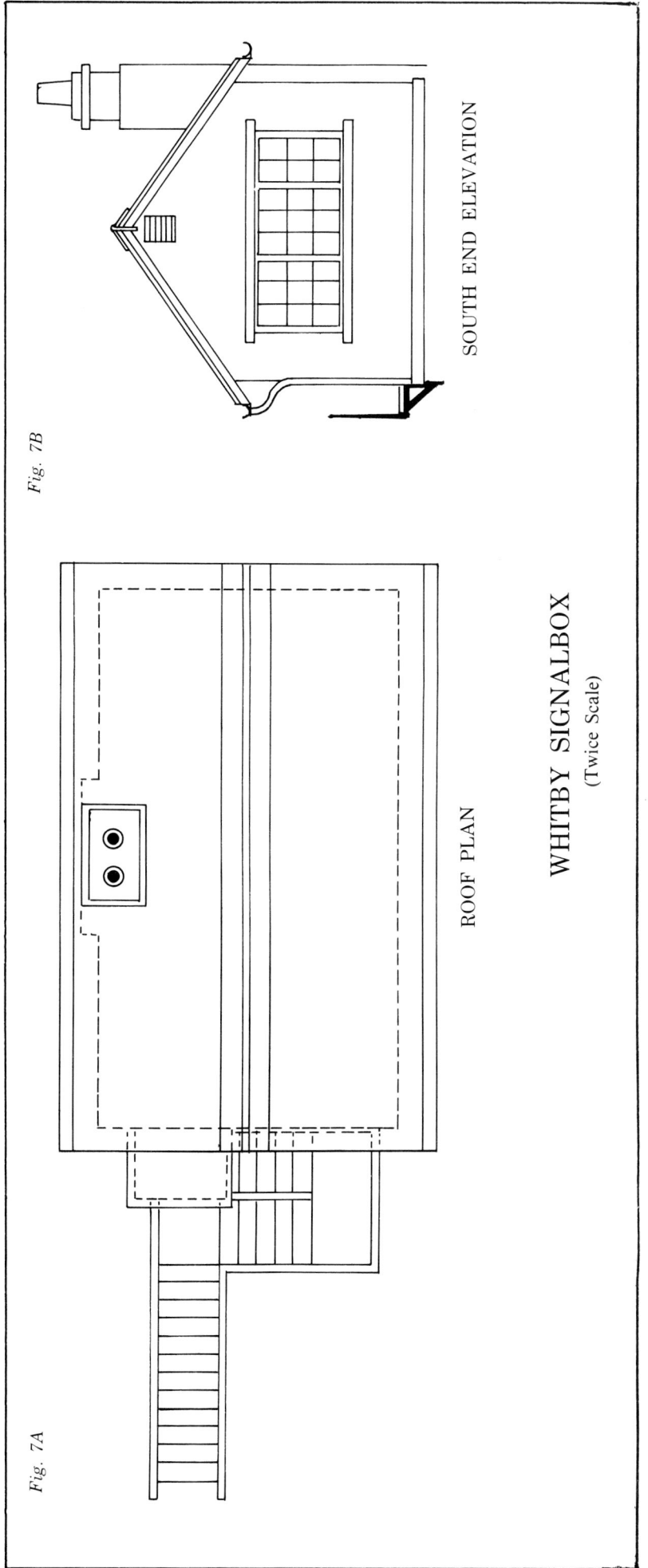

*Fig. 7B*

SOUTH END ELEVATION

*Fig. 7A*

ROOF PLAN

WHITBY SIGNALBOX

(Twice Scale)

**Signal box** (*Drawings 6 & 7*)

It is not known where the earlier box stood, but the 1884 cabin (in brick) was placed in a compromise position, because of its proximity to the goods warehouse. This necessitated an extra tall box which affected the goods office. Slight alterations to the drawing existed from the outset, as a standard round-headed 4ft. x 2ft. cast-iron framed window was placed in the north wall. The box was built with an external staircase to the first floor, and an internal staircase to the operating floor, but this arrangement was altered to that shown in *Fig. 6a* at some later date, when the frame was extended.

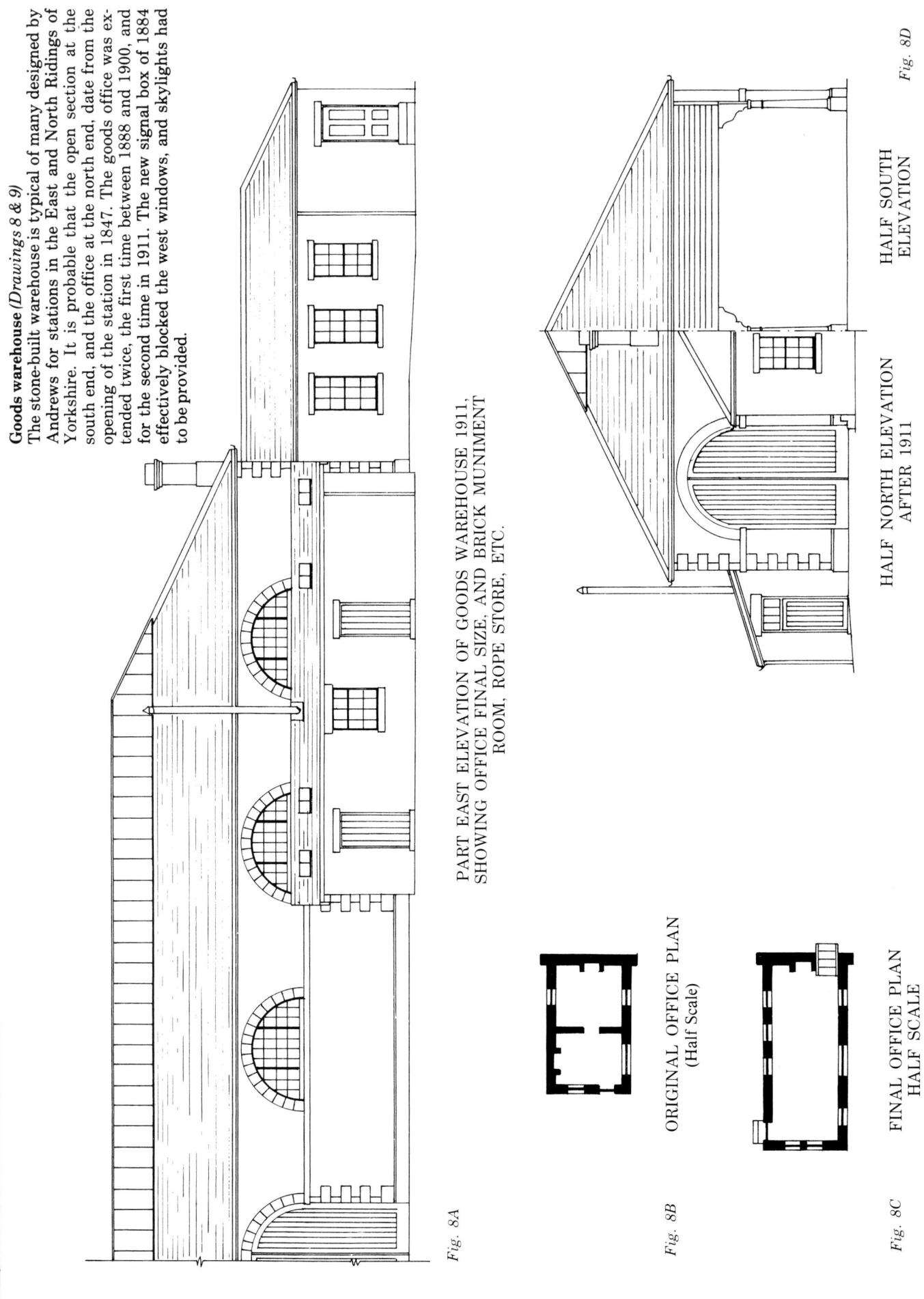

**Goods warehouse** *(Drawings 8 & 9)*

The stone-built warehouse is typical of many designed by Andrews for stations in the East and North Ridings of Yorkshire. It is probable that the open section at the south end, and the office at the north end, date from the opening of the station in 1847. The goods office was extended twice, the first time between 1888 and 1900, and for the second time in 1911. The new signal box of 1884 effectively blocked the west windows, and skylights had to be provided.

PART EAST ELEVATION OF GOODS WAREHOUSE 1911, SHOWING OFFICE FINAL SIZE, AND BRICK MUNIMENT ROOM, ROPE STORE, ETC.

*Fig. 8A*

ORIGINAL OFFICE PLAN (Half Scale)

*Fig. 8B*

FINAL OFFICE PLAN HALF SCALE

*Fig. 8C*

HALF SOUTH ELEVATION

*Fig. 8D*

HALF NORTH ELEVATION AFTER 1911

WHITBY WAREHOUSE

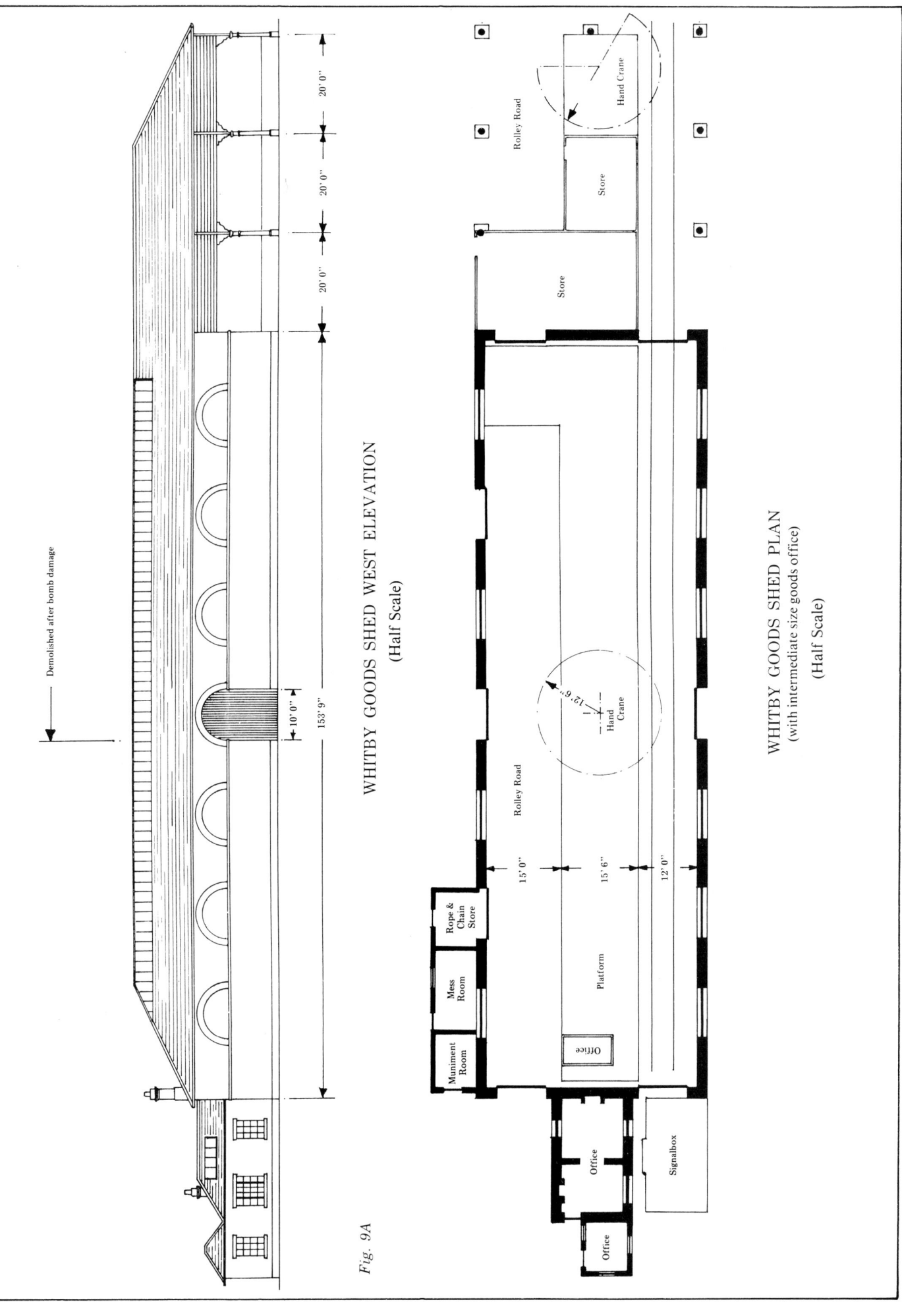

Demolished after bomb damage

WHITBY GOODS SHED WEST ELEVATION
(Half Scale)

Fig. 9A

WHITBY GOODS SHED PLAN
(with intermediate size goods office)
(Half Scale)

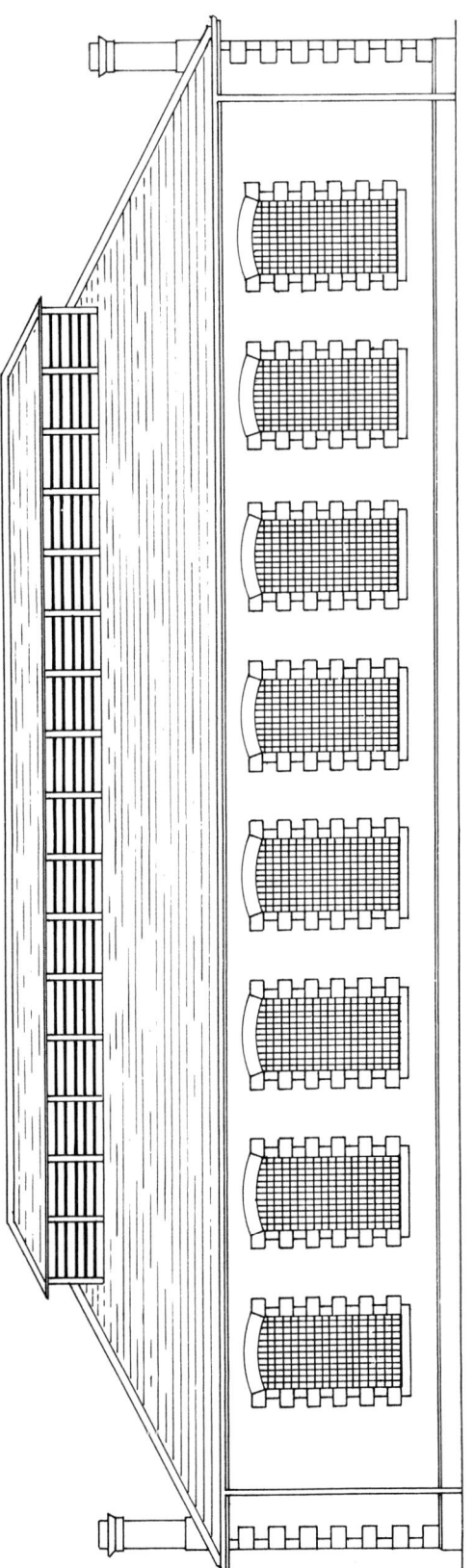

SIDE ELEVATION OF RICHMOND (1846) AND
WHITBY (1847) ENGINE SHEDS AS BUILT

(Note: Whitby had no windows in the west wall but Richmond had windows in both sides).

*Fig. 10A*

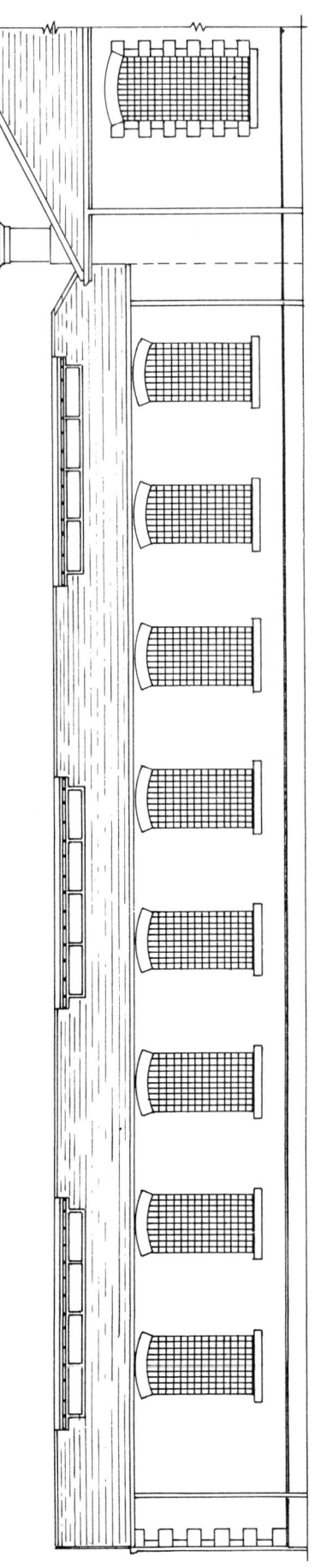

EAST SIDE ELEVATION OF WHITBY SHED EXTENSION
1867–1903

*Fig. 10B*

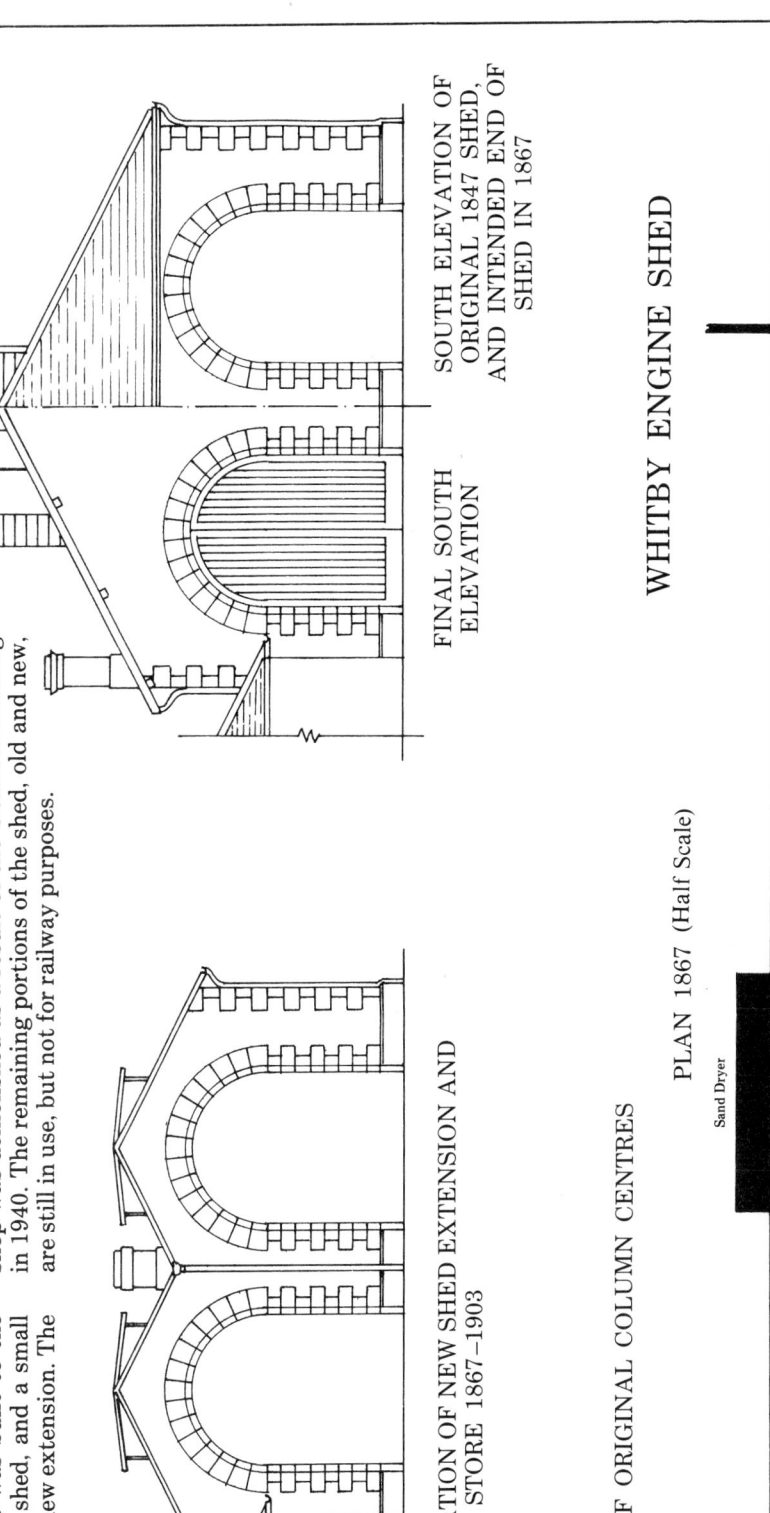

The shed was built in 1847 to the same design as Richmond, except that the west elevation was without windows, the roof ventilator was slightly smaller, and the chimney details differed. In March 1867, a contract was let for an extension of the shed, southwards, for 99ft. 8in. in identical style, together with a fitters' shop and stores in a building about 48ft. long, also at the south end, parallel to the western track.

A legal objection was raised by a local resident because the proposed extension affected his view of the River Esk, and he was successful in having the height of the shed reduced to a maximum of 19ft. 3in. The modified design is shown in *Fig. 10b*. The fitters' shop was built to the full height at the north end of the old shed, and a small store was built at the south end of the new extension. The

both extensions. In the engine shed, the new window sills were level with the old, but in the fitters' shop, because of the adjacent platform, the windows were placed with their tops level with the original windows. The floor level of the fitters' shop was 4ft. above rail level.

By 1903, the aggrieved resident must have departed because the shed was then rebuilt to full height, with a single large gable end instead of the two small gables, and a lower ridge ventilator than that proposed back in 1867. The small windows were retained, but the missing window at the junction of the old and new sheds was not inserted when the dividing wall was removed. The fitters' shop was demolished as a result of the German bombing in 1940. The remaining portions of the shed, old and new, are still in use, but not for railway purposes.

*Fig. 11B*

SOUTH ELEVATION OF ORIGINAL 1847 SHED, AND INTENDED END OF SHED IN 1867

FINAL SOUTH ELEVATION

*Fig. 11A*

SOUTH END ELEVATION OF NEW SHED EXTENSION AND STORE 1867–1903

*Fig. 11C*

WHITBY ENGINE SHED

-|- POSITION OF ORIGINAL COLUMN CENTRES

PLAN 1867 (Half Scale)

Store

Sand Dryer

Engine Pit

Wall end of original Shed (demolished 1903)

Engine Pit

Office

Forge

Workshop 1867–1940

Platform

Another class of locomotive which performed a large amount of work in the area was the McDonnell 4-4-0, later known as Class 38. This view shows No. 38 at Whitby Shed. It was built at Gateshead in October 1884 but it was not the pioneer engine of the class in spite of the classification. This number was allocated because No. 38 was the lowest numbered engine in the class.

*Author's Collection*

For local services another well-known Fletcher class engine, the BTP 0-4-4T, was used on normal trains and, from 1906, on push-and-pull 'autocars'. No. 1342 was one the engines built by R. & W. Hawthorn of Newcastle in 1875.

*Author's Collection*

At busy summer weekends, space was at a premium at Whitby and engines had to stand at various locations. Visible in this August 1930 view are at least eight engines and two Sentinel railcars. A visitor from Leeds was Class D21 4-4-0 No. 1244 (right).

*Author's Collection*

At the centre of this group of locomotives is former Hull & Barnsley Railway 0-6-0 No. 2459, a Whitby engine from July 1931 to September 1933, and railcar *Alexander,* a Stockton car, is seen in the background.

*Author's Collection*

As the largest of the six stations covered in this book, Whitby had a far greater variety of locomotives, including some types specially designed for work in the area. The first of these were the ten 'Whitby Bogies', a 4-4-0 design by Edward Fletcher, built by Robert Stephenson & Co. in 1864/5. No. 1810 was originally No. 501, and was withdrawn from service in November 1893 after covering a total distance of 749,699 miles.

*Author's Collection*

Also extensively used, even well into BR days, were the Class G5 0-4-4T engines, such as No. 1886, a Malton engine photographed at Whitby in 1938.

*Author's Collection*

Another design specially prepared for use in the Whitby area was the Class W 4-6-0T, which appeared in 1907. The small bunker proved to be inadequate and, between 1914 and 1917, the ten engines were rebuilt to 4-6-2T. This view is of the last to be built, No. 695, in its original condition.

*Author's Collection*

The first to be rebuilt was No. 688, in September 1914, and their best work around Whitby was performed in the 1920s. Early in the 1930s they were supplanted by larger engines, and especially by the newly-rebuilt Class A8 4-6-2T engines.

*Author's Collection*

Class A6 No. 692 seen in LNER black livery. The photograph was taken before vacuum brake equipment was fitted (in February 1929). Note the bogie brakes and shaped buffer heads. Seven of the class, including No. 692, were later fitted with superheated boilers.

*Author's Collection*

The first Class A8 4-6-2T engine appeared in the area in July 1931 and proved an immediate success. Eventually, as more were rebuilt from Class H1 4-4-4T, they worked virtually every train on the coast line between Middlesbrough, Whitby and Scarborough. No. 69881, photographed outside Whitby Station on 23rd June 1957, was a Scarborough engine and it had just assisted a railtour, headed by Class D49 No. 62731 *Selkirkshire*, over the severe grades on the Scarborough and Whitby line.

*P. B. Booth*

Tight curves on lines in the area, particularly on the Pickering route, restricted 6 coupled engines and, for many years, only short wheelbase engines were allowed, such as No. 1250, photographed here at Whitby Shed. The locomotive was built at Darlington in June 1873 and withdrawn in 1913.

*Author's Collection*

No. 1485 was a McDonnell engine of Class 59. It is seen photographed in August 1922 and was withdrawn from Whitby Shed in November 1928.

*T. Horn*

Throughout most of the LNER period the Class J24 0-6-0s were the mainstay of the goods traffic, such as No. 1958 photographed at the shed in the 1920s.

*Author's Collection*

# APPENDICES

## APPENDIX 1
### Acts of Parliament, opening and closing dates

| Station | Act | Opened Passengers | Opened Goods | Consent to Closure | Closed Passengers | Closed Goods | Note |
|---|---|---|---|---|---|---|---|
| Alnwick | 31.7.1845 | 19.8.1850 | 1.10.1850 | 28.9.1967 | 29.1.1968 | 2.10.1968 | 1 |
| Alston | 26.8.1846 | 17.11.1852 | 17.11.1852 | 10.1.1973 | 3.5.1976 | 6.9.1965 | |
| Guisborough | 17.6.1852 | 25.3.1854 | 11.11.1853 | 27.11.1963 | 2.3.1964 | 31.8.1964 | |
| Middleton-in-Teesdale | 19.6.1865 | 13.5.1868 | 13.5.1868 | 9.9.1964 | 30.11.1964 | 5.4.1965 | |
| Richmond | 21.7.1845 | 10.9.1846 | 10.9.1846 | 11.11.1968 | 3.3.1969 | 2.10.1967 | |
| Whitby | 6.3.1833 | 8.6.1836 | ? | — | — | — | 2 |

*Note 1:*   New station 1887
*Note 2:*   New station 1847
Whitby to Loftus (—Middlesbrough) closed 5.5.1958
Whitby to Scarborough closed 8.3.1965
(Whitby)—Grosmont—Pickering—Rillington (—Malton) closed 8.3.1965

## APPENDIX 2

### Summary of train services

In the early days of railways in the North-East, it was the practice to work branch lines with an engine and a set of coaches running between the junction station and the outlying terminus. Thus, the trains did not at first run beyond Alnmouth, but eventually a good service was established between Alnwick and Newcastle. The Alston branch trains, however, never seem to have ventured beyond Haltwhistle, where connections were given with the trains in both directions on the Newcastle and Carlisle line.

Until the changes of 1933, Guisborough was merely a stop on the local service between Middlesbrough and Saltburn, although some trains ran only between Guisborough and Middlesbrough but, with the rearrangement of the services, a number of trains ran through between Scarborough and Middlesbrough, calling at Guisborough, but still with some Guisborough to Middlesbrough trains in the intervals. The cutting back of the Scarborough service to Loftus in 1958, and eventually to Guisborough itself in 1960, meant that the service remaining at closure was between Guisborough and Middlesbrough, although a morning train was extended to Newcastle.

Middleton-in-Teesdale trains were eventually extended to Darlington and Sunderland, but Richmond branch trains usually terminated at Darlington. However, there was at one time a morning Richmond to Newcastle train and, in the 1960s, a 'Saturdays Only' Richmond to Newcastle, via Gateshead West Station and the High Level Bridge.

Trains from Whitby at first connected with Scarborough to York trains at Rillington, but this did not last long and Malton was found more suitable. In the summer months, Whitby to York and Leeds trains were found to be worthwhile, and there was, at one time, a through train

## Number of Passenger Trains on Weekdays (Mondays to Fridays) and Sundays: Departures Only

| Year | ALNWICK | | | | ALSTON | | GUISBOROUGH | | | | MIDDLETON-IN-TEESDALE | | RICHMOND | | WHITBY | | | | | | | |
|---|---|---|---|---|---|---|---|---|---|---|---|---|---|---|---|---|---|---|---|---|---|---|
| | To Alnmouth | | To Coldstream | | To Haltwhistle | | To Middlesbro' | | To Saltburn | | To Barnard Castle | | To Darlington | | To Malton | | To Battersby | | To Saltburn | | To Scarboro' | |
| | W | S | W | S | W | S | W | S | W | S | W | S | W | S | W | S | W | S | W | S | W | S |
| Nov. 1870 | 11 | 7 | — | — | 3 | — | 5 | — | — | — | 3 | — | 5 | 2 | 3 | 1 | 4 | — | — | — | — | — |
| Nov. 1900 | 18 | 8 | 3 | — | 4 | — | 10 | — | 8 | — | 5 | — | 6 | 2 | 6 | 1 | 5 | — | 6 | — | 5 | — |
| Nov. 1930 | 14 | 7 | — | — | 4 | — | 11 | — | 5 | — | 4 | 1 | 5 | 2 | 5 | — | 5* | — | 2** | — | 2** | — |
| Nov. 1960 | 12 | — | — | — | 6 | — | 7 | — | — | — | 5 | — | 12 | 2 | 7 | — | 5 | — | — | — | 4 | — |

Additional trains often ran on Saturdays and Market Days depending on local conditions. Some branches had a Sunday service in the summer months.

NOTES: * = Service to Egton (line cut by floods)

** = Connections with Scarborough to Saltburn and Saltburn to Scarborough trains given at West Cliff by four Whitby to West Cliff trains.

W = Weekdays      S = Sundays

---

between Whitby and King's Cross. With the completion of the Grosmont to Castleton section of the Esk Valley line in 1865, a Whitby to Stockton service was introduced, and this continued until the line closed between Battersby and Picton in 1954. However, over the years, some trains from Whitby reversed at Battersby, and continued to Middlesbrough via Great Ayton.

The Whitby, Redcar & Middlesbrough Union line allowed a Whitby to Saltburn service to be introduced in 1883, and this was connected with the section southwards to Scarborough when the Scarborough & Whitby line opened in 1885. Between 1933 and 1958, the northern terminus was Middlesbrough, but the closure of the West Cliff to Loftus section, in 1958, meant that all trains bound for Middlesbrough had to travel on the Esk Valley line and reverse at Battersby. From 1958 to 1965, a Middlesbrough to Scarborough service continued to be provided by additional reversals at West Cliff and Whitby Town but, when this was withdrawn due to the closure of the Whitby to Scarborough line, and with the simultaneous closure of the Grosmont—Pickering—Rillington line, Whitby was left with the Battersby to Middlesbrough service, the fate of which is also uncertain.

## Miscellaneous Notes on Train Services (See Table)

**1870**

Alnwick: Service between Alnwick and Alnmouth only.

Alston: 7.25a.m. and 5.25p.m. trains, First Class, Second Class and Government. 10.41a.m. train, First Class and Second Class

Middleton: 7.20a.m. train, First Class, Second Class and Government. 11.35a.m. and 4.45p.m. trains, First Class and Second Class

Whitby: All trains via Battersby through between Whitby and Stockton

**1900**

Alnwick: 8.18a.m. and 8.42a.m. trains through to Newcastle

**1930**

Alnwick: Six trains through to Newcastle

Whitby: 12.20p.m. from Whitby through train to York and Leeds, via Malton

**1960**

Alnwick: Four trains through to Newcastle

Guisborough: 8.12a.m. train through to Newcastle

Middleton: Four trains through to Darlington and one to Bishop Auckland

Whitby: 7.02a.m. and 3.15p.m. trains from Whitby to Malton ran through to York. 7.40:a.m. and 12.35p.m. trains to Goathland only.

# APPENDIX 3

## Goods Traffic Despatched Year Ending
## 31st December 1923

| *Alnwick* | *Tons* |
|---|---|
| Building stone | 2,304 |
| Grain | 1,976 |
| Flour and bran | 110 |
| Oil cake | 214 |
| Timber (other than round) | 401 |
| Creosote, tar and pitch | 159 |
| Scrap iron and steel | 180 |
| Bars, joists and girders | 100 |
| Iron ore | 118 |
| Livestock (2,129 wagons) | — |

| *Alston* | *Tons* |
|---|---|
| Ores | 1,956 |
| Lime | 1,359 |
| Roadstone | 25,318 |
| Manure | 2,930 |
| Scrap iron and steel | 122 |
| Spelter and zinc | 130 |
| Livestock (253 wagons) | — |

| *Guisborough* | *Tons* |
|---|---|
| Timber (round) | 852 |
| Iron and steel | 1,508 |
| Scrap iron and steel | 482 |
| Gas water | 454 |
| Barley | 198 |
| Creosote, tar and pitch | 136 |
| Cinder | 224 |
| Gravel and sand | 171 |
| Livestock (115 wagons) | — |

| *Middleton-in-Teesdale* | *Tons* |
|---|---|
| Roadstone | 92,860 |
| Building stone | 4,822 |
| Ores | 461 |
| Lime | 4,827 |
| Livestock (230 wagons) | — |

| *Richmond* | *Tons* |
|---|---|
| Minerals | 112 |
| Timber (round) | 387 |
| Timber (other than round) | 247 |
| Scrap iron and steel | 214 |
| Barley | 121 |
| Roadstone | 194 |
| Building stone | 860 |
| Livestock (362 wagons) | — |

| *Whitby* | *Tons* |
|---|---|
| Timber (other than round) | 385 |
| Gravel and sand | 700 |
| Gas water | 212 |
| Scrap iron and steel | 1,860 |
| Creosote, tar and pitch | 109 |
| Flour and bran | 226 |
| Fish | 260 |
| Ale and ale empties | 157 |
| Ashes and cinders | 266 |
| Cement | 147 |
| Roadstone | 142 |
| Livestock (39 wagons) | — |

# APPENDIX 4

## Population of Area Served by Station
## and Tickets Issued 1901

| *Station* | *Population* | *Tickets Issued* |
|---|---|---|
| Alnwick | 7,749 | 55,359 |
| Alston | 2,758 | 14,540 |
| Guisborough | 5,995 | 63,747 |
| Middleton-in-Teesdale | 3,439 | 22,188 |
| Richmond | 6,747 | 38,377 |
| Whitby | 11,316 | 134,750* |

*\* A further 65,880 tickets were issued at West Cliff Station.*

# APPENDIX 5

## Single line signalling

All the single lines serving the stations concerned in this work were worked originally on the staff and ticket system, but changes were made as technical developments came along, with all the relevant sections worked by electric tablet by 1939:

| Branch | | Position at |
|---|---|---|
| Alnwick North to Summit | 1892 | Staff and Ticket |
| | 1911 | Electric Staff |
| Alnwick North to Edlingham | 1922 | Electric Staff |
| Alnwick to Whittingham | 1931 | Electric Key Token |
| | 1939 | Electric Tablet |
| Alston to Lambley | 1892 | Staff and Ticket |
| | 1911 | Staff and Ticket |
| | 1922 | Staff and Ticket |
| | 1931 | Staff and Ticket |
| | 1939 | Electric Tablet |
| Middleton-in-Teesdale to to Tees Valley Junction | 1892 | Staff and Ticket |
| | 1911 | Staff and Ticket |
| | 1922 | Staff and Ticket |
| | 1931 | Staff and Ticket |
| | 1939 | Electric Tablet |
| Whitby (Bog Hall) to Prospect Hill | 1892 | Staff and Ticket |
| | 1911 | Electric Tablet |
| | 1922 | Electric Tablet |
| | 1931 | Electric Tablet |
| | 1939 | Electric Tablet |
| Guisborough Box to Passenger Station (Station Platform Line) | 1932 | No Token. Signals electrically interlocked |

The NER Appendix to the Working Timetable listed all the block telegraph signal stations (signal boxes) and the times they were open, amended as necessary according to the demands of traffic, but in 1911 the times were:

| Box | Closed |
|---|---|
| Alnwick Station | After traffic ceases to 6a.m., and on Saturdays after traffic ceases to 6a.m. Mondays. Sundays attends to passenger traffic. |
| Alston Station | During cessation of traffic. Sundays attends to passenger trains during summer months. |
| Guisborough Station | After traffic has ceased to 4.30a.m. Same time Saturdays to 4.30a.m. Mondays |
| Middleton-in-Teesdale Station | During cessation of traffic. Sundays attends to passenger trains. |
| Richmond Station | During cessation of traffic. Sundays attends to passenger trains. |
| Whitby Station | During cessation of traffic. |

# APPENDIX 6

## Engine Restrictions

The North Eastern Railway used a system whereby specific branches were listed, with the classes of engines not allowed to work on that branch, but it was not very comprehensive and occupied less than two pages in the Appendix to the Working Timetable. The scheme was extended in the early years of the LNER and amendments, still using the NER classifications, were issued at intervals, until in January 1929 when a change was made to the LNER system of locomotive classification. Further amendments were issued until September 1939 but, following World War II, the LNER introduced, in 1947, a route availability scheme, whereby all engines were included in groups numbered between 1 and 9, depending on the weight and size of the engine; RA1 being the lightest and RA9 the heaviest, and this scheme was perpetuated by British Railways.

The branches concerned were:

*Alnwick to Alnmouth*

| | Classes Prohibited |
|---|---|
| March 1922 | No restrictions |
| July 1925 | 4-6-2 (Pacific) restricted to 35m.p.h. |
| July 1929 | Classes A1, A2, A3 restricted to 35m.p.h. |
| July 1933 | Class W1 added |
| December 1936 | Classes A4 and V2 added |
| October 1947 | Line RA9. Engines in Group 9 restricted to 35m.p.h. |

*Alston to Haltwhistle*

| | |
|---|---|
| March 1922 | No restrictions |
| October 1947 | Line RA9. Engines in Groups 8 and 9 restricted to 30m.p.h. |

*Guisborough to Middlesbrough*

| | |
|---|---|
| March 1922 | No restrictions |
| October 1947 | Line RA9. No restrictions |

*Middleton-in-Teesdale*

| | |
|---|---|
| March 1922 | D, T2, T3, W, X, Y |
| July 1925 | Add 4-6-2 (Pacific) and 2-6-0 (GN Express Goods) |
| July 1929 | Revise: A1, A2, A3, A5, A6, A7, H1, K3, O4, Q6, Q7, T1 |
| December 1933 | Add W1 |
| March 1935 | Add A8 |
| March 1936 | Add A4 |
| December 1936 | Add B15, B16, C6, C7, C7/2, C9, D21, D49, V2. Delete A6 |
| July 1938 | Delete A8 |
| October 1947 | Line RA9 |

*Richmond to Eryholme*

| | |
|---|---|
| March 1922 | No restrictions |
| October 1947 | Line RA9. No restrictions. |

*Whitby to Pickering*

| | |
|---|---|
| March 1922 | B, C, E, E1, L, N, P, P1, P2, P3, S, S1, S2, S3, T, T1, T2, T3, U, V, X, Y, Z, 3cc, 4cc, 290, 398, 901, 1463 |

| January 1925 | Revise: B, C, N, P1, P2, P3, S3, T, T1, T2, T3, U, V, X, Y, Z, 4cc, 290, 398, 901, 1463, Pacific, R.O.D | June 1953 | Add WD 2-8-0, LMR 4MT tank 2-6-4T (LMS Standard taper boiler). (L1, V1 and V3 permitted between Grosmont and Whitby) |
| December 1925 | Add 2-6-0 (GN Express Goods) | | |
| January 1929 | Revise: A1, A2, A3, A7, B16, C6, C7, C8, E5, J21, J25, J26, J27, J39, J77, K3, N8, N9, N10, O4, Q5, Q6, Q7, T1 | | |
| July 1929 | Add J28, J35, J37 | | |
| December 1933 | Delete E5. Add C9, W1 | | |
| March 1936 | Add A4, N2 | | |
| March 1938 | Delete A2. Add V1, V2 | | |
| October 1947 | Line RA5. Additional classes permitted: D49/1, D49/2, D17, D20, O1, O2, O2/4, O3, O4/1, O4/2, O4/3, O4/4, O4/5, O4/6, O4/7, O4/8, O6, Q4, Q6, Q7 | | |

# APPENDIX 7

## Coal Staiths, Depots or Cells

Almost every North Eastern station had facilities for unloading coal for local distribution. This was usually a 'perk' of the stationmaster, who was allowed to trade as a coal merchant using the railway company's property as his base. There were certain conditions attached to this privilege, including the inspection of his account books by the railway auditors, but the stationmaster was allowed to retain the profit, which could be considerable at some stations, and even greater than his salary.

The coal was unloaded in the goods yard at the depots, where the rails climbed from yard level to run on beams or girders supported on brick or stone walls at right-angles to the track, so that when the bottom doors of the wagons were opened the coal fell into the individual cells formed by the supporting walls. There it was bagged, weighed and sold. At larger stations individual, or a complete set of cells, would be let to coal merchants, who could order the coal of their choice from any particular colliery, depending on local requirements and preferences.

In earlier days in the north east the term staiths was often used for a coal selling point, such as that in existence at Alnwick before the coming of the railway, but the NER reserved the title staiths . . . never staithes . . . for the large wooden jetties used for shipping coal at County Durham and Northumberland harbours and estuaries such as Tyne Dock, Percy Main, Blyth etc. The number of cells varied, again depending on local requirements, and those concerned were (in 1908):

| Station | Number of Cells | Capacity Per Cell Tons | Beams or Girders | Maximum Gross Weight Per Line Per Cell Tons |
| --- | --- | --- | --- | --- |
| Alnwick | 6 | 20 | Beams | 33 |
| Alston | 16 | 12¼ | Beams | 29 |
| Guisborough | 18 | 13½-15½ | Girders & beams | 33 |
| Middleton-in-Teesdale | 10 | 20 | Beams | 56 |
| Richmond | 27 | 27-30 | Girders, beams and steel joists | 20 |
| Whitby (West Cliff) | 6 | 13 | Beams | 20 |

Engines were allowed on depots only where a notice to that effect was displayed and, of the six stations listed, this applied only at Guisborough, where some of the coal cells still remain in existence within the confines of a local factory.

At Whitby, the coal-handling facilities were concentrated at West Cliff Station. It is presumed that there were originally coal cells at Town Station, but that these had been demolished after the opening of West Cliff Station in 1883.

# APPENDIX 8

## Yard cranes

At stations where goods traffic was handled, it was usual to have a fixed crane in the yard, and one or more in the warehouse/goods shed. I have details of the cranes at four stations dealt with in this work, where the cranes were maintained by the District Outdoor Machinery Engineer's Department at Darlington, and these are given in the following table. Of the other two stations,

Alnwick and Alston, NER and RCH records quote the maximum crane capacity at Alnwick as 3 tons, and Alston as 4 tons; both these, presumably, referred to the yard cranes.

For other than normal goods traffic, travelling cranes, either hand or steam, could be called upon; the former usually sufficed, and these were often used for loading round timber by gangs specially maintained for this task.

| | Guisborough | | Middleton-in-Teesdale | | Richmond | | Whitby | |
| | Yard | Warehouse | Yard | Warehouse | Yard | Warehouse | Yard | Warehouse |
|---|---|---|---|---|---|---|---|---|
| *Frame* | Cast-iron | Cast-iron | Cast-iron | Cast-iron | Cast-iron | Cast-iron | Cast-iron | Cast-iron |
| *Jib* | Wood (1) | Wood and iron | Wrought-iron | Wood | Steel | Wrought-iron | Wood | Wrought-iron |
| *Post* | Steel | Steel | Cast-iron (2) | Wood | Steel | Wrought-iron | Wood | (Wood clasped with iron) |
| *Foundations* | Stone | Wood | Stone | Stone | Concrete | Wood | Stone | Wood |
| *Capacity* | 6 tons | 1½ tons | 5 tons | 1½ tons | 3 tons | 1½ tons | 5 tons | 1 ton |
| *Radius* | 7ft. 5in. | 13ft. | 16ft. 6in. | 7ft. 10in. | 17ft. 8in. | 10ft. 6in. | 18ft. | 12ft. 11in. |
| *Length of jib* | 21ft. 10in. | 15ft. 5in. | 23ft. 3in. | 12ft. 8in. | 25ft. | 14ft. 4in. | 23ft. 3in | 16ft. 2in. |
| *Rope: diameter* | 3½in. | 2in. | 2¾in. | 2¾in. | 2¼in. | 2in. | 3in. | 1¾in. |
| *Rope: length* | 56ft. | 33ft. | 70ft. | 25ft. | 52ft. | 34ft. | 65ft. | 40ft. |
| *Maker* | Kitchin Warrington | Cowans, Sheldon, Carlisle, 1885 | Ianson, Darlington, 1867 | Kitchin 1867 | J. & E. Gledhills, Huddersfield, 1898 | J. Walker, York, 1846 (2 off) | Bray & Wadding-ton, Leeds | J. Walker, York (3) |

NOTES:

1: *Replaced by steel jib, 1939*

2: *Replaced by steel post, 11th September 1947*

3: *Dismantled after air raid, 1940*

# APPENDIX 9

## Water Supplies

### Water Columns (1911)

| Station | Where Situated | Type | Available From | Number | Notes |
|---|---|---|---|---|---|
| Alnwick | Near turntable | 6in. parachute | Turntable road | Alnmouth 5 | Cowans, Sheldon No. 1127 of 1885 2,000 gal. Capacity parachute tank built for two arms but only one fitted. Town supply. |
| Alston | Loco Yard | 8in. standard | Engine shed road | Carlisle 11 | |
| Middleton-in-Teesdale | Engine shed | 8in. swing pipe | Engine shed and turntable lines | Darlington 35 | Swing pipe on side of tank No. 9 |
| Richmond | Station, east end | 8in. standard | 'Up' line and siding | Darlington 39 | Cowans, Sheldon No. 1075 of 1886 |
| Whitby | Bog Hall | 8in. standard | Turntable line and goods yard | Whitby 7 | Cowans, Sheldon No. 1255 of 1893 |
| Whitby | Engine shed | 8in. standard | Engine shed line | Whitby 8 | — |

### Water Tanks (1911)

| Station | Maker and Date | Capacity | Source of Supply | Notes |
|---|---|---|---|---|
| Alnwick | — | 2,000gals. | Town mains | Parachute tank (see above) |
| Alston | J. & G. Joicey & Co. 1851 | 7,000gals. | Surface | — |
| Middleton-in-Teesdale | — | 10,000gals. | From reservoir on fells | Tank No. 9 (see above) |
| Middleton-in-Teesdale | — c 1884 | 6,000gals. | From reservoir on fells | Not in use. Tank No. 8 |
| Richmond | E. Thompson 1854 | 8,000gals. | Pumped from Sand Beck | — |
| Whitby | — 1902 | 18,000gals. | Whitby Water Co. | — |

The water supply at Richmond was obtained from Sand Beck, which joined the River Swale half a mile south-east of the station. The pump had an 8in. diameter piston with 10in. stroke, and it averaged 48 revolutions per minute. It was driven by a Carrick & Wardale vertical engine (No. 827 of 1892) with a cylinder, 10in. diameter x 10in. stroke. Steam was supplied by a vertical boiler which was built at Gateshead (No. 781 of 1909), which was 8ft. 4¹⁵/₁₆in. high and 3ft. 6in. diameter, working at 70p.s.i. The boiler was cut up in October 1945 and it is presumed that, at that time, an automatic electric pump was installed.

## Turntables

| Station | Location | Diameter | Maker and | Date | Remarks |
|---|---|---|---|---|---|
| nwick | In siding between Alnwick and Coldstream lines | 50ft. 0in. | Cowans, Sheldon No. 1590 | 1887 | Removed 1967 |
| ston | End of platform line | 42ft. 4in. | ? | ? | Removed 1952 |
| uisborough | Outside engine shed | 42ft. 1½in. | ? | 1887/8? | Removed and sold for scrap 1928. Realised £33 |
| iddleton-in-esdale | Outside engine shed | 45ft. 0in. | Cowans, Sheldon | 1867 | Removed 1940 or 1943 (both official dates) |
| chmond | Outside engine shed | 45ft. 0in. | Ianson | 1885 | Removed c 1956 |
| hitby | Outside engine shed | 42ft. 0in. | ? | ? | Replaced 1903 |
| | Bog Hall Sidings | 50ft. 0in. | Cowans, Sheldon No. 759 | 1876 | Ex-Church Fenton in 1903. Replaced 1936 |
| | Bog Hall Sidings | 60ft. 0in. | Cowans, Sheldon No. 2830 | 1912 | Ex-York in 1936. Removed 1966 |

## APPENDIX 11

### Ramps

The North Eastern Railway made extensive provision for rerailing wagons by providing sets of ramps at strategic locations, which were usually indicated by a horizontal white-painted board lettered 'Ramps' (in black), mounted on a short wooden post or on a convenient wall. The ramps, left-hand and right-hand, were made of cast iron, and were designed to provide a gradual slope up from ground level to the rail head for a derailed wheel, or wheels, as the vehicle was drawn forward. In 1922, the position was as follows:

| Location | Number of Sets | Single or double |
|---|---|---|
| Alnwick | 1 | Single |
| Alston | 1 | Single |
| Alston Loco Shed | ½ | Single |
| Guisborough Goods Yard | 1 | Single |
| Middleton-in-Teesdale | 1 | Single |
| Richmond Goods Yard | 1 | Single |
| Richmond Goods Yard | 1 | Double |
| Whitby Goods Yard | 1 | Single |

A set of single ramps was also carried in the brake vans working regularly over certain branches; from Alnwick the Coldstream branch van carried a set, and from Whitby the vans of the Scarborough, Loftus, Battersby and Malton pick-up goods trains all carried a set.

## Appendix 12

# The Alston Branch and the South Tynedale Railway Preservation Society

In 1973, with the impending closure of the Alston branch, the South Tynedale Railway Preservation Society was formed with the object of eventually purchasing and operating the line between Haltwhistle and Alston. This led to the formation of the South Tynedale Railway Co. (with Registered Offices in Hexham) to raise the necessary funds to purchase all or part of the line from British Rail, but this was unsuccessful. Consequently, in 1977, the Preservation Society adopted the revised aim of laying a narrow gauge line along all or part of the trackbed, as circumstances might permit.

Alston Station, and the 1½ miles of trackbed northwards to the county boundary at Gilderdale have been purchased from British Rail by Cumbria County Council, and part of the station area (including the goods warehouse) is being utilised for light industrial purposes. Another portion has been turned into a public car-park and picnic area, and it is intended to use the original station platform for the railway terminus, with the station buildings housing staff room, toilets, shop and a visitor centre. The south-west corner of the site is earmarked for a proposed railway museum.

Construction of the line is currently in progress, the station layout is complete and a start has been made on laying the running line northwards. The gauge is 2ft. Financial assistance has been given by the English Tourist Board on a 50 per cent basis, matching the amount raised by the Society. Passenger carrying services commenced in the summer of 1983 between Alston and Gildersdale.

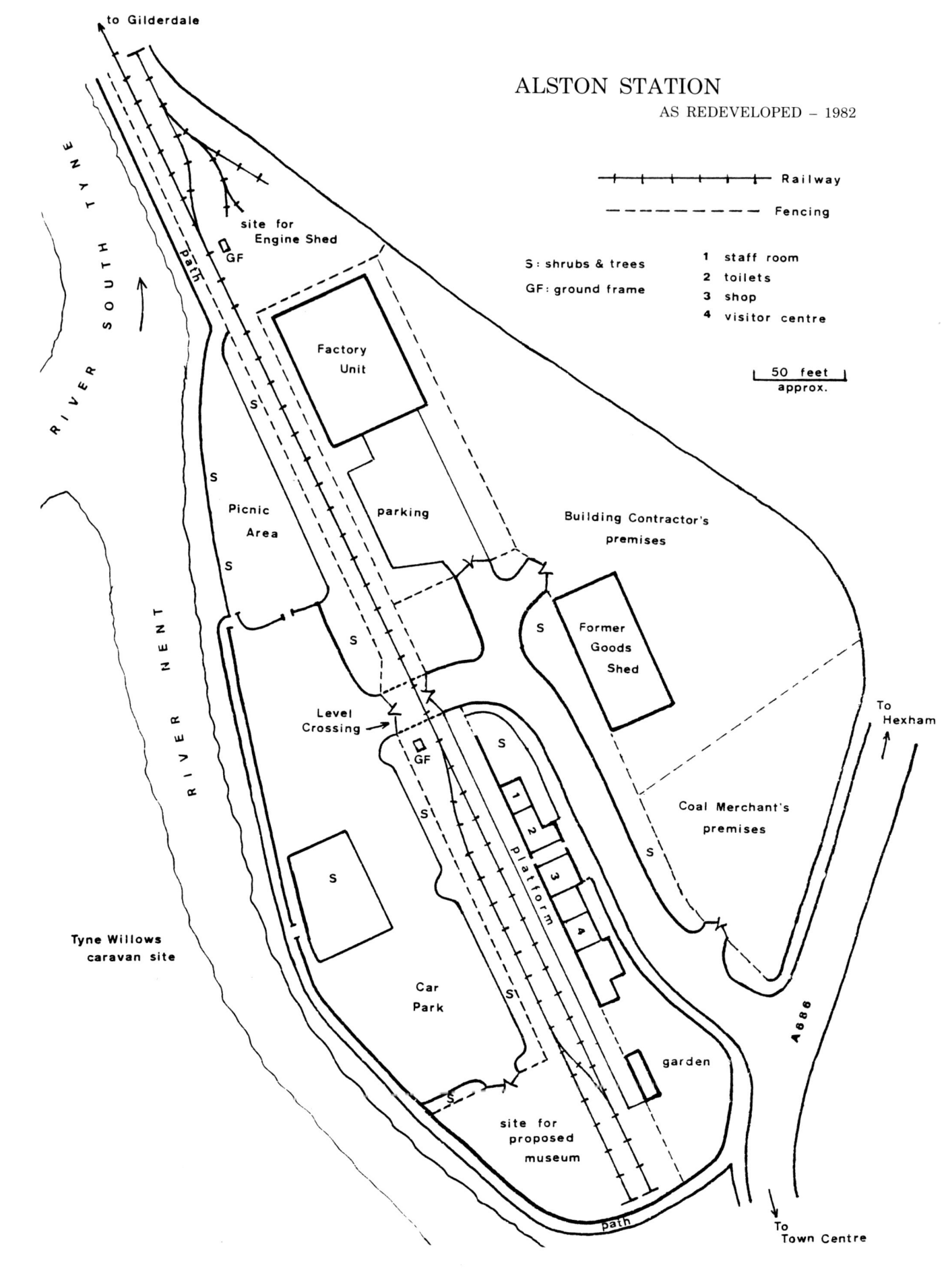

ALSTON STATION
AS REDEVELOPED – 1982

to Gilderdale

RIVER SOUTH TYNE

RIVER NENT

Path

site for
Engine Shed

GF

S

S

S

S

Picnic
Area

parking

Factory
Unit

Level
Crossing

GF

S

S

S

platform

1 2 3 4

S

S

S

Tyne Willows
caravan site

Car
Park

S

S

site for
proposed
museum

garden

path

Building Contractor's
premises

Former
Goods
Shed

S

Coal Merchant's
premises

S

A 686

To Hexham

To
Town Centre

Railway

Fencing

S : shrubs & trees

GF : ground frame

1  staff room
2  toilets
3  shop
4  visitor centre

50 feet
approx.

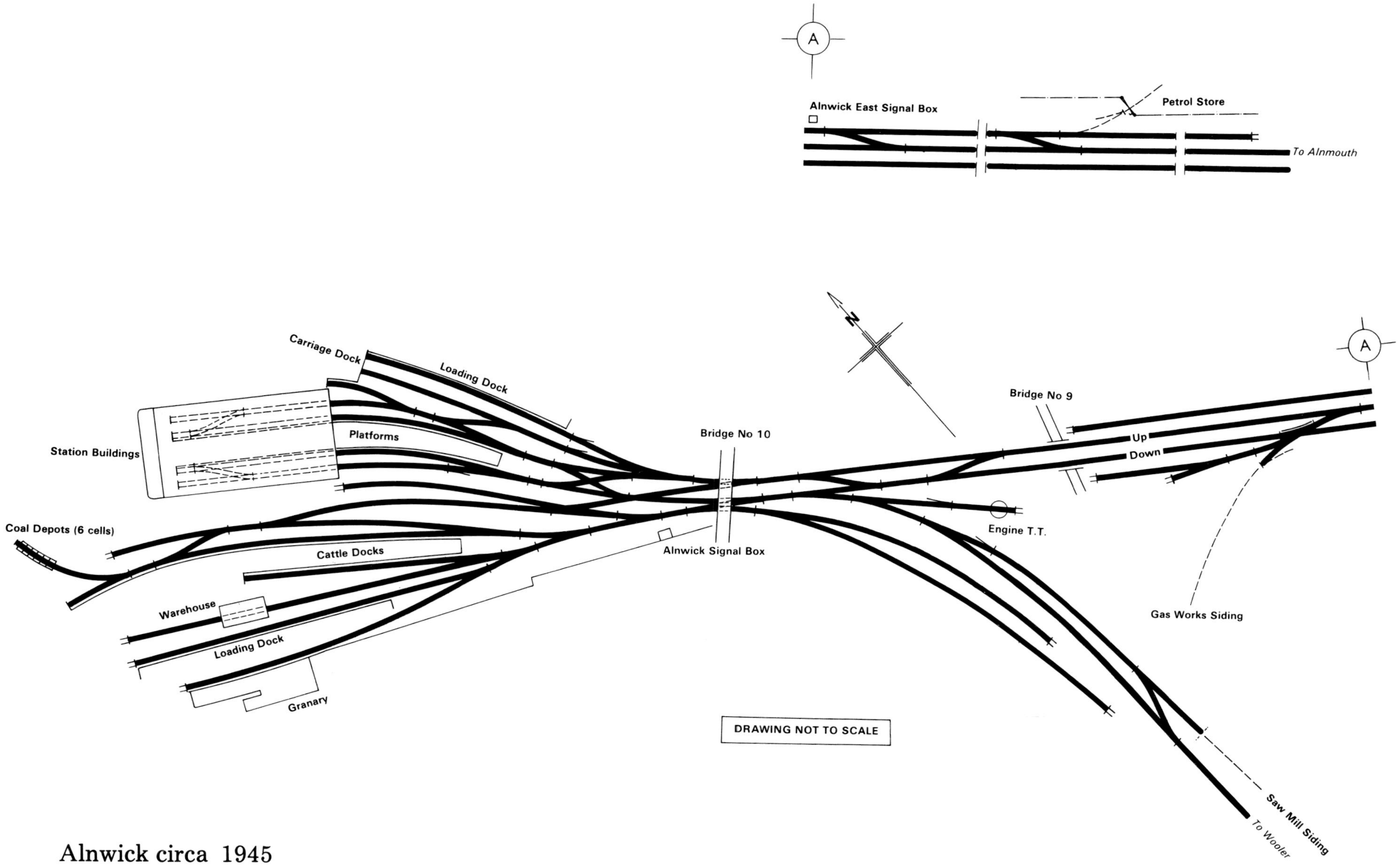

# Appendix 13: Track Plans

To Alnmouth

Petrol Store

Alnwick East Signal Box

A

A

Up

Down

Bridge No 9

Engine T.T.

N

Saw Mill Siding

To Wooler

Gas Works Siding

Bridge No 10

Alnwick Signal Box

DRAWING NOT TO SCALE

Loading Dock

Carriage Dock

Platforms

Station Buildings

Cattle Docks

Warehouse

Loading Dock

Granary

Coal Depots (6 cells)

## Alnwick circa 1945

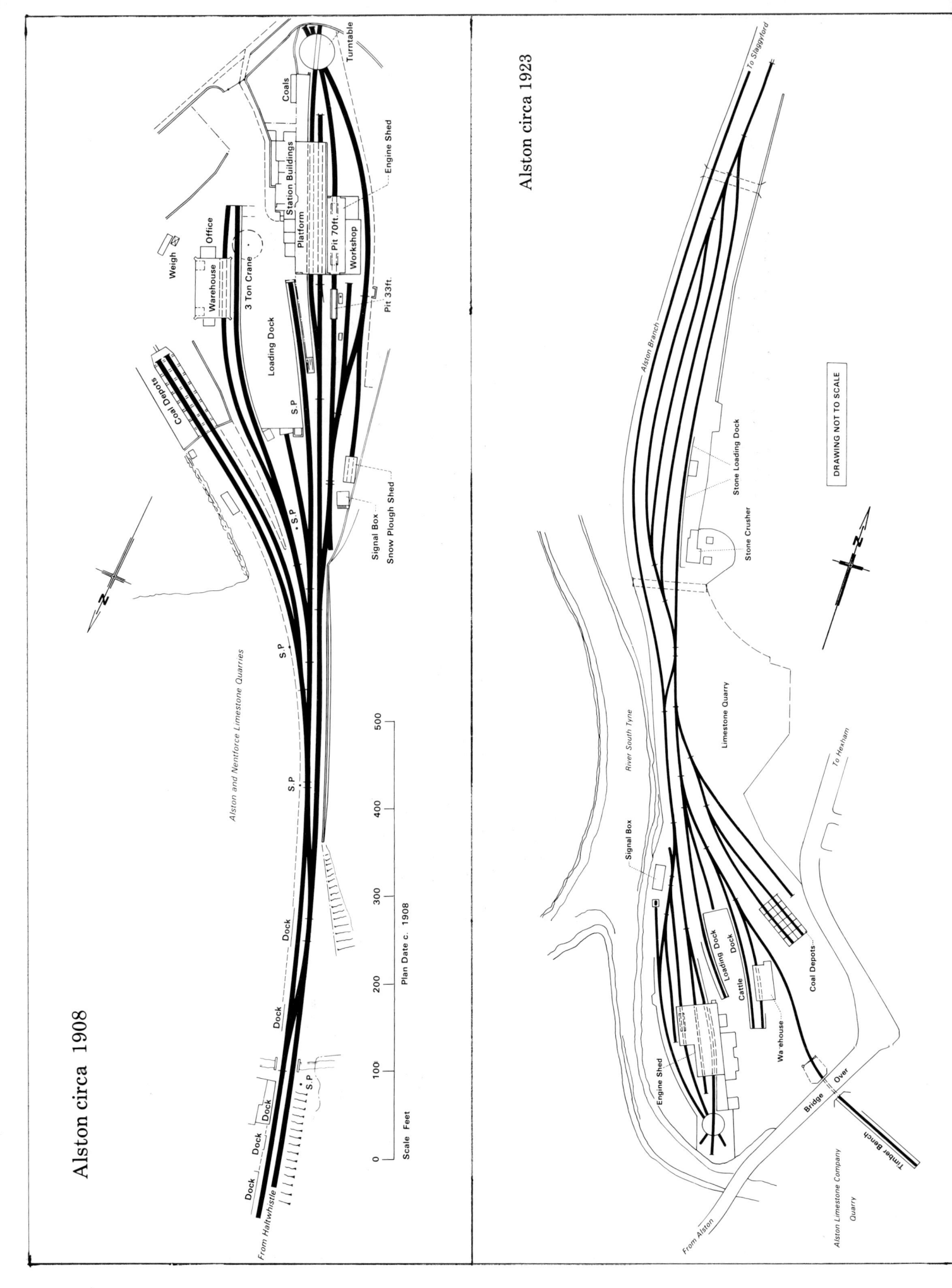

Alston circa 1908

From Haltwhistle

Dock
Dock
Dock
Dock
S.P
S.P
S.P
S.P
S.P

Alston and Nentforce Limestone Quarries

Coal Depots
Warehouse
Office
Weigh
3 Ton Crane
Station Buildings
Platform
Pit 70ft.
Workshop
Pit 33ft.
Loading Dock
Coals
Turntable
Engine Shed
Signal Box
Snow Plough Shed

N

Scale  Feet
0    100    200    300    400    500

Plan Date c. 1908

Alston circa 1923

To Slaggyford

Alston Branch

River South Tyne

Signal Box

Stone Loading Dock
Stone Crusher
Limestone Quarry

Engine Shed
Loading Dock
Cattle Dock
Warehouse
Coal Depots
Bridge Over

To Hexham

From Alston

Timber Bench

Alston Limestone Company Quarry

N

DRAWING NOT TO SCALE

# Guisborough

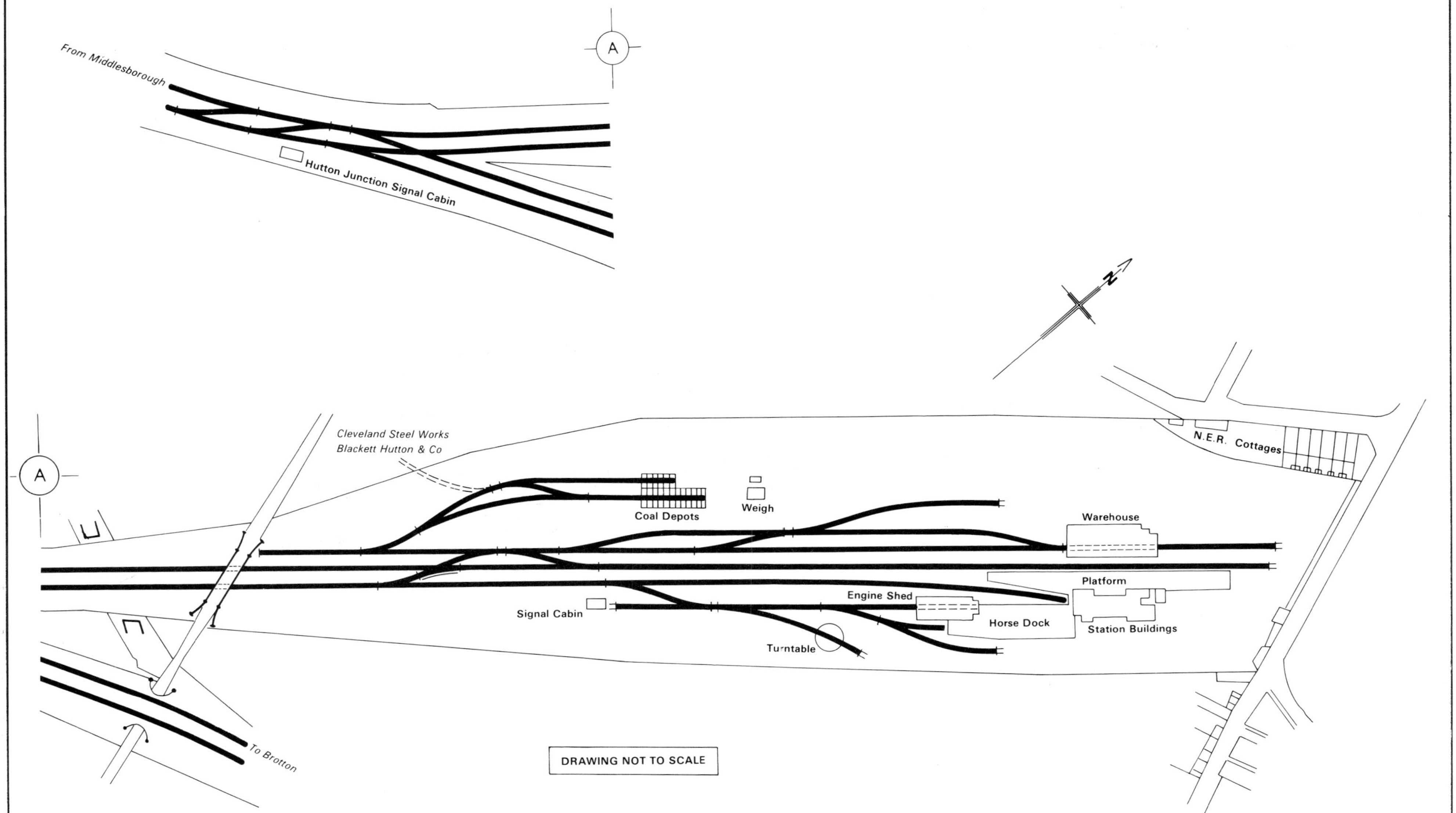

From Middlesborough

Hutton Junction Signal Cabin

A

N.E.R. Cottages

Warehouse

Platform

Station Buildings

Horse Dock

Engine Shed

Turntable

Weigh

Coal Depots

Cleveland Steel Works
Blackett Hutton & Co

Signal Cabin

To Brotton

A

DRAWING NOT TO SCALE

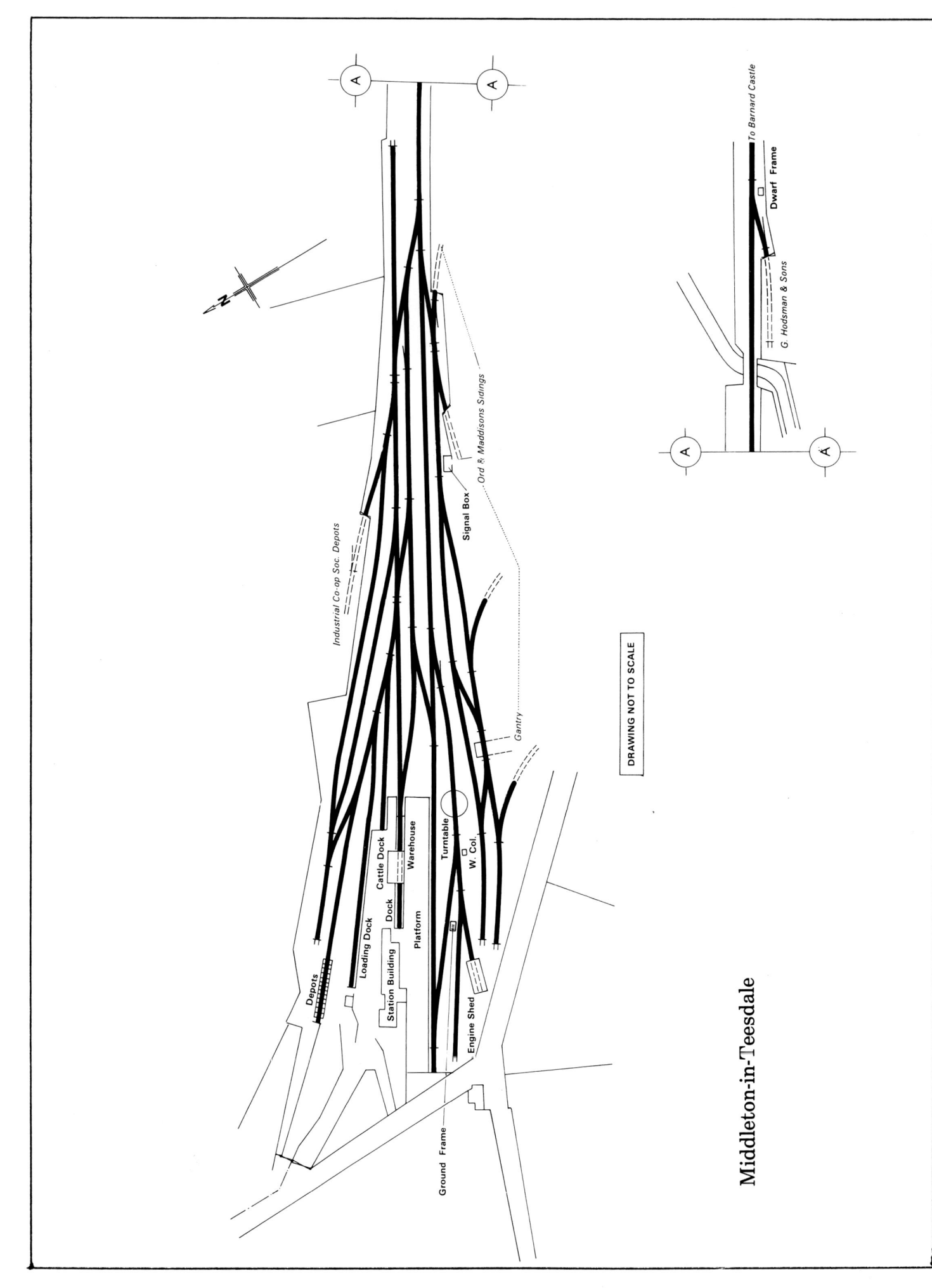

Middleton-in-Teesdale

DRAWING NOT TO SCALE

Industrial Co-op Soc. Depots

Ord. & Maddisons Sidings

Signal Box

Gantry

Depots

Loading Dock

Cattle Dock

Dock

Warehouse

Station Building

Platform

Turntable

W. Col.

Engine Shed

Ground Frame

To Barnard Castle

Dwarf Frame

G. Hodsman & Sons

A  A

A  A

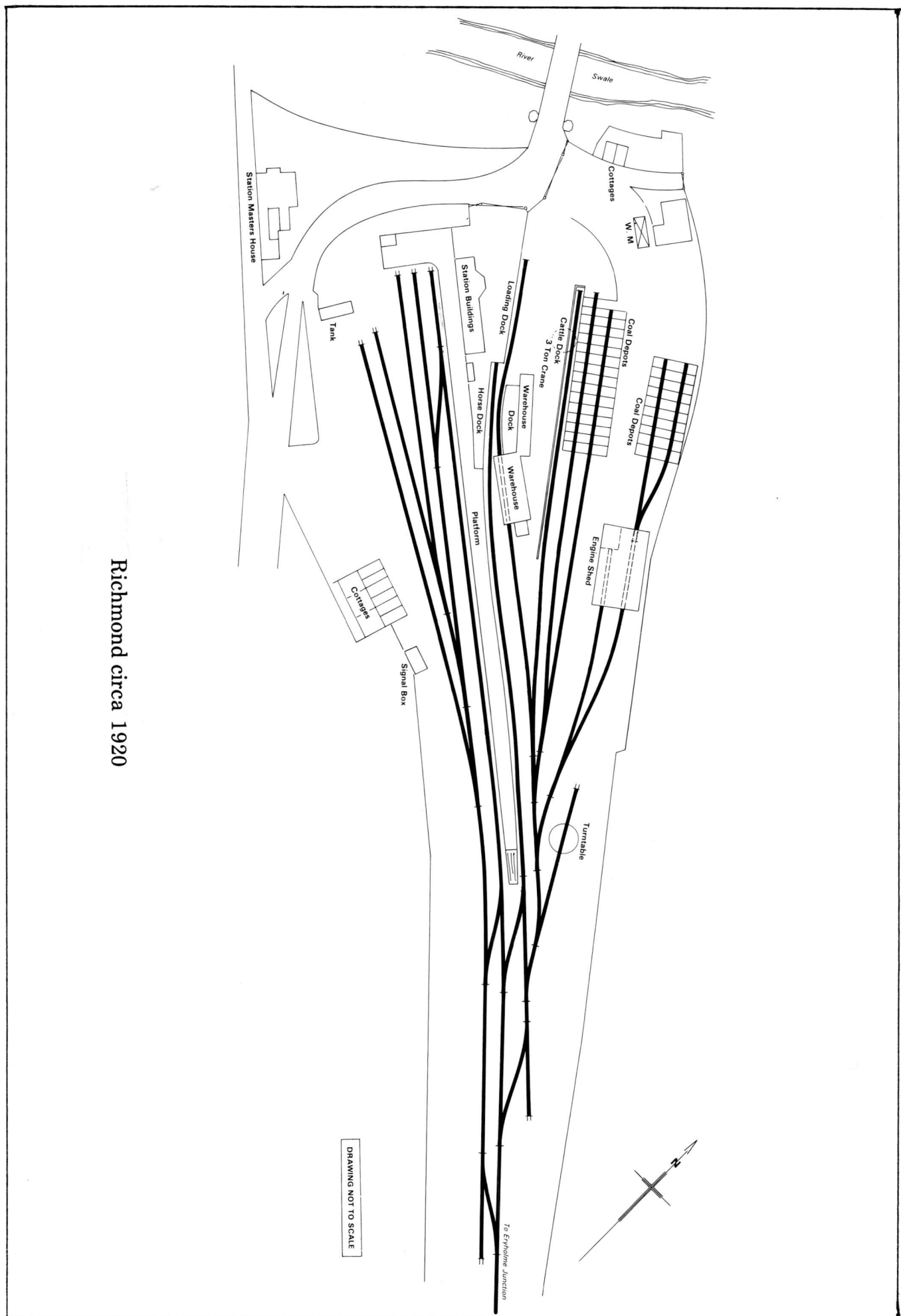

Richmond circa 1920

DRAWING NOT TO SCALE

River Swale

Cottages

W. M

Station Masters House

Tank

Station Buildings

Loading Dock

Horse Dock

Cattle Dock
3 Ton Crane

Warehouse Dock

Warehouse

Coal Depots

Coal Depots

Engine Shed

Platform

Cottages

Signal Box

Turntable

To Eryholme Junction

N

Whitby

Victoria Square

Office

Buildings

Station

5 Ton Crane

Timber Merchants

Station Masters House

Bog Hall Junction Signal Box

N.E.R. Stables

Crane

W.M. & W.O.

Coal Stack

Coal Stack

Coal Stack

Engine Turntable

S & T Stores

Waterstead Lane

P. Cabin

Carriage Sidings

Spring Hill

No 1 Platform

Platforms 2 & 3

No 4 Platform

Signal Box

Offices

Goods Office

Coal Stack

5 Ton Crane

Coal Stack

5 Ton Crane

Water Tank

P. Cabin

Windsor Terrace

Loco. Office

Goods Warehouse

N

Esk Terrace

Stores

Coal Stage

Engine Shed

Coal Stack

P. Cabin

Crane

From Prospect Hill Jc

From Grosmont

Cattle Dock

W.M. & W.O

0    100    200    300    400    500    600

Ⓐ

Ⓐ